STUDY GUIDE

to accompany

PHYSICAL GEOGRAPHY
THE GLOBAL ENVIRONMENT

STUDY GUIDE

Peter O. Muller
Elizabeth Muller Hames

to accompany

PHYSICAL GEOGRAPHY
THE GLOBAL ENVIRONMENT

THIRD EDITION

H. J. de Blij
Peter O. Muller
Richard S. Williams, Jr.

New York • Oxford
OXFORD UNIVERSITY PRESS
2004

Oxford University Press

Oxford   New York
Auckland Bangkok Buenos Aires Cape Town Chennai
Dar es Salaam Delhi Hong Kong Istanbul Karachi Kolkata
Kuala Lumpur Madrid Melbourne Mexico City Mumbai
Nairobi São Paulo Shanghai Taipei Tokyo Toronto

Published by Oxford University Press, Inc.
198 Madison Avenue, New York, New York, 10016
http://www.oup-usa.org

Oxford is a registered trademark of Oxford University Press

ISBN 0-19-517114-4

Printing number: 9 8 7 6 5 4 3 2 1

Printed in the United States of America
on acid-free paper

PREFACE

This Study Guide is designed to enhance your understanding of physical geography. It supplements, and will help you to build upon, your reading of the textbook's units and your classroom learning experiences.

Each unit of this Study Guide follows an identical format. The first section is the *Unit Summary* that presents a single-paragraph overview of the unit's contents. This is followed by a restatement of the *Unit Objectives*. Then comes the *Glossary of Key Terms*, a comprehensive, alphabetically arranged assemblage of all the bold-faced terms in the unit together with their definitions. A *Unit Outline* appears next, which provides a detailed guide to the flow of the subject matter in each unit. The next section consists of a set of *Review Questions* that focuses on the major ideas introduced in each unit; they would be a useful preparation for short-essay examinations. The concluding section is a *Self-Test* that can be used to prepare for short-answer examinations; for each unit, six multiple-choice and six true-false questions are provided (answers may be found at the end of the Study Guide).

The authors wish to acknowledge the central editorial role of Linda Harris of Oxford University Press in the preparation of this Study Guide. We are also grateful for the assistance and encouragement we received from her current and former colleagues at Oxford: Jenny Boully, Erin Clancy, Karen Shapiro, Eman Hudson, and Christopher Rogers.

Peter O. Muller
Elizabeth Muller Hames
Coral Gables, Florida

TABLE OF CONTENTS

STUDY GUIDE

to accompany

PHYSICAL GEOGRAPHY
THE GLOBAL ENVIRONMENT

UNIT SUMMARY

Geography is a holistic (integrative) discipline that synthesizes knowledge about the Earth's surface from many cognate disciplines. The broadest division of geography includes the subfields of human geography and physical geography. The history of physical geography is traced from early Greek and Roman times, and its subfields are defined. Emphasis is placed on the developments in physical geography during the last century. Systems and models in geography are defined, and their functions are examined. Orders of magnitude are described as they relate to scales commonly used in physical geography.

UNIT OBJECTIVES

1. To introduce and discuss the contemporary focus of physical geography.

2. To relate physical geography to the other natural and physical sciences.

3. To introduce the systems and modeling approaches to physical geography.

GLOSSARY OF KEY TERMS

Biogeography The geography of plants (*phytogeography*) and animals (*zoogeography*).

Climatology The geographic study of climates. This includes not only climate classification and the analysis of their regional distribution, but also broader environmental questions that concern climate change, interrelationships with soil and vegetation, and human-climate interaction.

Closed system A self-contained system exhibiting no exchange of energy or matter across its boundaries (interfaces).

Dynamic equilibrium State of a system in balance, when it is neither growing nor contracting but continues in full operation.

Feedback Occurs when a change in one part of a system causes a change in another part of the system.

Geomorphology Literally means *earth shape* or *form*. The geography of landscape and its evolution, a major subfield of physical geography.

Marine geography Physical side of this subfield treats coastlines and shores, beaches, and other landscape features associated with the oceanic margins of the continents.

Model The creation of an idealized representation of reality in order to demonstrate its most important properties.

Open system A system whose boundaries (interfaces) freely permit the transfer of energy and matter across them.

Orders of magnitude Sizes of geographic entities.

Phytogeography The geography of flora or plant life; where botany and physical geography overlap.

Soil geography Systematic study of the spatial patterns of soils, their distribution, and interrelationships with climate, vegetation, and humankind.

Spatial Pertaining to space on the Earth's surface; synonym for geographic(al).

Subsystem A component of a larger system; it can act independently, but operates within, and is linked to, the larger system.

System Any set of related objects or events and their interactions.

Water resources Subfield of physical geography involving its intersection with hydrology; systematic study of the surface and subsurface water supplies potentially available for human use.

Zoogeography The geography of animal life or fauna; where zoology and physical geography overlap.

UNIT OUTLINE

I. **Geography**
   A. Synthesis of knowledge about Earth's surface
   B. Concerned with organization of physical and human phenomena
   C. Holistic (all-inclusive), integrating discipline
   D. Fields of geography
       1. broad division into physical and human geography
       2. relations with cognate disciplines

II. **Physical Geography**
   A. Greek and Roman beginnings
   B. Arab leadership during the Dark Ages
   C. Renaissance after 1500 with age of exploration and discovery
   D. The rise of modern Physical Geography
   E. Subfields of physical geography
       1. geomorphology
       2. climatology

      3. phytogeography
      4. biogeography/ecology
      5. zoogeography
      6. soil geography
      7. marine geography
      8. water resources

III.   Advances in physical geography since 1900

IV.   Systems and models in physical geography
    A. Systems
      1. open systems
      2. closed systems
      3. subsystems
      4. dynamic equilibrium
      5. negative and positive feedback in systems
    B. Models
      1. idealized constructs
      2. representations of reality
      3. demonstrate workings of physical processes in relatively simple ways

V.   Geographic magnitude
    A. Orders of magnitude (Fig. 1.7)
    B. Sliding scale (box, p. 15)

REVIEW QUESTIONS

1. Contrast the mechanisms and effects of positive and negative feedback.

2. Trace some of the major developments in physical geography during the past century, mentioning a few of the most prominent physical geographers.

3. Write out in exponential notation the orders of magnitude from 1/1000 to 1 million.

SELF-TEST

Multiple-Choice Questions

1. The term <u>geography</u> was coined by:

    (a) Aristotle (b) von Humboldt (c) Eratosthenes (d) Davis (e) Geographicus

2. Which of the following is not a field of human geography?

    (a) cultural geography (b) physical geography (c) historical geography (d) economic geography (e) urban geography

3. Which of the following is not part of biogeography?

    (a) geomorphology (b) ecology (c) phytogeography (d) zoogeography (e) plant geography

4. Pedology is most closely related to:

    (a) marine geography (b) phytogeography (c) climatology (d) geomorphology (e) soil geography

5. Geomorphology is most closely related to the cognate discipline of:

    (a) hydrology (b) pedology (c) geology (d) ecology (e) meteorology

6. Which of the following is not an open system?

    (a) a completely self contained system
    (b) one that allows energy and matter to cross its boundaries
    (c) a system that contains more than two subsystems
    (d) one in which negative feedback occurs
    (e) a city

True-False Questions

___ 1. The word "spatial" refers only to terrestrial space.
___ 2. Climatology lies at the intersection of geography and meteorology.
___ 3. Phytogeography lies at the intersection of biogeography and zoogeography.
___ 4. A negative feedback mechanism operates to keep a system in its original condition.
___ 5. A model can never be an abstraction of the real world.
___ 6. A closed system is difficult to find on or near Earth's surface.

UNIT SUMMARY

The five interconnected spheres of the Earth System are described and include the atmosphere, lithosphere, hydrosphere, biosphere, and cryosphere. The term hemisphere is introduced, and exemplified by the Northern and Southern hemispheres, Eastern and Western hemispheres, and the land and water hemispheres. The six continental landmasses are described, as are the five major ocean basins. Attention is then focused on the physical forms that mark the continents and create the transitions to the seafloors. Seafloor features of interest include midoceanic ridges, seamounts, and abyssal plains.

UNIT OBJECTIVES

1. To define and highlight the five spheres of the Earth System.

2. To highlight the general characteristics of the Earth's continents.

3. To introduce the world's ocean basins and the topographic characteristics of the seafloor.

GLOSSARY OF KEY TERMS

Abyssal plains Large zones of relatively low-relief seafloor constituting one of the deepest areas of an ocean basin.

Atmosphere The blanket of air that adheres to the Earth's surface which contains the mixture of gases essential to the survival of all terrestrial life forms.

Biosphere The zone of terrestrial life, the habitat of all living things; include's the Earth's vegetation, animals, human beings, and the part of the soil layer below that hosts living organisms.

Continental rise Transitional zone of gently sloping seafloor that begins at the foot of the continental slope and leads downward to the lowest (abyssal) zone of an ocean basin.

Continental shelf The gently sloping, relatively shallow, submerged plain just off the coast of a continent, extending to a depth of ca. 180 m (600 ft/100 fathoms).

Continental slope The steeply plunging slope that begins at the outer edge of the continental shelf (ca. 180 m [600 ft.] below the sea surface) and ends in the depths of the ocean floor at the head of the continental rise.

Cryosphere The collective name for the ice system of the Earth.

Cultural landscapes The forms and artifacts sequentially placed on the natural landscape by the activities of various human occupants.

Earth System The shells or layers that make up the total Earth System range from those in the planet's deepest interior to those bordering outer space: this book focuses on the key Earth layers of the atmosphere, lithosphere, hydrosphere, biosphere, and cryosphere.

Ecumene The portion of the world's land surface that is permanently settled by human beings.

Hemisphere A half-sphere; used precisely, as in Northern Hemisphere (everything north of 0° latitude), or sometimes more generally, as in land hemisphere (the significant concentration of landmasses on roughly one side of the earth).

Hydrosphere The sphere of the Earth System that contains all the water that exists on and within the solid surface of our planet and in the atmosphere above.

Land hemisphere The roughly one-half of the Earth that contains most of the landmasses (*see* Fig 2.4); the opposite of the water (oceanic) hemisphere.

Lithosphere The outermost shell of the solid Earth, lying immediately below the land surface and ocean floor (*lithos* means rock).

Midoceanic ridge High submarine volcanic mountain ranges, part of a global system of such ranges, most often found in the central areas of the ocean basins; here new crust is formed by upwelling molten rock, which continuously moves away toward the margins of the ocean basins.

Natural landscapes The array of landforms that constitute the Earth's surface and the physical features that mark them.

Regional subsystem The particular interconnection, at any given place within the total Earth System, of the five spheres or subsystems (atmosphere, hydrosphere, cryosphere, lithosphere, and biosphere).

Water (oceanic) hemisphere The roughly one-half of the Earth that contains most of the surface water; the opposite of the *land hemisphere* (*see* Fig. 2.4).

UNIT OUTLINE

I. **Spheres of the Earth System (Figs. 2.1, 2.2)**
   A. The atmosphere
   B. The lithosphere
   C. The hydrosphere
   D. The biosphere

E. The cryosphere

II. **Hemispheres**
   A. Northern and Southern hemispheres
   B. Eastern and Western hemispheres
   C. Land and water hemispheres

III. **Continents and oceans**
   A. The six continental landmasses
      1. Africa
      2. South America
      3. North America
      4. Eurasia
      5. Australia
      6. Antarctica
   B. The five ocean basins
      1. Pacific Ocean
      2. Atlantic Ocean
      3. Indian Ocean
      4. Southern Ocean
      5. Arctic Ocean
   C. Ocean basin components
      1. continental margins
         a. continental shelf
         b. continental slope
         c. continental rise
      2. abyssal zone
         a. abyssal plains
         b. seamounts
         c. midoceanic ridges

REVIEW QUESTIONS

1. Draw and label the physical features that connect surface landmasses to the deepest abyssal zones of the ocean basins. Include the terms continental shelf, continental rise, and continental slope.

2. Describe the Earth's cryosphere, and its components.

3. State in very general terms the global distribution of population, using Fig. 2.5 as a reference.

SELF-TEST

Multiple-Choice Questions

1. The biosphere includes all of the following except:

    (a) vegetation (b) animals (c) human beings (d) air (e) plants

2. What percentage of Earth's surface is covered by water?

    (a) 29 % (b) 50% (c) 8% (d) 17% (e) 71%

3. What term is used for the gently sloping, submerged area at the edge of a landmass?

    (a) continental shelf (b) continental slope (c) continental rise (d) abyssal plain (e) oceanic ridge

4. Submarine volcanic mountain ranges are termed:

    (a) abyssal mounts (b) midoceanic ridges (c) continental rises (d) midoceanic mounts (e) continental shelves

5. The portion of Earth's surface where permanent settlement is possible is the:

    (a) land area (b) habitat (c) ecumene (d) biosphere (e) ecosystem

6. Which of the following is not a continent?

    (a) North America (b) Antarctica (c) Australia (d) Africa (e) Indonesia

True-False Questions

__ 1. The Earth is approximately 30 percent land.
__ 2. Australia is the world's smallest continent.
__ 3. The lithosphere does not continue beneath the oceans.
__ 4. The hydrosphere includes water in the atmosphere.
__ 5. Eurasia is the Earth's largest landmass.
__ 6. The continental slope is a gentle rise connecting continental margins to the abyssal zone.

UNIT SUMMARY

In order to map the Earth in an orderly fashion, the globe must be divided geometrically. The earth is spherical, and can be partitioned into units of degrees, hours, minutes, and seconds. Lines of longitude (meridians) map distances east or west of the arbitrarily drawn Prime Meridian that passes through Greenwich, England. Lines of latitude (parallels) map distances north or south of the Equator. All map projections have scale, area, and shape. Map projections can preserve one or two of these properties at a time, but only by distorting another factor. The major classes of map projections are cylindrical, conic, planar, and equal-area. Map interpretation is made possible through the use of symbols to represent point, line, area, and volume data. New cartographic techniques include the use of geographic information systems (GIS), global positioning systems (GPS), and environmental remote sensing.

UNIT OBJECTIVES

1. To introduce the reference system for locations on the Earth's surface.

2. To describe the most important characteristics of maps and the features of common classes of map projections.

3. To discuss the elements of map interpretation and contemporary cartographic techniques.

GLOSSARY OF KEY TERMS

Cartography The science, art, and technology of mapmaking and map use.

Conic projection One in which the transfer of the Earth grid is from a globe onto a cone, which is then cut and laid flat.

Contouring The representation of surface relief using isolines of elevation above sea level; an important basis of topographic mapping.

Cylindrical projection One in which the transfer of the Earth grid is from a globe onto a cylinder, which is then cut and laid flat.

Equal-area projection One in which all the areas mapped are represented in correct proportion to one another.

Equator The parallel of latitude running around the exact middle of the globe, defined as 0° latitude.

Geographic information system (GIS) A collection of computer hardware and software that permit spatial data to be collected, recorded, stored, retrieved, manipulated, analyzed, and displayed to the user.

Interactive Mapping In geographic information systems (GIS) methodology, the constant dialogue via computer demands and feedback to queries between the map user and the map.

Isarithmic (isoline) mapping A commonly-used cartographic device to represent three-dimensional volumetric data on a two-dimensional map; involves the use of isolines to show the surfaces that are mapped.

Isoline A line connecting all places possessing the same value of a given phenomenon, or "height" above the flat base of the surface being mapped.

Latitude The angular distance, measured in degrees north or south, of a point along a parallel from the Equator.

Legend The portion of a map where its point, line, area, and volume symbols are identified.

Longitude The angular distance, measured in degrees east or west, of a point along a meridian from the prime meridian.

Map projection An orderly arrangement of meridians and parallels, produced by any systematic method, that can be used for drawing a map of the spherical Earth on a flat surface.

Mercator projection The most famous of the cylindrical projections, the only one on which any straight line is a line of true compass direction.

Meridians On the Earth grid, a north-south line of longitude; these range from 0° (Prime Meridian) to 180° E and W.

Parallels On the Earth grid, an east-west line of latitude; parallels of latitude range from 0° (Equator) to 90° N and S (the North and South poles, respectively, where the east-west line shrinks to a point).

Planar projection One in which the transfer of the Earth grid is from a globe onto a plane, involving a single point of tangency.

Prime Meridian The north-south line on the Earth grid, passing through the Royal Observatory at Greenwich in London, defined as having a longitude of 0°.

Remote sensing A technique for imaging objects without the sensor being in immediate contact with the local scene.

Scale The ratio of the size of an object on a map to the actual size of the object it represents.

Standard parallel The parallel of tangency between a globe and the surface onto which it is projected.

UNIT OUTLINE

I. **The spherical Earth**
   A. Dividing the Earth
       1. degrees
       2. parallels
       3. meridians
   B. Latitude and Longitude
       1. the Equator
       2. latitude measures distance north or south of the Equator
       3. the Prime Meridian
       4. longitude measures distance east or west of the Prime Meridian

II. **Map projections**
   A. Properties of map projections
       1. scale
       2. area
       3. shape
   B. Types of map projections
       1. cylindrical projection
       2. mercator projection
       3. conic projection
       4. planar projections
       5. equal-area projections

III. **Map interpretation**
   A. Use of symbols in mapping
       1. point symbols map locations
       2. line symbols represent linkages
       3. area symbols map quantitative ranges
       4. volume symbols describe surfaces
           1. isarithmic (isoline) mapping
           2. contouring

IV. **New cartographic frontiers**
   A. Geographic information systems allow users to collect, store, analyze, and manipulate data to produce layered and integrated maps
   B. Remote sensing allows data to be collected from high-altitude locations
   C. Interactive mapping provides for dialogue between the user and the map

REVIEW QUESTIONS

1. Describe the properties of a Mercator projection, and why it is a valuable tool for navigation.

2. What is a global positioning system (GPS) and what are its uses in the field?

3. How is the Earth divided into a grid system of degrees, hours, and minutes?

SELF-TEST

Multiple-Choice Questions

1. The line running east-west on Earth's imaginary grid system are:

    (a) meridians (b) parallels (c) degrees (d) rhumb lines (e) mercators

2. In what type of map projection does the spacing of parallels increase towards the poles, producing polar distortion?

    (a) mercator projection (b) conic projection (c) planar projection (d) equal-area projection (e) magnified projection

3. The ratio of the size of an object on a map to its actual size is:

    (a) area (b) tangency (c) volume (d) contouring (e) scale

4. Lines on maps connecting areas with the same value of a given phenomenon are:

    (a) isolines (b) biolines (c) great circles (d) small circles (e) rhumb lines

5. Zero degrees latitude is represented by:

    (a) the Equator (b) the Prime Meridian (c) the north pole (d) the south pole (e) Greenwich, England

6. Degrees of longitude are measured from the starting point of:

   (a) the Equator (b) Greenwich, England (c) the north pole (d) present-day Iraq (e) the south pole

True-False Questions

___ 1. Earth's circumference is divided into 180 equal degrees for measurement purposes.
___ 2. The Prime Meridian runs north-south.
___ 3. Latitude measures degrees north or south of the Equator.
___ 4. Meridians and parallels appear as intersecting straight lines on a cylindrical projection.
___ 5. Isohyets display areas of equal rainfall.
___ 6. Equal-area projections do not show mapped areas in correct proportion to one another.

UNIT SUMMARY

The universe as a whole can be divided into a nested hierarchy of local superclusters, local groups, and galaxy groups. The Big Bang theory states that the origin of the universe was the result of a massive explosion, which produced all primordial matter and energy. Our galaxy, the Milky Way, contains the Sun and its nine planets. The Sun accounts for almost all of the mass of our solar system, and has a gravitational effect on the planets. The Inner Planets, in increasing distance from the Sun, are Mercury, Venus, Earth, and Mars. The Outer Planets, also in increasing distance from the Sun, are Jupiter, Saturn, Uranus, and Neptune. Pluto is treated separately, as a lesser body, due to its small size and unusual orbit. The smaller objects of the solar system include asteroids, comets, meteoroids, and dust.

UNIT OBJECTIVES

1. To introduce the basic structure of the universe, speculations about its origin, and the position of our home galaxy and star within it.

2. To describe the functions of the Sun as the dominant body of the solar system.

3. To briefly survey each of the Sun's nine planets and the lesser orbiting bodies that constitute the remainder of the solar system.

GLOSSARY OF KEY TERMS

Galaxy An organized, disk-like assemblage of billions of stars; our solar system belongs to the Milky Way galaxy, which measures about 120,000 light-years in diameter.

Gravity The force of attraction that acts among all physical objects as a result of their mass (the quantity of material they are composed of).

Light-year The distance traveled by a pulse of light in one year. Light travels at a speed of 300,000 km (186,000 mi) per second; a light-year thus involves a distance of 9.46 trillion km (5.88 trillion mi).

Moon Satellite that orbits a planet, probably originating from the clustering of planetesimals. All planets except Mercury and Venus have such bodies; our Moon orbits the Earth once every 27.3 days at an average distance of 385,000 km (240,000 mi).

Planet   A dark solid body, much smaller in size than a star, whose movements in space are controlled by the gravitational effects of a nearby star.

Revolution   One complete circling of the Sun by a planet; it takes Earth precisely one year to complete such an orbit.

Rotation   The spinning of a planet on its axis, the imaginary line passing through its center and both poles; it takes Earth one calendar day to complete one full rotation.

Solar system   The Sun and its nine orbiting planets (plus their orbiting satellites). In order of increasing distance from the Sun, these planets are Mercury, Venus, Earth, Mars. Jupiter, Saturn, Uranus, Neptune, and Pluto.

Universe   The entity containing all of the matter and energy that exists anywhere in space and time.

UNIT OUTLINE

I.   **The universe**
        A. A light-year measures distances and is about 9.46 trillion km or 5.88 trillion mi
        B. Galaxies
                1. Milky Way
                2. local group
                3. local supercluster
        C. Big Bang Theory
                1. explosion expelling all primordial energy and matter
                2. gravity is the force of attraction among all objects due to their mass

II.   **The solar system**
        A. The Sun
                1. solar wind
                2. sunspots
        B. The planets
                1. revolution
                2. the inner planets
                        a. Mercury
                        b. Venus
                        c. Earth
                        d. Mars
                3. the outer planets
                        a.   Jupiter
                        b.   Saturn
                        c.   Uranus
                        d.   Neptune
        C. The lesser bodies of the solar system

1. Pluto
2. moons
D. Smaller objects of the solar system
    1. asteroids
    2. comets
    3. meteoroids (and meteorites)
    4. dust

REVIEW QUESTIONS

1. Compare and contrast the relative sizes and distances from the Sun of the nine planets of our solar system.

2. List the critical variables that make Earth a habitable environment - use Table 4.1 as a guide.

3. Define the term sunspots, and describe some of their possible effects on Earth.

SELF-TEST

Multiple-Choice Questions

1. The planet closest in size and mass to Earth is:

    (a) Mars (b) Neptune (c) Venus (d) Pluto (e) Saturn

2. The force of attraction between objects due to their mass is:

    (a) density (b) gravity (c) weight (d) magnetism (e) polarity

3. An organized, disk-shaped assembly of billions of stars is a:

    (a) galaxy (b) universe (c) local group (d) local supercluster (e) supernova

4. Which of the following planets is an outer (major) planet?

   (a) Jupiter (b) Mercury (c) Pluto (d) Earth (e) Venus

5. The dark areas on the sun's surface are:

   (a) sunspots (b) sun streaks (c) solar holes (d) quasars (e) black holes

6. Saturn's rings are composed of icy particles of:

   (a) sulfur and magnesium (b) water and rock (c) acids and rock (d) nitrogen (e) carbon dioxide and iron

True-False Questions

___ 1. Moons are satellites that orbit all nine planets.
___ 2. One complete circling of the sun is called a revolution.
___ 3. The Sun accounts for over 99 percent of the mass in the solar system.
___ 4. Mercury is the hottest planet because it is closest to the Sun.
___ 5. The red spot on Jupiter is actually a hurricane-like storm.
___ 6. The gaseous flow of energy radiating from the Sun is called solar wind.

UNIT 5: EARTH-SUN RELATIONSHIPS

UNIT SUMMARY

Earth's natural environment is largely a product of Earth-Sun relationships. The earth rotates on its axis approximately once every 24 hours, and revolves around the Sun approximately once every 365¼ days. Earth's seasonality is a result of the 66½-degree tilt of its axis with respect to the plane of the ecliptic, which causes varying amounts of solar radiation to reach different parts of the Earth. At the solstices, (June 22 and December 22), the maximum northern or southern positions of overhead noontime sun are reached, while at the equinoxes (March 21 and September 23), the Earth receives 12 hours of daylight and 12 hours of darkness at all latitudes. The dates of the four seasons (in the Northern Hemisphere) are as follows: spring, March 21-June 22; summer, June 22- Sept. 23; fall, Sept. 23- Dec.22; winter, Dec. 22- March 21.

UNIT OBJECTIVES

1. To examine the Earth's motions relative to the Sun.

2. To demonstrate the consequences of the Earth's axis tilt for the annual march of the seasons.

3. To introduce the time and spatial variations in solar radiation received at surface locations.

GLOSSARY OF KEY TERMS

Antarctic circle The latitude (66½°) marking the northern boundary of the Southern Hemisphere portion of the Earth's surface that receives a 24-hour period of sunlight at least once a year.

Aphelion The point in the Earth's orbit, which occurs every July 4th, where the distance to the Sun is maximized.

Arctic Circle The latitude (66½°N) marking the southern boundary of the Northern Hemisphere portion of the Earth's surface that receives a 24-hour period of sunlight at least once each year.

Axis The imaginary line that extends from the North Pole to the South Pole through the center of the Earth; the planet's rotation occurs with respect to this axis.

Circle of illumination At any given moment on our constantly rotating planet, the boundary between the halves of the Earth that are in sunlight and darkness.

Daylight-saving time By law, all clocks in a time zone are set one hour forward from standard time for at least part of the year.

Equinox One of the two days (March 21 and Sept. 21) in the year when the Sun's noontime rays strike the Earth vertically at the Equator; in Northern Hemisphere terminology, the March 21 event is called the spring (vernal) equinox and the September 23 event is called the fall (autumnal) equinox.

Fall (autumnal) equinox The equinox that occurs when the Sun's noontime rays strike the Equator vertically on ca. September 23.

Insolation Incoming solar radiation.

International date line For the most part is antipodal to the Prime Meridian and follows the 180th meridian; crossing the line toward the west involves skipping a day, while crossing the line toward the east means repeating a day.

Perihelion The point in the Earth's orbit, which occurs every January 3, where the distance to the Sun is minimized.

Plane of the ecliptic The plane formed by the Sun and the Earth's orbital path.

Revolution One complete circling of the Sun by a planet; it takes the Earth precisely one year to complete such an orbit.

Rotation The spinning of a planet on its axis, the imaginary line passing through its center and both poles; it takes the Earth one calendar day to complete one full rotation.

Solar elevation The number of degrees above the horizon of the noontime Sun, the position at which the solar rays strike the surface at their highest daily angle. Also called the angle of incidence.

Solstice (see summer solstice; winter solstice).

Spring (vernal) equinox n Northern Hemisphere terminology, the equinox that occurs when the Sun's noontime rays strike the Equator vertically on ca. March 21.

Summer solstice The day each year of the poleward extreme in the latitude where the Sun's noontime rays strike the Earth's surface vertically. In the Northern Hemisphere, that latitude is 23½°N (the Tropic of Cancer) and the date is June 22; in the Southern Hemisphere, that latitude is 23½°S (the Tropic of Capricorn) and the date is December 22.

Tropic of Cancer The most northerly latitude (23½°N) where the Sun's noontime rays strike the Equator vertically (June 22).

Tropic of Capricorn   The most southerly latitude (23½°S) where the Sun's noontime rays strike the Earth's surface vertically (December 22).

Winter solstice The day each year of the poleward extreme in latitude in the opposite hemisphere where the Sun's noontime rays strike the Earth's surface vertically. In the Northern Hemisphere, that latitude is 23½°S and the date is December 22; in the Southern Hemisphere, that latitude is 23½°N and the date is June 22.

Zenith The point in the sky directly overhead, 90° above the horizon

---

UNIT OUTLINE

I.   **Earth's planetary motions**
     A. Revolution is movement of a planet around the Sun
               1. perihelion
               2. aphelion
     B. Rotation is the spinning motion of a planet on its own axis
               1. Coriolis force is a product of rotation

II.   **Seasonality**
     A. Axis tilt
               1. plane of the ecliptic
               2. Tropic of Cancer 23½ degrees N latitude
               3. Arctic circle 66½ degrees N latitude
               4. Tropic of Capricorn 23½ degrees S latitude
               5. Antarctic circle 66½ degrees S latitude
     B. Solstices and equinoxes
               1. summer solstice (June 22)
               2. winter solstice (December 22)
               3. earth receives 12 hours light and 12 hours darkness at equinoxes
                         a. vernal equinox (March 21)
                         b. autumnal equinox (September 23)
     C. The four seasons
               1. spring (March 21-June 22)
               2. summer (June 22-September 23)
               3. autumn (September 23- December 22)
               4. winter (December 22-March 21)

III.   **Insolation and its variation**
     A. Circle of illumination
     B. Insolation factors
               1. solar elevation (angle of incidence)
               2. duration of daily sunlight
     C. Global profiles for insolation

REVIEW QUESTIONS

1. Trace the path of the Earth as it travels on its yearly revolution around the Sun. What are the dates of the solstices and the equinoxes?

2. Describe the *Coriolis force*.

SELF-TEST

Multiple-Choice Questions

1. The Earth's axis is always tilted at an angle of _____ to the plane of the ecliptic.

    (a) 23½ degrees (b) 66½ degrees (c) 90 degrees (d) 180 degrees (e) 360 degrees

2. The actual plane in space, tracing Earth's elliptical orbit is the:

    (a) plane of rotation (b) plane of revolution (c) plane of the ecliptic (d) plane of Capricorn (e) plane of the eclipse

3. The point at which the most intense insolation is directly overhead at 90 degrees is:

    (a) the perihelion (b) the north pole (c) the ecliptic (d) the horizon (e) the zenith

4. Autumn's dates range between:

    (a) August 1 - November 30 (b) September 23 - December 22 (c) September 1 - January 1 (d) September 15 - November 1 (e) October 31-November 31)

5. The point during its revolution that the earth is farthest from the Sun is:

    (a) perihelion (b) aphelion (c) isohelion (d) winter (e) autumn

6. The southern-most latitude where the Sun's noon rays can strike the Earth at 90 degrees is:

    (a) Tropic of Cancer (b) Equator (c) Antarctic Circle (d) Tropic of Capricorn (e) South Pole

True-False Questions

__ 1. The angle of solar elevation is one factor that determines annual insolation.
__ 2. Insolation is a contraction for incoming solar radiation.
__ 3. The summer solstice is reached on July 1 of each year.
__ 4. The equinoxes occur halfway between each solstice date.
__ 5. The Earth's axis is always tilted 23½ degrees towards the plane of the ecliptic.
__ 6. The Earth is not always half in light and half in darkness.

UNIT 6: COMPOSITION AND STRUCTURE OF THE ATMOSPHERE

UNIT SUMMARY

Weather represents the short-term conditions in a given place, whereas climate reflects long-term trends of weather patterns for a given location. The atmosphere is divided into the homosphere and the heterosphere; the homosphere contains constant and variable gases. Constant gases include nitrogen and oxygen, while the most important variable gases are carbon dioxide, water vapor, and ozone. The four vital atmospheric cycles are the hydrologic cycle, oxygen cycle, nitrogen cycle, and carbon dioxide cycle. The atmosphere's vertical temperature layering, with increasing height above the Earth, includes the troposphere, stratosphere, mesosphere, and thermosphere. The protective ozone layer, or ozonosphere is contained within the stratosphere. This thin and critical layer is threatened by the presence of the ozone hole centered above Antarctica (see Perspective: Ozone Holes in the Stratosphere). The ozone-depletion crisis has unleashed new research frontiers.

UNIT OBJECTIVES

1. To describe the constituents of the atmosphere and their relative concentrations.

2. To survey the four temperature layers of the atmosphere together with their major properties.

3. To discuss the problem of ozone depletion and its consequences.

GLOSSARY OF KEY TERMS

Aerosols Tiny solid or liquid particles suspended in the atmosphere.

Carbon dioxide cycle Dominated by exchanges occurring between the air and the sea; carbon dioxide is directly absorbed by the ocean from the atmosphere and is released during the photosynthesis of billions of small organisms known as plankton.

Chlorofluorocarbons (CFCs) Ozone-depleting chemicals widely used as coolants, propellents, cleaning solvents, and as components in plastic foam prior to 1990.

Climate The long- term conditions (over at least 30 years) of aggregate weather over a region, summarized by averages and measures of variability; a synthesis of the succession of weather events we have learned to expect at any given location.

Constant gases Atmospheric gases always found in the same proportions; two of them constitute over 99 percent of the air, nitrogen (78 percent) and oxygen (21 percent).

Hydrologic cycle The complex system of exchange involving water in its various forms as it continually circulates among the atmosphere, lithosphere, hydrosphere, biosphere, and cryosphere.

Impurities Solid particles floating in the atmosphere whose quantities vary in time and space; among other things, they play an active role in the formation of raindrops.

Lapse rate The rate of decline in temperature as altitude increases; the average lapse rate of temperature with height in the troposphere is 0.65°C/100 m (3.5°F/1000 ft).

Mesopause The upper boundary of the mesosphere, lying approximately 80 km (50 mi) above the surface.

Mesosphere The third layer of the atmosphere, lying above the troposphere and stratosphere; here temperatures again decline with increasing elevation as they do in the troposphere.

Nitrogen cycle Cycle in which nitrogen-fixing bacteria convert atmospheric nitrogen into the organic compounds in plants. This organic material is consumed by animals (including humans) when the plants are eaten. When animals die, organic proteins are transformed by other bacteria and microorganisms to ammonia, urea, nitrates, and finally back into gaseous nitrogen.

Oxygen cycle Oxygen is put back onto the atmosphere as a by-product of photosynthesis, and is lost when it is inhaled by animals or chemically combined with other materials during oxidation.

Ozone layer Also known as the ozonosphere, the ozone-rich layer of the atmosphere that extends between 15 and 50 km (9 and 31 mi) above the surface; the highest concentrations of ozone are usually found at the level between 20 and 25 km (12 and 15 mi).

Stratopause The upper boundary of the stratosphere, lying approximately 52 km (32 mi) above the surface.

Stratosphere The atmospheric layer lying above the troposphere; here temperatures are either constant or start increasing with altitude.

Temperature inversion Condition in which temperature increases with altitude rather than decreases - a positive lapse rate; it inverts what we, on the surface, believe to be the "normal" behavior of temperature change with increasing height.

Thermosphere The fourth layer of the atmosphere, lying respectively above the troposphere, stratosphere, and mesosphere; in this layer, temperatures increase as altitude increases.

Tropopause   The upper boundary of the troposphere along which temperatures stop decreasing with height.

Troposphere   The bottom layer of the atmosphere in which temperature usually decreases with altitude.

Variable gases   Atmospheric gases present in differing quantities at different times and places; three are essential to human well-being: carbon dioxide, water vapor, and ozone.

Water vapor   The invisible gaseous form of water; the most widely distributed variable gas of the atmosphere.

Weather   The immediate and short-term conditions of the atmosphere that impinge on daily human activities.

UNIT OUTLINE

I. Weather and climate
   A. Weather represents the short-term conditions of the atmospheric system
   B. Climate is the long-term weather averages for a region

II. Contents of the atmosphere
   A. Homosphere (surface to 50-63 mi above)
   B. Heterosphere (above the homosphere)
   C. Homospheric gases
     1.   constant gases
         a. nitrogen (78% of air)
         b. oxygen (21% of air)
         c. respiration
         d. fossil fuels
         e. inert gases
     2. variable gases
         a. carbon dioxide
         b. water vapor
         c. ozone
     3. variable gases in minute quantities
         a. hydrogen
         b. helium
         c. sulfur dioxide
         d. oxides of nitrogen
         e. ammonia
         f. methane
         g. carbon monoxide
   D. Impurities (aerosols)
     1. smoke

2. dust
3. bacteria
4. plant spores
5. salt crystals

E. Atmospheric cycles
    1. atmosphere in dynamic equilibrium
    2. hydrologic cycle
    3. oxygen cycle
    4. nitrogen cycle
    5. carbon dioxide cycle

III. The layered temperature structure of the atmosphere

A. Troposphere (bottom of atmosphere)
B. Tropopause (at approximately 7.5 mi or 12 km above surface)
C. Stratosphere (7.5 mi or 12 km to 31 mi or 50 km)
D. Stratopause (at mi or 50 km above surface)
E. Mesosphere (31 mi or 50 km to 50 mi or 80 km)
F. Mesopause (at 50 mi or 80 km above surface)
G. Thermosphere (top of atmosphere - above 50 mi or 80 km)

REVIEW QUESTIONS

1. What are chlorofluorocarbons and how do they effect the atmosphere?

2. List the constant gases and variable gases of Earth's atmosphere.

3. Define and contrast the terms *weather* and *climate*.

SELF-TEST

Multiple-Choice Questions

1. Which of the following is a constant gas of the atmosphere?

    (a) helium (b) hydrogen (c) carbon dioxide (d) nitrogen (e) water vapor

2. Which of the following is a variable gas of the atmosphere?

    (a) oxygen (b) nitrogen (c) carbon dioxide (d)argon (e) neon

3. The nitrogen cycle is maintained largely by:

(a) mammals (b) plants (c) the atmosphere (d) water (e) rocks

4. In which layer of the atmosphere does the ozone layer lie?

    (a) troposphere (b) thermosphere (c) stratosphere (d) mesosphere (e) mesopause

5. What approximate percentage of air does oxygen comprise?

    (a) 78 % (b) 12 % (c) 50 % (d) 93 % (e) 21%

6. The carbon dioxide cycle consists largely of exchanges between air and:

    (a) land (b) oceans (c) bacteria (d) animals (e) humans

True-False Questions

__ 1. Ozone is confined mainly to the ozonosphere.
__ 2. The hydrologic cycle refers to the cycling of hydrogen through the atmosphere.
__ 3. The mesosphere lies directly above the troposphere.
__ 4. The rate of a decline in temperature with increasing altitude is called the lapse rate.
__ 5. The highest layer of the atmosphere is called the thermosphere.
__ 6. Climate tends to exhibit rapid adjustments in response to atmospheric changes.

UNIT 7: RADIATION AND THE HEAT BALANCE OF THE ATMOSPHERE

UNIT SUMMARY

Radiation is the transmission of electromagnetic waves. The Sun produces shortwave, high-energy radiation, while the Earth radiates longwave, lower-energy radiation. Approximately 31 percent of the Sun's incoming solar energy is received at the Earth's surface as direct radiation. Approximately 30 percent of incoming radiation is reflected and scattered back into space. Some of these scattered rays eventually reach the Earth as diffuse radiation. Earth's atmosphere is heated by longwave radiation from below, and not directly by the Sun. This process is described as the greenhouse effect. Earth's heat balance is maintained by four different kinds of flows -- radiant heat, latent heat, sensible heat, and ground heat. Significant variations in these flows create the global patterns of climate variation.

UNIT OBJECTIVES

1. To understand the Sun-generated flows of energy that affect the Earth and its atmosphere.

2. To link the greenhouse effect to the Earth's habitability and climatic variation.

3. To introduce the Earth's heat flows and their spatial patterns.

GLOSSARY OF KEY TERMS

Albedo The proportion of incoming solar radiation that is reflected by a surface; the whiter the color of the surface (albedo derives from the Latin word *albus*, meaning white), the higher the albedo.

Conduction The transport of heat energy from one molecule to the next.

Convection Spontaneous vertical air movement in the atmosphere.

Counter-radiation Longwave radiation emitted by the Earth's surface that is absorbed by the atmosphere and re-radiated (also as longwave radiation) back down to the surface.

Diffuse radiation The proportion of incoming solar energy (22 percent) that reaches the Earth's surface after first being scattered in the atmosphere by clouds, dust particles, and other airborne materials.

Direct radiation The proportion of incoming solar energy that travels directly to the earth's surface; globally, this averages 31 percent.

Global warming The notion, popular among scientists in the late 1980s and early 1990s, that human fossil-fuel consumption is causing atmospheric warming that will melt glaciers; raise sea levels, and inundate low-lying coastal areas. In the mid-1990s, however, competing theories of climate change are receiving considerable attention and gaining new proponents.

Greenhouse effect The widely used analogy describing the blanket-like effect of the atmosphere in the heating of Earth's surface; shortwave insolation passes through the "glass" of the atmospheric "greenhouse," heats the surface, is converted to longwave radiation that cannot penetrate the "glass," and thereby results in trapping of heat that raises the temperature inside the "greenhouse."

Ground heat flow The heat that is conducted into and out of the Earth's surface; also known as *soil heat flow*.

Longwave radiation Radiation emitted by the Earth, which has much longer wavelengths - and involves much lower energy - than solar (shortwave, higher energy) radiation emitted by the Sun.

Net radiation The amount of radiation left over when all the incoming and outgoing radiation flows have been tallied; totals about one-fourth of the shortwave radiation originally arriving at the top of the atmosphere.

Radiation The transmission of energy in the form of electromagnetic waves; a wide range of energy occurs within the electromagnetic spectrum.

Sensible heat flow The environmental heat we feel or sense on our skins.

Shortwave radiation Radiation coming from the Sun, which has much shorter wavelengths - and involves much higher energy - than the terrestrial (longwave, lower energy) radiation emitted by the Earth.

UNIT OUTLINE

I. The radiation balance
    A. Shortwave radiation emitted from Sun
        1. direct radiation
        2. diffuse radiation
        3. albedo (reflectivity)
    B. Longwave radiation emitted from Earth
        1. counter-radiation
        2. greenhouse effect
    C. Net radiation

II. The Heat Balance
    A. Sensible heat flow
        1. convection
    B. Ground heat flow
        1. conduction
    C. Climates and heat balance
        1. net radiation
        2. latent heat flow
        3. seasonal variation due to location

III. Global distribution of heat flows
    A. Distribution of latent heat loss (Fig. 7.7)
    B. Distribution of sensible heat loss (Fig. 7.8)

REVIEW QUESTIONS

1. Describe generally the global patterns of latent heat loss, using Figure 7.7 from your textbook as a guide.

2. Define the terms direct radiation, diffuse radiation, and net radiation.

SELF-TEST

Multiple-Choice Questions

1. Radiation coming from the Sun is known as:

    (a) shortwave radiation (b) longwave radiation (c) infrared radiation (d) counter-radiaiton (e) gamma radiation

2. Approximately what percentage of direct radiation from the Sun reaches Earth's surface?

    (a) 10 % (b) 30% (c) 90 % (d) 75 % (e) 100%

3. The proportion of radiation that is reflected by a surface is called its:

    (a) insolation (b) solar constant (c) diffuse radiation (d) net radiation (e) albedo

4. When warm air rises in a vertical heat-transfer process, this is known as:

    (a) conduction (b) conversion (c) convection (d) condensation (e) contraction

5. What type of radiation is trapped by the greenhouse effect, consequently producing heat?

   (a) longwave radiation (b) shortwave radiation (c) diffuse radiation (d) net radiation (e) transverse radiation

6. Net radiation is usually greatest at:

   (a) high latitudes (b) low latitudes (c) the poles (d) on mountain peaks (e) sea level

True-False Questions

___ 1. The atmosphere is actually heated from below, not directly from the Sun.
___ 2. Counter-radiation is shortwave radiation.
___ 3. The heat that you feel on your skin is called sensible heat.
___ 4. The largest amount of latent heat loss occurs at Earth's poles.
___ 5. Ground heat flow depends upon conduction.
___ 6. Radiation is the transmission of energy as electromagnetic waves.

UNIT 8: ATMOSPHERIC AND SURFACE TEMPERATURE

UNIT SUMMARY

Temperature is actually the measurement of kinetic energy, or movement of molecules. Several scales are used for temperature measurement, including the Celsius, Fahrenheit, and Kelvin scales. The rate of change of temperature with height is known as the lapse rate, and this rate determines the relative stability or instability of an air mass. Several lapse rates mark temperature differences in the atmosphere, including the dry adiabatic lapse rate (DALR), saturated adiabatic lapse rate (SALR), and the environmental lapse rate (ELR). Temperature inversions are associated with the increase of temperature with increasing height, the opposite of "normal" decreases of temperature with height. Air pollution can become trapped above urban areas when temperature inversions occur, creating smog and dust domes. The horizontal distribution of temperature across landmasses is influenced by insolation, nature of the surface (land or water), altitude, cloud cover, advection, and local currents in coastal areas. Diurnal (daily) and annual cycles of temperature change are observed, and depend on the factors just mentioned. Land and water heat differently, which is expressed by the terms maritime effect and continental effect. A seasonal march of latitudinal temperature belts can be seen most clearly when January and July isotherm patterns are compared, where belts are shifted to the "high-Sun" hemispheres (Northern Hemisphere in July, and Southern Hemisphere in January).

UNIT OBJECTIVES

1. To discuss the measurement and characteristics of temperature and heat.

2. To explain the adiabatic process whereby vertically moving air heats and cools.

3. To discuss the global distribution of temperatures and their variation in time and space.

GLOSSARY OF KEY TERMS

Adiabatic With air being a poor conductor of heat, a parcel of air at one temperature that is surrounded by air at another temperature will neither gain nor lose heat energy over a short period of time; when such non-transfer of heat occurs, the process is called *adiabatic*.

Adiabatic lapse rate When a given mass of air is forced to expand, its temperature decreases. If a parcel of air rises to a higher altitude, it expands and cools adiabatically; its lapse rate is therefore referred to as an *adiabatic lapse rate*.

Advection The horizontal movement of material in the atmosphere.

Annual (temperature) cycle   The pattern of temperature change during the course of a year.

Celsius scale   Metric temperature scale most commonly used throughout the world (the United States is an exception); the boiling point of water is set a 100°C and its freezing point at 0°C.

Continentality (continental effect)   The variation of the continental effect on air temperatures in the interior portions of the world's landmasses; the further the distance from the moderating influences of an ocean (known as the *maritime effect*), the greater the extreme in summer and winter temperatures.

Diurnal (temperature) cycle   The pattern of temperature change during the course of a day.

Dry adiabatic lapse rate (DALR)   The lapse rate of an air parcel not saturated with water vapor: (1°C/100m (5.5°F/1000ft).

Dust dome   The characteristic shape taken by the large quantities of dust and gaseous pollutants in a city's atmosphere.

Environmental lapse rate (ELR)   The non-adiabatic lapse rate at any particular time or place; the troposphere's (non-adiabatic) normal lapse rate averages .65°C/100m (3.5°F/1000ft).

Fahrenheit scale   Temperature scale presently used in the United States; water boils at 212°F (100°C) and freezes at 32°F (0°C).

Isotherms   Lines connecting all points experiencing identical temperatures.

Kelvin scale   The absolute temperature scale used by scientists, based on the temperature of absolute zero (-273°C/-459.4°F); a Kelvin degree is identical to a Celsius degree, so that water boils at 373°K (100°C) and freezes at 273°K.

Kinetic energy   The energy of movement.

Maritime effect   The moderating influence of the ocean on air temperature, which produces cooler summers and milder winters relative to inland locations at similar latitudes.

Saturated adiabatic lapse rate (SALR)   The lapse rate of an air parcel saturated with water vapor in which condensation is occurring; unlike the *dry adiabatic lapse rate* (DALR) the value of the SALR is variable, depending on the amount of water condensed and latent heat released.

Stability (of air) A parcel of air whose vertical movement is such that it returns to its original position after receiving some upward force; however, if an air parcel continues moving upward after receiving such a force, it is said to be unstable.

Temperature The index used to measure the kinetic energy possessed by molecules; the more kinetic energy they have, the faster they move. Temperature, therefore, is an abstract term that describes the energy (speed of movement) of molecules.

Temperature gradient The horizontal rate of temperature change over distance.

Temperature inversion Condition in which temperature increases with altitude rather than decreases - a positive lapse rate; it inverts what we, on the surface believe to be the "normal" behavior of temperature change with increasing height.

Thermometer An instrument for measuring temperature; most commonly, these measurements are made by observing the expansion and contraction of mercury inside a glass tube.

UNIT OUTLINE

I. What is temperature?
    A. Kinetic energy and its measurement

II. Temperature scales
    A. Fahrenheit scale
    B. Celsius scale
    C Kelvin scale

III. The vertical distribution of temperature
    A. Tropospheric temperature and air stability
        1. lapse rate
        2. stability vs. instability
    B. Adiabatic lapse rates
        1. adiabatic processes do not gain heat from or lose heat to surrounding air
        2. air rises, expands, and cools as it moves to higher altitudes; it does not gain heat from or lose heat to surrounding air
        3. dry adiabatic lapse rate (DALR)
        4. environmental lapse rate (ELR)
        5. saturated adiabatic lapse rate (SALR)
    C. Temperature inversions and air pollution
        1. temperature of tropospheric air normally decreases with height, as air rises it expands, and cools
        2. temperature inversions show an increase in tropospheric air temperature with height
        3. In an inversion, warm air lies on top of cool air and traps dust and pollutants

    a. dust domes

    b. smog

IV. The horizontal distribution of temperature

  A. Diurnal cycle

    1. balance between radiation and radiant loss

  B. Annual cycle

    1. similar balance as diurnal cycle, between radiation and radiant loss

  C. Land/water heating differences

    1. land requires less time to heat and cool than water

    2. land has greater annual temperature ranges than water

      a. maritime effect

      b. continental effect

    3. air temperature is affected by heat balance and advection, the horizontal movement of air by wind

  D. Global temperature variations

    1. isotherms, lines connecting all points with the same temperature, used for maps

    2. temperature gradient is the horizontal rate of temperature change over distance

    3. flow patterns associated with ocean currents and air movement

REVIEW QUESTIONS

1. Compare and contrast the dry adiabatic lapse rate (DALR), saturated adaibatic lapse rate (SALR), and environmental lapse rate (ELR).

2. Discuss the general trends of the seasonal march of the latitudinal temperature belts.

3. Define the term temperature and discuss what it actually measures.

SELF-TEST

Multiple-Choice Questions

1. On the Kelvin temperature scale, what is absolute zero in degrees Celsius?

  (a) 273 degrees C (b) -273 degrees C (c) 0 degrees C (d) -32 degrees C (e) -373 degrees C

2. In what process is heat given off when water changes from a gas to a liquid?

   (a) evaporation (b) inversion (c) condensation (d) displacement (e) sublimation

3. When an air parcel cools with height at a constant rate, and is not saturated with water vapor, this phenomenon is:

   (a) temperature inversion (b) the saturated adiabatic lapse rate (c) the environmental lapse rate (d) the dry adiabatic lapse rate (e) unsaturated temperature inversion

4. A thermometer actually measures:

   (a) gravitational energy (b) potential energy (c) relative energy (d) displaced energy (e) kinetic energy

5. In July, toward which hemisphere do latitudinal temperature belts shift?

   (a) Northern Hemisphere (b) Southern Hemisphere (c) no shift occurs (d) water hemisphere (e) land hemisphere

6. A dust dome is the result of:

   (a) increased air pollution (b) a traveling dust cloud (c) a temperature inversion (d) a solar eclipse (e) acid rain

True-False Questions

___ 1. In a temperature inversion, tropospheric temperature decreases with height.
___ 2. A temperature gradient is the horizontal rate of temperature change over distance.
___ 3. Advection is the vertical movement of air through the atmosphere with wind.
___ 4. The oceans have a moderating effect on air temperature.
___ 5. The lapse rate determines stability of air.
___ 6. The air above an ocean is warmer in summer and cooler in winter than air over land at the same latitude.

UNIT SUMMARY

Wind is the movement of air relative to Earth's surface. Gravity is the primary force exerting influence on air molecules. The combined weight of air molecules exerts a force on Earth's surface, which is defined as pressure. Pressure decreases rapidly with increasing height above the surface of Earth. Circulation of the atmosphere is caused by two basic factors, the unequal heat received at different latitudes, and Earth's rotation on its axis. Because Earth is a rotating object, it experiences the Coriolis force, which deflects moving objects from a straight-line path. The pressure-gradient force (difference in surface pressure between two locations) is the true trigger for air movement. Many large- and small-scale wind systems are seen globally. Local wind systems include sea/land breeze systems, mountain/valley breeze systems, katabatic winds, Chinook winds, and Santa Ana winds.

UNIT OBJECTIVES

1. To explain atmospheric pressure and its altitudinal variation.

2. To relate atmospheric pressure to windflow at the surface and aloft.

3. To apply these relationships to the operation of local wind systems.

GLOSSARY OF KEY TERMS

Anticyclone An atmospheric high-pressure cell involving the divergence of air, which subsides at and flows spirally out of the center; the isobars around an anticyclone are generally circular in shape, with their values increasing toward the center. In the Northern Hemisphere, winds flow clockwise around an anticyclone; in the Southern Hemisphere, winds flow counterclockwise around an anticyclone.

Barometer Instrument that measures atmospheric pressure; invented by Torricelli in 1643.

Chinook wind Name given to the *foehn* winds that affect the leeward areas of mountain zones in the western plateaus of North America.

Cold-air drainage A category of local-scale wind systems governed by the downward oozing of heavy, dense, cold air along steep slopes under the influence of gravity; produces katabatic winds (such as southeastern France's *mistral*) that are fed by massive pools of icy air that accumulate over such major upland regions as the Alps and the Rocky Mountains.

Coriolis force   The force that, owing to the rotation of the Earth, tends to deflect all objects moving over the surface of the Earth away from their original path. In the absence of any other forces, the deflection is to the right in the Northern Hemisphere and to the left in the Southern Hemisphere; the higher the latitude, the stronger the deflection.

Cyclone   An atmospheric low-pressure cell involving the convergence of air, which flows into and spirally rises at the center; the isobars around a cyclone are generally circular in shape, with their values decreasing toward the center. In the Northern Hemisphere, winds flow counterclockwise around a cyclone; in the Southern Hemisphere, winds flow clockwise around a cyclone.

Frictional force   The drag that slows the movement of air molecules in contact with, or close to, the Earth's surface. Varies with the "roughness" of the surface; there is less friction with movement across a smooth water surface than across the ragged skyline of a city center.

Geostrophic wind   A wind that results when the Coriolis and pressure-gradient forces balance themselves out; follows a relatively straight path that minimizes deflection and lies parallel to the isobars.

Isobar A line connecting all points having the identical atmospheric pressure.

Katabatic wind   The winds that result from cold-air drainage; especially prominent under clear conditions where the edges of highlands plunge sharply toward lower-lying terrain.

Land breeze   An offshore airflow affecting a coastal zone, resulting from a nighttime pressure gradient that steers local winds from cooler (higher-pressure) land surface to the warmer (lower-pressure) sea surface.

Leeward   The protected side of a topographic barrier with respect to the winds that flow across it; often refers to the area downwind from the barrier as well, which is said to be in the "shadow" of that highland zone.

Pressure   The weight of a column of air at a given location, determined by the force of gravity and the composition and properties of the atmosphere at that location. Standard sea-level air pressure produces a reading of 760mm (29.92 in) on the mercury barometer; in terms of weight, it is also given as 1013.25 millibars (mb) or 14.7 lb per sq in.

Pressure-gradient force   The difference in surface pressure over a given distance between two locations is called the pressure gradient; when that pressure gradient exists, it acts as a force that causes air to move (as wind) from the place of higher pressure to that of lower pressure.

Santa Ana wind A hot, dry, *foehn*-type wind that occasionally affects Southern California; its unpleasantness is heightened by the downward funneling of this airflow from the high inland desert through narrow passes in the mountains that line the Pacific coast.

Sea breeze An onshore airflow affecting a coastal zone, resulting from a daytime pressure gradient that steers local winds from the cooler (higher-pressure) sea surface onto the warmer (lower-pressure) land surface.

Wind The movement of air relative to the Earth's surface; winds are always named according to the direction from which they blow.

Wind chill temperature (WCT) index An index that tells us subjectively how cold we would feel under given combinations of wind speed and air temperature.

Windward The exposed, upwind side of a topographic barrier that faces the winds that flow across it.

UNIT OUTLINE

I. Atmospheric pressure
    A. Wind is created by an imbalance of forces that act on air molecules
    B. Pressure is a result of the combined weight of air molecules in a given area exerting a force
        1. standard sea level air pressure is 1013 millibars
    C. Atmospheric pressure and altitude
        1. air pressure is highest at low altitudes, and lowest at high altitudes

II. Air movement in the atmosphere
    A. Causes of atmospheric circulation
        1. unequal heat energy distribution
        2. rotation of Earth
        3. Coriolis force is the deflective force that acts on rotating objects
        4. winds are always named for the direction from which they come
    B. Forces on an air molecule
        1. pressure-gradient force due to gravity
        2. Coriolis force greatest at poles
        2. frictional force near Earth's surface slows molecules

III. Large- and smaller-scale wind systems
    A. Geostrophic winds
        1. follow relatively straight path, deflection minimized in upper atmosphere
        2. flows parallel to isobars
    B. Frictional surface winds
        1. near Earth's surface, friction reduces wind speed and alters its direction

2. surface winds converge towards a cyclone (low pressure cell); air rises in center
3. surface winds diverge away from an anticyclone (high pressure cell); air subsides in center

IV. Local wind systems
A. Sea/land breeze systems
    1. during the day, warmer, lower pressure air is over land -- air moves from high to low pressure, from water to land
    2. at night, warmer, lower pressure air is over water, so air flows from land to sea
B. Mountain/valley breeze systems
    1. during the day, warmer, lower pressure air develops on mountain slopes, triggering a valley breeze
    2. at night, mountain slopes cool more rapidly, creating higher pressure on slopes than in the valley, and a mountain breeze results
C. Other local wind systems
    1. cold air drainage on steep slopes cause katabatic winds
    2. local winds created by forced passage of air across mountains
        a. Chinook winds
        b. Santa Ana winds

REVIEW QUESTIONS

1. What are katabatic winds? Santa Ana winds? Chinook winds?

2. Describe the general formation of valley and mountain breezes.

3. Define the terms windward and leeward, and describe the role that winds play in our lives.

SELF-TEST

Multiple-Choice Questions

1. Standard sea level air pressure is equivalent to:

    (a) 1013 mb (b) 500 mb (c) -1013 mb (d) 273 mb (e) 760 mb

2. Air circulates due to Earth's rotational forces and which other factor?

(a) seasonality (b) equal heating at different latitudes (c) unequal heating at different latitudes (d) saturation of air (e) equal heating at the poles

3. In the Northern Hemisphere, the Coriolis force deflects moving air:

    (a) to the left (b) to the right (c) does not deflect moving air (d) to both the left and right (e) upward and downward

4. Air converging toward a cyclone (low pressure cell) then:

    (a) rises vertically in the cell (b) sinks vertically in the cell (c) is deflected away from the cyclone (d) is transported horizontally across the cyclone (e) remains stationary in the center of the cyclone

5. A sea breeze generally occurs:

    (a) during the night (b) when the Coriolis force subsides (c) in winter (d) in summer (e) during the day

6. Cold air drainage results in the formation of:

    (a) a Coriolis wind (b) a geostrophic wind (c) a sea breeze (d) a katabatic wind (e) a cyclone

True-False Questions

__ 1. As altitude increases, air pressure increases.
__ 2. The pressure-gradient force actually triggers air movement.
__ 3. Geostrophic winds are most common near the Earth's surface.
__ 4. An anticyclone is a low pressure cell.
__ 5. Frictional force does not affect speed of surface winds.
__ 6. Winds are always named according to the direction from which they come.

UNIT 10: CIRCULATION PATTERNS
OF THE ATMOSPHERE

UNIT SUMMARY

The primary cause of atmospheric circulation is heat imbalance between polar and tropical regions. The Equatorial Low, or Inter-Tropical Convergence Zone (ITCZ) is produced by year-round heating of the equatorial region. Warm air rises in the ITCZ, and then flows poleward, cools, and subsides around 30 degrees north and south latitude at the Subtropical Highs. Surface air returning equatorward from the Subtropical Highs forms the Northeast and Southeast Trades. The Polar Highs are large high-pressure cells centered over each pole, and air flowing out of them toward the Equator gets sharply deflected, and becomes the Polar Easterlies. The Polar Front occurs where the Polar Easterlies meet the Westerlies, creating a belt of low pressure, called the Upper-Midlatitude Low. The general, or primary circulation of the atmosphere includes wind belts and semipermanent pressure cells: the ITCZ, the Bermuda and Pacific Highs, the Canadian and Siberian Highs, and the Aleutian, Icelandic, and Southern Hemisphere Upper-Midlatitude Lows. The regional, or secondary circulation consists of shifting surface windbelts, such as the Asian monsoon phenomenon. Windflow in the upper atmosphere is geostrophic, or perpendicular to the pressure gradient. Zonal flow dominates the upper atmosphere, and is westerly in its configuration in both hemispheres. Azonal flow helps to correct the latitudinal heat imbalance by causing meridional (north-south) air exchange.

UNIT OBJECTIVES

1. To develop a simple model of the global atmospheric circulation.

2. To discuss the pressure systems and wind belts that constitute that model circulation, and the complications that arise when the model is compared to the actual atmospheric circulation.

3. To introduce the basic workings of the upper atmosphere's circulation.

GLOSSARY OF KEY TERMS

Azonal flow The meridional (north-south) flow of upper atmospheric winds (poleward of 15 degrees of latitude), particularly the subtropical and Polar Front jet streams; periodic departures from the zonal (west-to-east) flow of these air currents are important because they help to correct the heat imbalance between the polar and equatorial regions.

Equatorial low The Inter-Tropical Convergence Zone (ITCZ) or thermal low-pressure belt of rising air that straddles the equatorial latitudinal zone; fed by the windflows of the converging Northeast and Southeast Trades.

General circulation The global atmospheric circulation system of windbelts and semipermanent pressure cells. In each hemisphere, the windbelts include the Trades, Westerlies, and Polar Easterlies. The pressure cells include the Equatorial Low (ITCZ), and, in each hemisphere, the Subtropical High, Upper-Midlatitude Low, and Polar High.

Inter-Tropical Convergence Zone (ITCZ) The thermal low-pressure belt of rising air that straddles the equatorial latitudinal zone, which is fed by the windflows of the converging Northeast and Southeast Trades.

Jet stream The two concentrated, high-altitude, west-to-east flowing "rivers" of air that are major features of the upper atmospheric circulation system poleward of latitude 15 degrees in both the Northern and Southern Hemispheres; because of their general occurrence above the subtropical and subpolar latitudes, they are respectively known as the subtropical jet stream and the Polar Front jet stream. A third such corridor of high-altitude, concentrated windflow is the tropical easterly jet stream, a major feature of the upper-air circulation equatorward of 15 degrees North. This third jet stream, however, flows in the opposite, east-to-west direction and occurs only above the tropics of the Northern Hemisphere.

Monsoon Derived from the Arabic word for "season," a regional windflow that streams onto and off certain landmasses on a seasonal basis; the moist onshore winds of summer bring the *wet monsoon*, whereas the offshore winds of winter are associated with the *dry monsoon*.

Northeast Trades The surface wind belt that generally lies between the Equator and 30 degrees North; the Coriolis force deflects equatorward-flowing winds to the right, thus recurving north winds into northeast winds.

Polar Easterlies The high-latitude wind belt in each hemisphere, lying between 60 and 90 degrees of latitude; the Coriolis force is strongest in these polar latitudes, and the equatorward-moving air that emanates from the Polar High is sharply deflected in each hemisphere to form the Polar Easterlies.

Polar Front The latitudinal zone, lying at approximately 60 degrees north and south, where the equatorward-flowing Polar Easterlies meet the poleward-flowingWesterlies; the warmer Westerlies are forced to rise above the colder Easterlies, producing a semipermanent surface low-pressure belt known as the *Upper-Midlatitude Low*.

Polar High Large semipermanent high-pressure cell centered approximately over the pole in the uppermost latitudes of each hemisphere.

Southeast Trades The surface wind belt that generally lies between the Equator and 30 degrees South; the Coriolis force deflects equatorward-flowing winds to the left, thus recurving south winds into southeast winds.

Subtropical High The semipermanent belt of high pressure that is found at approximately 30 degrees of latitude in both the Northern and Southern Hemispheres; the subsiding air at its center flows outward toward both the lower and higher latitudes.

Upper-Midlatitude Low The semipermanent surface low-pressure belt, lying at approximately 60 degrees north and south, where the equatorward-flowing Polar Easterlies meet the poleward-flowing Westerlies; at this sharp atmospheric boundary, known as the Polar Front, the warmer Westerlies are forced to rise above the colder Easterlies.

Westerlies The two broad midlatitude belts of prevailing westerly winds, lying between approximately 30 and 60 degrees in both hemispheres; fed by the Coriolis-force-deflected, poleward windflow emanating from the Subtropical High on the equatorward margin of the Westerlies wind belt.

Zonal flow The westerly flow of winds that dominates the upper atmospheric circulation system poleward of 15 degrees latitude in each hemisphere.

UNIT OUTLINE

I. A model of the surface circulation
   A. The Equatorial Low and Subtropical High
      1. Equatorial Low (ITCZ) is a region of low pressure and rising air
      2. Air from ITCZ rises, expand, cools, and subsides in the high pressure Subtropical Highs at 30 degrees N and S
   B. The Trade Winds and the Westerlies
      1. Northeast trades of northern hemisphere created by air returning toward Equator, deflected to the right
      2. Southeast Trades of Southern Hemisphere created by air returning toward Equator, deflected to the left
      3. Westerlies from 30 to 60 degrees N and S produced by air moving poleward from Subtropical Highs
   C. The Polar high, Polar Easterlies, and Polar Front
      1. Polar Highs are pressure cells over each pole
      2. Air moving toward Equator from poles directed to create Polar Easterlies
      3. Polar Front (upper mid-latitude low) created by converging air from the Polar Easterlies and the Westerlies (Fig. 10.2)

II. Actual surface circulation pattern
   A. Actual circulation more complex than idealized models
   B. The Equatorial Low (ITCZ)
      1. The ITCZ migrates into the "summer" hemisphere more prominently over land than water

2. ITCZ migrates generally less towards Southern Hemisphere because there are fewer landmasses

C. The Bermuda and Pacific highs
1. Subtropical Highs are actually more cellular than belt-like
2. Bermuda (Azores) High in North Atlantic
3. Pacific High in North Pacific

D. The Canadian and Siberian Highs
1. The Polar High in the Northern Hemisphere actually consists of two cells
a. weaker Canadian High
b. stronger Siberian High

E. The Aleutian, Icelandic, and Southern Hemisphere Upper Mid-latitude Lows (Polar Fronts)
1. Polar Front (Upper Mid-latitude Low) in Northern Hemisphere in January is actually two cells
a. Aleutian Low in North Pacific
b. Icelandic Low in North Atlantic

III. Secondary surface circulation: monsoonal windflows
A. Monsoon is a regional wind that blows onto and off certain land areas seasonally
1. In coastal Asia, summer wind reversal brings moist onshore winds: the wet monsoon
2. In coastal Asia, winter offshore winds produce the dry monsoon

IV. Circulation of the upper atmosphere
A. Zonal flow maintains westerly (west-to-east) winds
B. Jet streams located at subtropics and polar fronts, due to pressure gradients in upper atmosphere
C. Azonal flow to correct global heat imbalance
1. Troughs of low pressure
2. Ridges of high pressure

REVIEW QUESTIONS

1. Describe the Bermuda and Pacific Highs, using Fig. 10.3 in your textbook as a guide.

2. Compare and contrast the Polar Easterlies, Polar Highs, and the Polar Fronts.

3. What would the hypothetical atmospheric circulation patterns look like on an Earth that had no topographic relief and did not rotate? Use Fig. 10.1 in your textbook as a reference.

SELF-TEST

Multiple-Choice Questions

1. The Equatorial Low (ITCZ) is an area of :

    (a) rising air (b) sinking air (c) cooled air (d) relatively stationary air (e) polluted air

2. The Westerlies are located in both the Northern and Southern Hemispheres in belts at:

    (a)60-90 degrees N&S (b) 30-60 degrees N&S (c)30-90 degrees N&S (d)10 degrees N&S (e) 0-5 degrees N&S

3. The upper atmosphere is dominated by a westerly air movement called:

    (a) troughs (b) azonal flow (c) ridges (d) solar flow (e) zonal flow

4. In summer in coastal Asia, reversing winds bring the:

    (a) dry monsoon (b) wet monsoon (c) chinook winds (d) Aleutian low (e) Aleutian high

5. The subtropical highs at 30 degrees north and south latitudes are regions where air:

    (a) is warmed and subsides (b) is cooled and rises (c) is cooled and subsides (d) is warmed and rises (e) is fairly stationary

6. The boundary in both hemispheres where air converges from the Polar Easterlies and the Westerlies is the:

    (a) subtropical high (b) polar front (c) polar high (d) ITCZ (e) midlatitude high

True-False Questions

__ 1. The ITCZ is a region of low pressure.
__ 2. A polar high is only found in the Northern Hemisphere.
__ 3. Air deflected sharply from the polar highs forms the polar easterlies.
__ 4. The ITCZ migrates seasonally less into the Southern Hemisphere than the Northern Hemisphere.
__ 5. The Canadian High is stronger than the Siberian High.
__ 6. The jet streams are tube-like areas of westerly air flow in the upper atmosphere.

UNIT 11: HYDROSPHERE: CIRCULATION OF THE WORLD OCEAN

UNIT SUMMARY

Ocean currents form the counterpart to the atmospheric wind belts and semipermanent pressure cells. The majority of heat from equatorial to polar regions is transported in the atmosphere; surface ocean currents transfer the remainder of the heat from low latitudes. Ocean currents are mainly generated by the frictional drag of surface winds that blow above them; they can also be generated by relative differences in sea level, density variation in seawater, and differences in water salinity. Gyres, which can be large enough to encompass an entire ocean basin, are characterized by continuous clockwise or counterclockwise circulation. In both the Northern and Southern Hemispheres, subtropical gyres dominate surface ocean flow. Subtropical gyres are maintained by the wind belts that exist above them in the atmosphere. Tropical gyres are reinforced by the Northeast and Southeast Trades. Upwelling is characterized by the rising of cold deep sea water, and subsequent deflection of ocean currents from coastlines. Deep-sea water movement is characterized by thermohaline circulation, which is regulated by differences in water temperature and/or salinity. The thermohaline circulation is represented as a "global conveyor belt" which moves deep-sea water from high to low latitudes. The El Niño-Southern Oscillation is a phenomenon of low-latitude waters of the eastern Pacific. Abnormally warm sea surface waters causes currents to reverse direction as well as the winds that blow above them. During periodic strong El Niños, weather changes in many parts of the world are pronounced.

UNIT OBJECTIVES

1. To relate the surface oceanic circulation to the general circulation of the atmosphere.

2. To describe the major currents that constitute the oceanic circulation.

3. To demonstrate the role of oceanic circulation in the transport of heat at the Earth's surface.

GLOSSARY OF KEY TERMS

Drift A term often used as a synonym for an ocean current, whose rate of movement usually lags well behind the average speeds of surface winds blowing in the same direction; currents are characterized by a slow and steady movement that very rarely exceeds 8 kph (5 mph).

El Niño A periodic, large-scale, abnormal warming of the sea surface in the low latitudes of the eastern Pacific Ocean that produces a (temporary) reversal of surface ocean currents and airflows throughout the equatorial Pacific; these regional events have global implications, disturbing normal weather patterns in many parts of the world.

ENSO Acronym for El Niño-Southern Oscillation; the reversal of the flow of ocean currents and prevailing winds in the equatorial Pacific Ocean that disturbs global weather patterns.

Global conveyor belt Ocean circulation which moves masses of cold, deep-sea water from high to lower latitudes (see Fig. 11.7).

Gyre The cell-like circulation of surface currents that often encompasses an entire ocean basin; for example, the subtropical gyre of the North Atlantic Ocean consists of the huge loop formed by four individual, continuous legs - the North Equatorial, Gulf Stream, North Atlantic Drift, and Canaries currents.

La Nina The lull or cool ebb in low-latitude Pacific Ocean surface temperatures that occurs between El Niño peaks of anomalous sea-surface warming.

North Atlantic Oscillation (NAO) The alternating pressure gradient between the Icelandic Low and the Bermuda High, especially its eastern segment, the Azores High. See Perspectives: The North Atlantic Oscillation.

Ocean current Large-scale movements of ocean water.

Southern Oscillation The periodic, anomalous reversal of the pressure zones in the atmosphere overlying the equatorial Pacific; associated with the occurrence of the El Niño phenomenon. As the sea-surface temperatures change and water currents reverse, corresponding shifts occur in the windflows above.

Subpolar gyre Oceanic circulation loop found only in the Northern Hemisphere; its southern limb is a warm current steered by prevailing westerly winds, but the complex, cold returning flows to the north are complicated by sea-ice blockages and the configuration of landmasses vis-a-vis outlets for the introduction of frigid Arctic waters.

Subtropical gyre Circulates around the Subtropical High that is located above the center of the ocean basin; dominates the oceanic circulation of both hemispheres, flowing clockwise in the Northern Hemisphere and counterclockwise in the Southern Hemisphere.

Thermohaline circulation Describes the deep-sea system of oceanic circulation, which is controlled by differences in the temperature and salinity of subsurface water masses.

Tropical gyre Narrow, low-latitude oceanic circulation loop, in both the Northern and Southern Hemisphere, comprised of the equatorial currents and returning counter-currents; reinforced by the converging winds of the Northeast and Southeast Trades.

Upwelling The rising of cold water from the ocean depths to the surface; affects the local climatic environment because cold water lowers air temperatures and the rate of evaporation.

UNIT OUTLINE

I. Surface currents
A. Ocean currents are large-scale water movements, the counterparts of wind belts and pressure cells
B. A vital role of ocean currents is to adjust Earth's surface heat imbalance
C. "Warm" currents travel from tropics to poles
D. "Cold" currents travel from poles to tropics
E. Most currents referred to as drifts because they move slowly and steadily

II. Generation of ocean currents
A. Main trigger is the frictional drag of winds that blow across the ocean surface
B. Water piles up along up along coastlines, creating higher sea levels than surrounding water
C. Variation in density of seawater; cool water sinks and spreads toward the Equator
D. Variation in salinity of seawater; saltier/denser water sinks and spreads toward the Equator

III. Flow behavior of ocean currents
A. Meanders of currents become such pronounced curves, they can detach into eddies
B. Gyre circulations
    1. gyres are continuously moving loops that can be clockwise or counterclockwise
    2. created by prevailing winds, the Coriolis force, and landmasses
    3. subtropical gyres in both hemispheres around subtropical highs
    4. tropical gyres from equatorial currents
    5. subpolar gyres in northern hemisphere
    6. upwelling in subtropical gyres is the rising of deep, cold water at coastlines in the eastern parts of ocean basins
C. The geography of ocean currents
    1. Pacific Ocean currents dominated by subtropical gyres
    2. Atlantic Ocean currents dominated by subtropical gyres
    3. Indian Ocean currents controlled by both subtropical and equatorial gyres

III. Deep-sea currents
A. Deep-sea movement is thermohaline circulation
    1. dependent upon temperature and salinity
    2. dominant global movement is flow from higher to lower latitudes

IV. The coupled ocean-atmosphere system
    A. Larger amounts of heat moved by ocean at lower and middle latitudes
    B. Sea is a vast heat reservoir
    C. Latent heat from evaporation of oceans powers the general circulation of the atmosphere

V. El Niño - Southern Oscillation
    A. Temperature anomalies in eastern equatorial waters of the Pacific Ocean
    B. Reversal of ocean currents and atmospheric conditions
    C. Disturbance of weather patterns, local fishing industries

REVIEW QUESTIONS

1. Describe the general features of the North Atlantic Oscillation.

2. What is meant by the term *global conveyor belt*?

3. Describe upwelling and list some its consequences on weather patterns.

SELF-TEST

Multiple-Choice Questions

1. Oceanic circulation can be produced by a variation in all of the following except:

    (a) density (b) salinity (c) sea level (d) relative size of water molecules (e) frictional drag

2. Thermohaline circulation characterizes:

    (a) polar currents (b) deep-sea currents (c) surface currents (d) currents only in the Northern Hemisphere (e) currents only in the Southern Hemisphere

3. What is the term for the rising of deep, cold ocean water that is diverted by the Coriolis force near coastlines?

    (a) upwelling (b) subduction (c) monsoon (d) reverse drift (e) upduction

4. The oceans transport approximately how much heat from the low and higher latitudes?

(a) 13% (b) under 1% (c) 97% (d) 52% (e) 25%

5. The El Niño-Southern Oscillation (ENSO) occurs when:

    (a) equatorial winds and water flow reverse (b) subtropical winds reverse
    (b) drought occurs (d) equatorial winds cease (e) equatorial currents cease

6. The latent heat of seawater is released in the process of:

    (a) upwelling (b) condensation (c) evaporation (d) El Niño (e) sublimation

True-False Questions

__ 1. There is at least one subtropical gyre in each hemisphere.
__ 2. The Atlantic Ocean really consists of two ocean basins.
__ 3. Eddies occur when a current develops meanders that detach.
__ 4. Upwelling has no effect upon El Niño.
__ 5. Tropical gyres are reinforced by the Northeast and Southeast Trade Winds.
__ 6. Most of the poleward movement of heat is done by the atmosphere.

UNIT 12: ATMOSPHERIC MOISTURE
AND THE WATER BALANCE

UNIT SUMMARY

Water has the ability to exist in the solid, liquid, and gaseous states. When water changes state, there are associated latent heats: the heat involved in melting is the latent heat of fusion, and the heat required for evaporation to occur is the latent heat of vaporization. Water vapor is measured in terms of vapor pressure, relative and specific humidity, and the mixing ratio. The hydrologic cycle is responsible for continuously moving water from the atmosphere to the land, plants, ocean, and freshwater bodies--and ultimately back to the atmosphere. Evaporation requires both a vapor-pressure gradient and a heat source. Evapotranspiration is the passage of moisture from the land to the atmosphere through evaporation and transpiration, and includes potential and actual evapotranspiration (PE and AE). Clouds are visible masses of suspended water droplets and/or ice crystals. Clouds are classified based on structure, appearance, and altitude. These classifications include the general groupings of stratus, cumulus, and cirrus clouds. Precipitation includes rain, snow sleet, freezing rain, and hail. Earth's water balance is measured at its surface, and is the net difference between all forms of precipitation (water gain) and the sum of runoff and evapotranspiration (water loss). Near the Equator, stronger radiant energy leads to high evaporation rates and large amounts of precipitation. In higher midlatitudes, there is a moderate amount of precipitation, and less solar energy available for evaporation. In high latitudes cold air cannot hold much water vapor, and there is little precipitation. Most large population clusters exist where there are neither large surpluses or deficits in the water balance.

UNIT OBJECTIVES

1. To discuss the various forms of water and to understand the important heat transfers that accompany changes of these physical states.

2. To explain the various measures of atmospheric humidity, and how they are related, and the processes responsible for condensation.

3. To outline the hydrologic cycle and the relative amounts of water that flow within this cycle.

4. To introduce the concept of precipitation.

5. To describe the Earth's surface water balance and its variations.

GLOSSARY OF KEY TERMS

Actual evapotranspiration (AE) The amount of water that can be lost to the atmosphere from a land surface with any particular soil-moisture conditions.

Cirrus clouds The cloud-type category that encompasses thin, wispy, streak-like clouds that consist of ice particles, rather than water droplets; occur only at altitudes higher than 6000 m (20,000 ft).

Cloud A visible mass of suspended, minute water droplets or ice crystals.

Condensation The process by which a substance is transformed from the gaseous to the liquid state.

Condensation nuclei Small airborne particles around which liquid droplets can form when water vapor condenses; almost always present in the atmosphere in the form of dust or salt particles.

Cumulus clouds The cloud-category type that encompasses thick, puffy, billowing masses that often develop to great heights; subclassified according to height.

Dew The fine water droplets that condense on surfaces at and near the ground when saturated air is cooled; the source of this condensate is excess water vapor beyond the saturation level of that air parcel, whose capacity to contain water decreases as its temperature drops.

Dew point The temperature at which air becomes saturated and below which condensation forms.

Evaporation Also known as vaporization, the process by which water changes from the liquid to the gaseous (water vapor) state; it takes 597 cal of heat energy to change the state of 1 g (.04 oz) of water at 0°C (32°F) from a liquid to a gas.

Evapotranspiration The combined processes by which water (1) evaporates from the land surface and (2) passes into the atmosphere through the leaf pores of plants (transpiration).

Freezing The process by which a substance is transformed from the liquid to the solid state.

Hydrologic cycle The complex system of exchange involving water in its various forms as it continually circulates among the atmosphere, lithosphere, hydrosphere, cryosphere, and biosphere.

Latent heat of fusion The heat energy involved melting, the transformation of a solid into a liquid; a similar amount of heat is given off when a liquid freezes into a solid.

Latent heat of vaporization The heat energy involved in the transformation of a liquid into a gas or vice versa.

Melting A change from the solid state to the liquid state; at 0°C (32°F) it takes ca. 80 cal of heat energy to change 1 g (.04 oz) of water from a solid into a liquid.

Potential evapotranspiration(PE) The maximum amount of water that can be lost to the atmosphere from a land surface with abundant available water.

Precipitation Any liquid water or ice that falls to the Earth's surface through the atmosphere (rain, snow, sleet, and hail).

Relative humidity The proportion of water vapor present in a parcel of air relative to the maximum amount of water vapor that air could hold at the same temperature.

Runoff The removal - as overland flow via the network of streams and rivers - of the surplus precipitation at the land surface that does not infiltrate the soil or accumulate on the ground through surface detention.

Stratus clouds The cloud-type category that encompasses layered and fairly thin clouds that cover an extensive geographic area; subclassified according to height.

Sublimation   The process whereby a solid can change directly into a gas; the reverse process is also called sublimation (or deposition); the heat required to produce these transformations is the sum of latent heats of fusion and vaporization.

Water balance Analogous to an accountant's record (which tallies income, expenditures, and the bottom-line balance), the measurement of the inflow (precipitation), outflow (evapotranspiration), and net annual surplus or deficit of water at a given location.

Water vapor The invisible gaseous form of water; the most widely distributed variable gas of the atmosphere.

UNIT OUTLINE

I. Physical properties of water
    A. Ability to exist as a solid, liquid, or gas
    B. Melting: solid to liquid
        1. latent heat of fusion
    C. Evaporation: liquid to vapor
        1. latent heat of vaporization
    D. Sublimation: solid to vapor
        1. sum of latent heat of fusion and vaporization
    E. Condensation: vapor to liquid
    F. Freezing: liquid to solid
    G. Deposition (or also sublimation): vapor to solid

II. Measuring water vapor
  A. Vapor pressure is the pressure exerted by molecules of water vapor in the air
  B. Saturated air is air holding all possible water vapor molecules at a given temperature
  C. Dew is formed by condensation of over-saturated air
    1. the dew point is the temperature at which air becomes saturated, and below it condensation will form
  D. Relative humidity shows how close a parcel of air is to its dewpoint
    1. a proportion of water vapor present in air relative to the maximum amount of water vapor it can hold
  E. Specific humidity and the mixing ratio
    1. specific humidity is the ratio of the weight of water vapor in the air to the combined weight of the vapor plus air itself
    2. Mixing ratio is the ratio of the mass of water vapor to the mass of the dry air containing the vapor
      a. psychrometer
      b. wet-bulb temperature
      c. dry-bulb temperature

III. The hydrologic cycle
  A. Moves water from the air to the land, plants, oceans, freshwater bodies, and back to air
  B. Precipitation is any water or ice that falls from the atmosphere to Earth's surface
    1. transpiration
    2. evapotranspiration
    3. runoff
    4. advection

IV. Evaporation
  A. Occurs when heat energy is available at the water surface and the air is not saturated
    1. a vapor-pressure gradient exists
  B. Evapotranspiration is transfer of moisture from land to the atmosphere by a combination of evaporation and transpiration (photosynthesis)
    1. potential evapotranspiration (PE)
    2. actual evapotranspiration (AE)

V. Condensation and clouds
  A. Clouds are masses of suspended water droplets or ice crystals
  B. Cloud formation requires saturated air and a large amount of condensation nuclei
  C. Cloud classification
    1. stratus
      a. nimbostratus
      b. cirrostratus

    2. cumulus

        a. stratocumulus

        b. altocumulus

        c. cirrocumulus

        d. cumulonimbus

    3. cirrus

VI. Precipitation

    A. Formation processes

        1. ice-crystal process

        2. coalescence process

    B. Forms of precipitation

        1. rain

        2. snow

        3. sleet

        4. freezing rain (glaze)

        5. hail

VII. The surface water balance

    A. Range of water balance conditions

        1. runoff cannot exceed precipitation in a given area

    B. Water balance variations and latitude

        1. evaporation greatest in subtropical and low latitudes

        2. water surplus in upper midlatitudes

        3. precipitation, runoff, and evaporation lowest in highest latitudes

    C. Population and water balance

        1. most people live where there is not a great deficit or surplus of water balance

REVIEW QUESTIONS

1. Define evaporation, condensation, sublimation, and deposition.

2. Generally describe the global pattern of precipitation using Fig. 12.11 as a guide.

SELF-TEST

Multiple-Choice Questions

1. The heat associated with evaporation is:

(a) latent heat of vaporization (b) latent heat of fusion (c) melting (d) transpiration (e) potential vaporization

2. The hydrologic cycle involves all of the following except:

    (a) precipitation (b) evapotranspiration (c) runoff (d) hydrogen transfer (e) rain and snow

3. When air is completely saturated, it has reached its:

    (a) melting point (b) dew point (c) boiling point (d) water balance point (e) deposition point

4. Clouds in the higher levels of the atmosphere are called:

    (a) cumulus (b) cumulonimbus (c) cirrus (d) stratus (e) altostratus

5. The upper midlatitudes exhibit:

    (a) water surpluses (b) water deficits (c) lowest precipitation totals (d) no evaporation (e) highest precipitation totals

6. Precipitation is lowest at:

    (a) the Equator (b) the Prime Meridian (c) subtropical latitudes (d) lower latitudes (e) the highest latitudes

True-False Questions

___ 1. Clouds require condensation nuclei.
___ 2. Water cannot change form directly from ice to water vapor.
___ 3. Evapotranspiration does not include moisture lost from photosynthesis.
___ 4. Globally, most people live where there are great water balance surpluses.
___ 5. Hail is a form of precipitation.
___ 6. Evaporation requires a vapor-pressure gradient.

UNIT 13: PRECIPITATION, AIR MASSES, AND FRONTS

UNIT SUMMARY

All precipitation occurs when moist air is adiabatically cooled below its condensation level (dew-point) as a result of the lifting of this air from the surface to higher altitudes. The four mechanisms that produce precipitation include (1) the forced lifting of air where low-level windflows converge; (2) convection, or spontaneous rise of air; (3) forced uplift of air as it crosses mountain barriers; and (4) forced uplift of air at the edges of colliding air masses. These types of precipitation are called, respectively, (1) convergent-lifting; (2) convectional; (3) orographic; and (4) frontal (cyclonic). Convectional precipitation often includes thunderstorms, which exhibit a definite life cycle through developing, mature, and dissipating stages (see Fig. 13.3).Orographic precipitation also exhibits a regular sequence, with cooling of air at the dry adiabatic lapse rate (DALR) upon ascent on the windward side of a barrier, subsequent saturation and cooling at the saturated adiabatic lapse rate (SALR) farther up the slope, and finally descent and warming at the dry adiabatic lapse rate (DALR). Frontal (cyclonic) precipitation is noticeably more violent with cold fronts than with warm fronts, because cold air wedges itself below warmer air, creating a steep slope and rapid cooling and condensation. Air masses are classified as maritime (m), continental (c), tropical (T), Polar (P), Arctic (A), Antarctic (AA), Equatorial (E), colder (k), warmer (w), stable (s), and unstable (u).

UNIT OBJECTIVES

1. To discuss the four basic mechanisms for producing precipitation.

2. To develop the concept of air masses - their character, movement patterns, and influence on precipitation.

3. To distinguish between cold fronts and warm fronts, and to describe their structure and behavior as they advance.

GLOSSARY OF KEY TERMS

Air mass A very large parcel of air (more than 1600 km [1000 mi] across) in the boundary layer of the troposphere that possesses relatively uniform qualities of density, temperature, and humidity in the horizontal dimension; it is also bound together as an organized whole, a vital cohesion because air masses routinely migrate as distinct entities for hundreds of kilometers.

Cold front Produced when an advancing cold-air mass hugs the surface and displaces all other air as it wedges itself beneath the preexisting warmer air mass; cold fronts have much steeper slopes than warm fronts and thus produce more abrupt cooling and condensation (and more intense precipitation).

Convection Spontaneous vertical air movement in the atmosphere.

Convectional-precipitation Convection is the spontaneous vertical movement of air in the atmosphere; convectional precipitation occurs after condensation of this rising air.

Convergent-lifting precipitation Precipitation produced by the forced lifting of warm, moist air where low-level windflows converge; most pronounced in the equatorial latitudes where the Northeast and Southeast Trades come together in the Inter-Tropical Convergence Zone (ITCZ), especially over the oceans.

Front The surface that bounds an air mass, along which contact occurs with a neighboring air mass possessing different qualities; this narrow boundary zone usually marks an abrupt transition in air density, temperature, and humidity. A moving front is the leading edge of the air mass built up behind it.

Frontal precipitation Precipitation that results from the movement of fronts whereby warm air is lifted, cooled, and condensed; also frequently called *cyclonic precipitation.*

Life cycle of a thunderstorm The stages marking the formation, progression, and termination of a thunderstorm: the developing stage, mature stage, and dissipating stage.

Orographic precipitation The rainfall (and sometimes snowfall) produced by moist air parcels that are forced to rise over a mountain range or other highland zone; such air parcels move in this manner because they are propelled both by steering winds and the push of other air parcels piling up behind them.

Rain shadow effect The dry conditions - often at a regional scale as in the U.S. interior West - that occur on the leeward side of a mountain barrier that experiences orographic precipitation; the passage of moist air across that barrier wrests most of the moisture from the air, whose adiabatic warming as it plunges downslope sharply lowers the dew point and precipitation possibilities.

Source region An extensive geographic area, possessing relatively uniform characteristics of temperature and moisture, where large air masses can form.

Tornado A small vortex of air, averaging 100 to 500 m (330 to 1650 ft) in diameter, that descends to the ground from rotating clouds at the base of a severe thunderstorm, accompanied by winds whose speeds range from 50 to 130 m per second (110 to 300 mph); as tornadoes move across the land surface, they evince nature's most violent weather and can produce truly awesome destruction in the natural and cultural landscapes.

Warm front Produced when an advancing warm air mass infringes on a preexisting cooler one; when they meet, the lighter, warmer air overrides the cooler air mass, forming the gently sloping, upward-sloping warm front (producing far more moderate precipitation than that associated with steeply sloped cold fronts).

UNIT OUTLINE

I. Precipitation - producing processes
   A. All precipitation is from moist air that has been cooled adiabatically to below its condensation (dew) point

II. Precipitation Processes
   A. Convergent-lifting precipitation occurs when warm, moist air converges, rises, expands, and condenses into precipitation
      1. Inter-Tropical Convergence Zone (ITCZ)
   B. Convectional precipitation occurs when a column of air (convection cell) rises spontaneously, expands, cools, and condenses into precipitation
   C. Thunderstorms are produced by convectional precipitation, common in low and mid-latitudes where there is a large amount of latent heat
      1. developing stage
      2. mature stage (anvil top)
      3. dissipating stage
   D. Thunderstorm-related phenomena
      1. hail in squall-line storms
      2. lightning
      3. thunder
      4. supercells
      5. mesoscale convective complexes

IV. Classifying air masses
   A. Maritime (m) or continental (c)
   B. Tropical (T)
   C. Polar (P)
   D. Maritime Tropical (mT)
   E. Continental Polar (cP)
   F. Maritime Polar (mP)
   G. Continental Arctic (cA) or Continental Antarctic (cAA)
   H. Maritime Equatorial (mE)
   I. Colder (k)
   J. Warmer (w)
   K. Stable (s)
   L. Unstable (u)

V. Movements of air masses
   A. Air masses are somewhat affected by their contacts with the surface, but retain many of their original characteristics far from their origin

---

REVIEW QUESTIONS

1. Describe the life cycle of a thunderstorm, using Fig. 13.3 as a reference.

2. Compare and contrast orographic and frontal precipitation.

3. What conditions characterize the windward slope of a mountain barrier?

SELF-TEST

Multiple-Choice Questions

1. The most prominent type of precipitation in the tropics is:

    (a) orographic (b) convergent-lifting (c) frontal (d) acid (e) cumulus

2. In what stage does a thunderstorm produce cumulonimbus clouds?

    (a) mature stage (b) developing stage (c) orographic stage (d) dissipating stage (e) no cumulonimbus clouds are formed

3. What type of precipitation is associated with an air mass rising over a mountain range?

    (a) convergent-lifting (b) leeward (c) convective (d) frontal (e) orographic

4. A large parcel of air with relatively uniform characteristics is termed a(n):

    (a) supercell (b) convective cell (c) air mass (d) air cell (e) low pressure cell

5. Air descending a mountain range is usually:

    (a) colder and moister (b) colder and drier (c) warmer and moister (d) warmer and drier (e) identical in temperature and moisture to that ascending a peak

6. All of the following are types of precipitation except:

    (a) convergent-lifting (b) orographic (c) frontal (d) condensative (e) convectional

True-False Questions

__ 1. A cold front is produces more violent weather than a warm front.
__ 2. Lightning and thunder are a result of a thunderstorm's horizontal air currents.
__ 3. A spontaneously rising column of air is called a convection cell.
__ 4. Thunderstorms never tend to cluster.
__ 5. Hailstones are common in squall-line thunderstorms.
__ 6. If a tornado forms over a water surface, it is called a windspout.

UNIT 14: WEATHER SYSTEMS

UNIT SUMMARY

Weather systems are transient features of the atmosphere, with constant inputs and outputs and changes of energy and moisture. Low-latitude weather systems include easterly waves, tropical depressions, tropical storms, and hurricanes. Hurricanes are also known as typhoons in the western Northern Pacific, and (tropical) cyclones in the Indian Ocean. Mature hurricanes are characterized by a well-defined eye containing cool, descending air. The eye wall contains the most damaging winds and heaviest rains of a hurricane. Hurricanes originate between 5 and 25 degrees latitude, and feed on warm tropical waters for development and intensification. Most destruction from hurricanes is caused by the storm surge. Weather systems of the middle and higher latitudes are primarily influenced by the Polar Front jet stream, and include the formation of midlatitude cyclones. Midlatitude cyclones are characterized by a life cycle of four stages: early (stationary front), open-wave, occlusion, and dissipation. Each weather system has a characteristic internal organization, with inputs of warm air carrying latent heat, and moisture in the form of water vapor. Warm air is transformed into faster moving air, and moisture becomes precipitation (see Fig. 14.12).

UNIT OBJECTIVES

1. To demonstrate the importance of migrating weather systems in the global weather picture.

2. To discuss the significant tropical weather systems, particularly hurricanes.

3. To explain how midlatitude cyclones are formed, and to describe the weather patterns associated with them.

GLOSSARY OF KEY TERMS

Cyclogenesis The formation, evolution, and movement of midlatitude cyclones.

Easterly wave A wave-like perturbation in the constant easterly flow of the Northeast and Southeast Trade winds that produces this type of distinctive weather system; westward-moving air is forced to rise on the upwind side (producing often heavy rainfall) and descend on the fair-weather down-wind side of the low-pressure wave trough.

Eye The open vertical tube that marks the center of a hurricane, often reaching an altitude of 16 km (10 mi).

Eye wall The rim of the eye or open vertical tube that marks the center of a well-developed hurricane; the tropical cyclone's strongest winds and heaviest rainfall occur here.

Hurricane A tropical cyclone capable of inflicting great damage. A tightly organized, moving low-pressure system, normally originating at sea in the warm moist air of the tropical atmosphere, exhibiting wind speeds in excess of 33m per second (74 mph); as with all cyclonic storms, it has a distinctly circular and pressure field.

Occluded front The surface boundary between cold and cool air in a mature midlatitude cyclone; caused by the cold front undercutting and lifting the warm air entirely off the ground as in Fig. 14.10c.

Open wave The early-maturity stage in the development of a midlatitude cyclone; surface cyclonic air motion transforms the original kink on the stationary front into an open wave, around which cold and warm air interact in the distinct ways shown in Fig 14.10b.

Polar Front jet stream The upper atmosphere jet stream located above the subpolar latitudes, specifically the Polar Front; at its strongest during the half-year centered on winter.

Stationary front The boundary between two stationary air masses.

Storm An organized, moving atmospheric disturbance.

Storm surge The wind-driven wall of water hurled ashore by the approaching center of a hurricane, which can surpass normal high tide levels by more than 5 m (16 ft); often associated with a hurricane's greatest destruction.

Weather system Organized phenomena of the atmosphere, with inputs, outputs, and changes of energy and moisture.

UNIT OUTLINE

I. Low-latitude weather systems
    A. Weather systems are organized phenomena with inputs, outputs, and changes in energy and moisture
        1. storms are moving disturbances of the atmosphere
    B. Easterly (tropical) waves
        1. result of the trade winds in tropical latitudes
    C. Tropical depressions
        1. low-pressure troughs with cyclonic organization
    D. Tropical storms
        1. sustained winds exceed 39 mi/hr (63 km/hr)
    E. Hurricanes (tropical cyclones)
        1. sustained winds exceed 74 mi/hr (119 km/hr)
        2. called hurricanes in western Atlantic and eastern Pacific
        3. called typhoons in western north Pacific
        4. called (tropical) cyclones in Indian Ocean

          5. open eye structure in center

          6. strongest winds and rain in eye wall

    F. Hurricane development

          1. develop between 5 and 25 degrees latitude

    G. Hurricane destruction

          1. storm surge

          2. tornadoes

II. Weather systems of the middle and higher latitudes

    A. The polar front jet stream

          1. important implications for surface pressure patterns and weather

    B. Cyclogenesis

          1. formation, evolution, and movement of midlatitude cyclones

          2. called depressions or extratropical cyclones

          3. stages of development

               a. stationary

               b. open-wave

               c. occluded front

               d. dissipation

          4. atmospheric events

               a. steady rain and falling pressure as cyclone approaches

               b. warm front passes, winds shift, pressure steady, occasional showers

               c. cold front arrives, intense rain, wind shifts, abrupt cold temperatures

III. Energy and moisture within weather systems

    A. Inputs into weather systems

          1. warm air carrying latent heat

          2. water vapor

REVIEW QUESTIONS

1. Describe the process of mid-latitude cyclogenesis.

2. List the differences between a tropical depression, tropical storm, and hurricane.

SELF-TEST

Multiple-Choice Questions

1. A hurricane must have sustained winds over:

    (a) 74 mph (b) 50 mph (c) 47 mph (d) 34 mph (e) 100 mph

2. In the northern Pacific, hurricanes are called:

    (a) willy-willies (b) monsoons (c) cyclones (d) hurricanes (e) typhoons

3. Hurricanes originate between _____ degrees latitude.

    (a) 20 and 30 (b) 5 and 55 (c) 5 and 25 (d) 30 and 50 (e) 50 and 75

4. The earliest stage of the development of a midlatitude cyclone is the:

    (a) stationary front (b) open-wave (c) occluded front (d) closed wave (e) easterly
    wave

5. Hurricanes form originally from:

    (a) the polar jet stream (b) easterly waves (c) occluded fronts (d) typhoons (e)
    stationary fronts

6. Within the eye of a hurricane, there is:

    (a) warm, rising air (b) warm, descending air (c) cool, rising air (d) cool,
    descending air (e) warm, stationary air

True-False Questions

___ 1. The weather is more changeable in the tropics than the midlatitudes.
___ 2. A tropical depression has higher sustained wind speeds than a tropical storm.
___ 3. The strongest winds and rains are contained within the eye wall of a hurricane.
___ 4. Cyclogenesis refers to the life cycle of midlatitude cyclones.
___ 5. A tropical storm must have sustained winds between 39 and 74 mph.
___ 6. An easterly wave generally advances in a westerly direction in the North Atlantic.

UNIT 15: WEATHER TRACKING AND FORECASTING

UNIT SUMMARY

The World Meteorological Organization maintains the World Weather Watch, a global network of weather stations. Synoptic weather charts map meteorological conditions at any given moment over large geographic areas. Observations of surface conditions, radiosonde, and satellites are all involved in weather data collection. Processing centers around the world collect and organize these raw data, so forecasters can interpret them and advise the public. The National Weather Service issues a daily 500-mb Height Contours map based on radiosonde data. The configuration of the 500-mb surface closely resembles ground-level pressure patterns. The National Weather Service uses numerical weather prediction, a computer-based forecasting method using projections over small increments of time. This unit also includes a practical application of forecasting the progress of a midlatitude cyclone across the central United States.

UNIT OBJECTIVES

1. To discuss the general network of weather stations and the types of data collected from each.

2. To illustrate typical weather maps compiled from weather data and to provide some elementary interpretations of them.

3. To outline weather forecasting methods and comment on their formulation and reliability.

GLOSSARY OF KEY TERMS

Geosynchronous satellite Satellite whose revolution of the Earth is identical to the planet's rotational speed; therefore, the satellite is "fixed" in a stationary position above the same point on the Earth's surface.

Numerical weather prediction The computer weather forecasting method used by the National Weather Service, based on projections by small increments of time up to 48 hours into the future.

Polar orbit Longitudinal orbits that repeatedly pass close to both poles, surveying a different, complete meridional segment of the surface during each revolution.

Radiosonde Radio-equipped weather instrument packages that are carried aloft by balloon.

Synoptic weather chart A map of weather conditions covering a wide geographic area at a given moment in time.

UNIT OUTLINE	

I. Weather data acquisition
    A. Weather stations
        1. instrumentation
        2. synoptic weather chart
        3. radiosondes
        4. rawinsonde observations
    B. Weather satellites
        1. geosynchronous orbits

II. Mapping weather data
    A. The surface weather map
        1. open-wave cyclone
        2. storm track
    B. The upper-air weather map
        1. correspondence between the upper air and surface conditions

III. Weather Forecasting
    A. The forecasting industry
        1. numerical weather prediction
        2. National Weather Service
        3. American Meteorological Society
    B. Long-range forecasting
        1. 30- and 90-day forecasts for temperature and precipitation, error rate high

REVIEW QUESTIONS

1. List the types of symbols used for representing ongoing precipitation, wind direction, wind speed, and isobars on weather maps.

2. What is a geosynchronous satellite, and approximately how much of the Earth's surface can it monitor?

3. Briefly describe the process of numerical weather prediction, used by the National Weather Service.

SELF-TEST

Multiple-Choice Questions

1. Rawinsonde observations are:

   (a) radar trackings of radiosonde balloons (b) radar trackings of geosynchronous satellites (c) sonar trackings (d) not useful for weather prediction (e) only useful in winter months

2. Satellites that revolve at the same speed as the Earth's rotation are called:

   (a) rotational (b) numerical (c) geosynchronous (d) synoptic (e) revolutionary

3. On a surface weather map, wind direction is represented as:

   (a) dashed lines (b) a line extending from a circle (c) a triangle (d) squares (e) small dots

4. In its forecasts, the National Weather Service uses which temperature scale?

   (a) Fahrenheit (b) kelvin (c) absolute (d) Celsius (e) radiosonde

5. On a surface weather map, fronts and isobars are represented by:

   (a) circles (b) dashes (c) triangles (d) squares (e) line symbols

6. The World Weather Watch is maintained by:

   (a) National Weather Service (b) American Meteorological Society (c) NOAA (d) The World Meteorological Organization (e) The Weather Channel

True-False Questions

___ 1. Hurricane forecasts are issued at the main National Weather Services facility.
___ 2. Geosynchronous satellites revolve around the Earth faster than the planet rotates.
___ 3. The numerical weather prediction method is based on projections by small increments in time.
___ 4. In the upper atmosphere, the higher the altitude of the 500-mb level, the cooler the surface temperature of the air beneath it.
___ 5. Weather prediction is still an art as well as a science.
___ 6. The configuration of the 500-mb surface generally follows the ground-level pressure pattern.

UNIT 16: CLIMATE CLASSIFICATION AND REGIONALIZATION

UNIT SUMMARY

The ideal climate classification should clearly differentiate among all climate types, show the relationships between them, apply to the world as a whole, provide a framework for subdivision, and demonstrate the controls causing climate change. While it does not perform all of the tasks completely, the Köppen climate classification system provides a balanced approach to define Earth's climate types. The major climate groups are **A** (Tropical), **B** (Arid), **C** (Mesothermal), **D** (Microthermal), **E** (Polar), **H** (Highland). The lowercase letters **f**, **m**, **w**, and **s** describe precipitation in **A**, **C**, and **D** climates. Capital letters **S** and **W** indicate the degree of aridity in **B** climates. A hypothetical continent of low uniform elevation is used as a model to display the global pattern of climate type location. Tropical (**A**) climates reach from the Equator to approximately 25 degrees latitude. Arid (**B**) climates exist poleward of **A** climates, and on the western sides of continents. Mesothermal (**C**) climates are located in the middle latitudes. Microthermal (**D**) climates are found only in the Northern Hemisphere, generally north of 50 degrees latitude. Polar (**E**) climates are located in both hemispheres, poleward of 66 ½ degrees latitude. Highland (**H**) climates are located in high-altitude regions, and are too cold to support vegetation. The Köppen climate classification system is most useful at the global or regional scale.

UNIT OBJECTIVES

1. To define climate and discuss the general problems of climate classification based on dynamic phenomena.

2. To outline a useful climate classification scheme devised by Köppen, based on temperatures and precipitation amounts and totals.

3. To apply the modified Köppen classification system to the Earth, and briefly describe appropriate climate regions as they appear on a hypothetical continent and the world map.

GLOSSARY OF KEY TERMS

Climate The long-term conditions (over at least 30 years) of aggregate weather over a region, summarized by averages and measures of variability; a synthesis of the succession of weather events we have learned to expect at any given location.

Hypothetical continent The Earth's landmasses generalized into a single, idealized, shield-shaped continent of uniform low elevation.

Köppen climate calssification system A descriptive classification of the world's climates, based its association with plant life, devised by Wladimir P. Köppen.

UNIT OUTLINE

I. Classifying Climates
    A. Climate is defined as the average values of weather components, such as temperature and precipitation, for at least a thirty-year period

    B. Koppen climate classification system

        1. six major climate groups

            a. tropical (A)

            b. arid (B)

            c. mesothermal (C)

            d. microthermal (D)

            e. polar (E)

            f. highland (H)

        2. precipitation indicators: f, m, w, s

II. The regional distribution of climate types
    A. Hypothetical continent of uniform elevation used as model

    B. **A** climates near equator, extend about 25 degrees in either direction from it

        1. tropical rainforest (Af)

        2. savanna (Aw)

        3. monsoon (Am)

    C. **B** climates are poleward of **A** climates and on west coasts of continents, associated with subsiding air of subtropical highs

        1. desert (BW)

        2. steppe (BS)

    D. **C** climates are located in the middle latitudes and are mesothermal (moderate temps.)

        1. Mediterranean (Cs)

        2. humid climates with moist winters (Cf)

        3. subtropical monsoon (Cw)

    E. **D** climates are cold, and are located in upper-middle and subpolar latitudes

        1. precipitation throughout the year (Df)

        2. drier, harsher winters (Dw)

    F. **E** climates are located poleward of the Arctic and Antarctic Circles (66 ½ degrees)

        1. tundra (ET)

        2. ice cap or frost (EF)

    G. **H** (highland) climates are found in the upper regions of mountainous areas, too cold to support vegetation

III. Boundaries of climate regions
    A. Köppen system does not really consider causes of climate and some links to vegetation are not very strong

    B. Köppen system best for global or regional, large-scale patterns

        C. At the micro-level, climate boundaries are constantly changing

REVIEW QUESTIONS

1. Compare and contrast the **B** and **C** climate classifications. List the major subclasses of each, and the type of vegetation associated with them.

2. Why can highland (**H**) climates not support vegetation?

3. Describe generally the pattern of climate types across a hypothetical continent of uniform low elevation, using Fig 16.2 as a guide.

SELF-TEST

Multiple-Choice Questions

1. What is the Köppen designation for a steppe climate?

   (a) BW (b) BS (c) B (d) Bw (e) Bf

2. Tropical (**A**) climates extend approximately how many degrees north and south of the Equator?

   (a) 60 (b) 10 (c) 45 (d) 75 (e) 25

3. **C** climates are associated with:

   (a) moderate temperatures (b) severe cold (c) no precipitation (d) mountain peaks (e) enormous rainfall totals

4. In the Northern Hemisphere, polar (**E**) climates are located north of:

   (a) 30 degrees latitude (b) 66 ½ degrees latitude (c) 23 ½ degrees latitude (d) 80 degrees latitude (e) 66 ½ degrees longitude

5. The hypothetical continent used as a model to plot climate types has:

   (a) uniform elevation (b) varying elevation (c) no use in climatology (d) Eurasia's shape (e) greatly varied relief

6. The Koppen letters f, m, w, and s refer to:

   (a) temperature (b) vegetation (c) pressure (d) precipitation (e) plant species

True-False Questions

___ 1. The **Aw** (savanna) climate exhibits a distinct dry season.
___ 2. **B** climates generally have harsher winters than **D** climates.
___ 3. The Mediterranean climate is an **A** climate.
___ 4. Highland (**H**) climates are generally too cold to support vegetation.
___ 5. Climates are highly dynamic, and change markedly from year to year.
___ 6. The **Dw** climate is harsher than the **Df** climate.

UNIT SUMMARY

The tropical (**A**) climates extend from the Equator in 30-50 degree-wide latitudinal belts in both hemispheres. The **A** climate subtypes include the tropical rainforest (**Af**) climate with relatively constant warm temperatures and copious rainfall. The monsoon rainforest (**Am**) climate exists exclusively on tropical coasts, with a long wet season and a short dry season. The savanna climate (**Aw**) is found in transition areas to higher latitudes, and has a relatively extended dry season. The arid (**B**) climates exist poleward of the **A** climates, and their subdivisions are based on precipitation totals. The desert climate (**BW**) is fully arid, with only small amounts of winter rainfall. The steppe (**BS**) climate is transitional between deserts and the subhumid areas of the **A**, **C**, and **D** climate margins. Drought is an ever-present problem in semiarid areas, as evidenced by recurring drought in the Great Plains and the growing problem of desertification.

UNIT OBJECTIVES

1. To expand the discussion of tropical (**A**) and arid (**B**) climates using climographs developed for actual weather stations.

2. To highlight climate-related environmental problems within tropical and arid climate zones.

3. To examine the causes and consequences of tropical deforestation and desertification.

GLOSSARY OF KEY TERMS

Arid climate Dry climate where potential evaporation always exceeds the moisture supplied by precipitation; found in areas dominated by the subtropical high-pressure cells, in the interiors of continents far from oceanic moisture sources, and in conjunction with rain-shadow zones downwind from certain mountain ranges.

Climograph A graph that simultaneously displays, for a given location, its key climatic variables of average temperature and precipitation, showing how they change monthly throughout the year.

Desertification The process of desert expansion into neighboring steppelands as a result of human degradation of fragile semiarid environments.

Tropical climate Climate dominated by warmth (due to low-latitude location) and moisture (from the rains of the *Inter-Tropical Convergence Zone*); contained within a continuous east-west belt astride the Equator, varying latitudinally from 30 to 50 degrees wide.

Tropical deforestation The clearing and destruction of tropical rainforests to make way for expanding settlement frontiers and the exploitation of new economic opportunities.

UNIT OUTLINE

I. The major tropical (A) climates
  A. The tropical rainforest climate (**Af**)
    1. located close to Equator
    2. high temperatures and large amounts of rainfall
    3. convectional thunderstorms
    4. dense canopy of tropical forest
  B. The monsoon rainforest climate (**Am**)
    1. located on tropical coasts, often near highlands
    2. distinct short dry season in winter
    3. evergreens and some grasslands
  C. The savanna climate (**Aw**)
    1. located in transitional area between subtropical highs and equatorial low
       pressure belts
    2. extended dry season in winter
    3. tall grasses, individual trees, thorny bushes

II. The major arid (B) climates
  A. The desert (**BW**) climate
    1. located near 30 degrees north and south at the subtropical highs
    2. minimal precipitation
    3. sparse vegetation
  B. The steppe (**BS**) climate
    1. located on the edges of the most arid (**BW**) deserts
    2. semiarid, rainfall varying with latitude (more in lower latitudes)
    3. short-grass prairie vegetation
  C. Human activities in **B** climates
    1. Virgin and Idle Lands Program (former Soviet Union)
    2. Great Plains droughts
    3. Nile Valley
    4. desertification

REVIEW QUESTIONS

1. Compare and contrast the general types of plant life found in **A** and **B** climate zones.

2. What is a climograph?

SELF-TEST

Multiple-Choice Questions

1. A climograph displays average:

   (a) temperature and precipitation (b) rainfall only (c) temperature and pressure (d) isobars (e) wind speeds and direction

2. Which of the following is not a type of **A** climate?

   (a) tropical monsoon (b) monsoon rainforest (c) savanna (d) steppe (e) tropical rainforest

3. The driest deserts are generally located around:

   (a) 30 degrees N&S latitude (b) 30 degrees N&S longitude (c) 60 degrees N&S latitude (d) 15 degrees N&S latitude (e) 55 degrees N&S latitude

4. An intensifying problem at the edges of arid zones is:

   (a) deforestation (b) hybridization (c) overpopulation (d) mechanized agriculture (e) desertification

5. The short-grass prairie is associated with which climate type?

   (a) **Af** (b) **BS** (c) **BW** (d) **Am** (e) **AS**

6. An arid climate may result from its location:

   (a) on the windward side of a mountain (b) on the coast (c) on the leeward side of a mountain (d) in forests (e) on mountain tops

True-False Questions

___ 1. **B** climates are always dry year round.
___ 2. The monsoon rainforest is usually limited to tropical coasts.
___ 3. Tropical rainforests actually have very little undergrowth.
___ 4. The savanna is a **B** climate.
___ 5. The Virgin and Idle Lands Program was a huge success.
___ 6. Deforestation of tropical rainforests poses a large environmental threat.

UNIT 18: HUMID MESOTHERMAL (C) CLIMATES

UNIT SUMMARY

Mesothermal (**C**) climates dominate the globe in east-west bands between the Equator and the middle latitudes, and are considered transitional from the tropics to the upper midlatitude zones. These are generally moderate climates, and the regions they occupy contain some of the world's large population clusters. The perpetually moist (**Cf**) climates include the humid subtropical (**Cfa**) climate and the marine west coast (**Cfb**, **Cfc**) climate. The dry summer (**Cs**) climate is also called the Mediterranean climate. The warmer variety of this climate (**Csa**) is found in the Mediterranean Basin and other interior areas. The cooler type (**Csb**) is found on coastlines near cool ocean currents. The dry winter (**Cw**) climate most resembles the tropical savanna climate type, only with more of a dip in temperature in the cool season and lass rainfall. Drought is a natural hazard, which occurs unpredictably due to a decrease in precipitation and warmer temperatures with consequent shrinking amounts of surface and soil water. Drought can have devastating effects, which are highlighted in *Perspectives: The Drought of '88*.

UNIT OBJECTIVES

1. To widen understanding of the various **C** climates.

2. To interpret representative climographs depicting actual conditions in these **C** climate areas.

3. To highlight a major environmental-climatic problem of many **C** climate areas – drought.

GLOSSARY OF KEY TERMS

Drought The below-average availability of water in a given area over a period lasting several months.

Mesothermal climate The moderately heated climates that are found on the equatorward side of the middle latitudes, where they are generally aligned as interrupted east-west belts; transitional between the climates of the tropics and those of the upper midlatitudes where polar influences begin to produce harsh winters.

UNIT OUTLINE

I. C climates are located on the equator's side of the middle latitudes
   A. Average temperature below 18° C (64.4° F) but not below 0 degrees C (32° F) in winter, and an average temperature not less than 10°C (50° F) for at least one month out of the year

II. The perpetually moist (Cf) climate
    A. **(Cfa)** humid subtropical climate created by warm, moist air traveling around the western margins of the subtropical highs
        1. located in southeastern corners of 5 major continents
        2. rainfall totals almost as high as tropical rainforests
    B. The marine west coast **(Cfb, Cfc)** climate
        1. occurs on coasts affected by the westerlies year round
        2. **Cfb** climate is warmer than **Cfc** climate

III. The dry-summer (Cs) climates
    A. Mediterranean climate, abundant sunshine and long, dry summers
        1. **Csa** climate is warmer than **Csb**
    B. The dry-winter **(Cw)** climates
        1. similar to the tropical savanna climate, but more rainfall and cooler mean temperatures
        2. winter dry season, sometimes called the subtropical monsoon climate
    3. **Cwa** associated with high elevations in tropical latitudes, **Cwb** is cooler

REVIEW QUESTIONS

1. Describe generally the global distribution of **C** climates.

2. Compare and contrast the **Cf**, **Cs**, and **Cw** climates.

3. What were the causes and effects of the Drought of 1988?

SELF-TEST

Multiple-Choice Questions

1. The marine west coast climate (**Cfb, Cfc**) is associated with which winds?

    (a) Northeast Trades (b) Southeast Trades (c) Westerlies (d) Jet Stream (e) Easterlies

2. The humid subtropical climate is:

    (a) **Cw** (b) **Cfa** (c) **Aw** (d) **Cs** (e) **Bfa**

3. Mesothermal climates are transitional between the tropics and:

    (a) upper-midlatitudes (b) polar regions (c) the Equator (d) the subtropical highs
    (e) the desert latitudes

4. Mesothermal climates cannot have an average winter temperature below
    approximately:

    (a) 64° F (b) 32° F (c) 78 ° F (d) 45° F (e) 0° F

5. When an area experiences below-average water availability for several months, it is
    termed a(n):

    (a) water shortage (b) drought (c) hydrolysis (d) dry climate (e) arid region

6.Globally, mesothermal (**C**) climates resemble:

    (a) north-south belts (b) small randomly spaced patches (c) east-west belts
    (d) large circles (e) north-south belts

True-False Questions

___ 1. Mesothermal climates are marked by harsh winters and short summers.
___ 2. Not much of the world's population lives in the **C** climate zones.
___ 3. The **Cf** climate is perpetually moist.
___ 4. Temperature extremes in the marine west coast climate are unusual.
___ 5. The humid mesothermal climate (**Cw**) is most like the tropical savanna climate.
___ 6. The **Cw** climate is only associated with low altitudes.

UNIT 19: HIGHER LATITUDE (D,E) AND HIGH-ALTITUDE (H) CLIMATES

UNIT SUMMARY

Microthermal (**D**) climates exist poleward of mesothermal (**C**) climates in the Northern Hemisphere. The humid microthermal climates include the humid continental (**Dfa/Dwa and Dfb/Dwb**) climates in the upper middle latitudes, and the taiga (**Dfc/Dwc** and **Dfd/Dwd**) climates farther to the north. Permafrost in these areas can reach 300 m (1000 ft) in depth. A serious environmental problem in **D**-climate areas is acid precipitation, caused by the spread of pollutants from industrial sources in the middle latitudes. The polar (**E**) climates exist poleward of 66½° in both hemispheres, and include the tundra (**ET**) climate (primarily in the Northern Hemisphere), and the ice cap (**EF**) climate near the poles. Ice cap climates exhibit the lowest temperatures on Earth, and contain snow year-round. Highland (**H**) climates exhibit vertical zonation according to altitude. These climate layers, moving increasingly upwards from the surface, include tropical and desert, subtropical, mesothermal, microthermal, and polar conditions.

UNIT OBJECTIVES

1. To expand the discussion of typical **D**, **E**, and **H** climates and to interpret representative climographs for these zones.

2. To highlight a major environmental-climatic problem of many **D** climate regions – acid precipitation.

3. To characterize the general influence of altitude on climatic conditions.

GLOSSARY OF KEY TERMS

Acid precipitation Abnormally acidic rain, snow, or fog resulting from high levels of the oxides of sulfurs and nitrogen that exist as industrial pollutants in the air.

Highland climate Climate of high-elevation areas that exhibit characteristics of climates located poleward of those found at the base of those highlands; the higher one climbs, the colder the climate becomes – even in the low latitudes. Thus **H** climate areas are marked by the vertical zonation of climates.

Humid microthermal climate The weakly heated continental climates of the Northern Hemisphere's upper midlatitudes, where the seasonal rhythms swing from short, decidedly warm summers to long, often harsh winters; mostly confined to the vast interior expanses of North America and Eurasia poleward of 45° N.

Permafrost The permanently frozen layer of subsoil that is characteristic of the colder portions of the **D**-climate zone as well as the entire **E**-climate zone; can exceed 300 m (1000 ft) in depth.

pH scale Used to measure acidity and alkalinity of substances on a scale ranging from 0 to 14, with 7 being neutral; below 7 increasing acidity is observed as 0 is approached, while above 7 increasing alkalinity is observed as 14 is approached.

Polar climate Climate in which the mean temperature of the warmest month is less than 10° C (50° F); the tundra (**ET**) subtype exhibits warmest-month temperatures between 0° C (32° F) and 10° C (50° F), while in the (coldest) icecap (**EF**) subtype the average temperature of the warmest month does not reach 0° C (32° F).

Vertical zonation Characteristic of **H** climates, the distinct arrangement of climate zones according to altitudinal position; the higher one climbs, the colder and harsher the climate becomes.

UNIT OUTLINE

I. The major humid microthermal (D) climates
  A. Located poleward of mesothermal climates in Northern Hemisphere
  B. Harsh winters and warm summers
  C. Period longer than a month when temperature is below 0°C (32°F)
  D. Humid continental (**Dfa/Dwa/,Dfb/Dwb**) and taiga (**Dfc/Dwc, Dfd, Dwd**) climates
    1. humid continental climates in upper-midlatitudes
    2. taiga climate is subarctic
    3. both humid continental and taiga are moist year round (**Df**)
    4. on interiors of large landmasses, dry-winter climates occur (**Dw**)
        a. permafrost is a permanently frozen layer of topsoil
    5. environmental problem of acid precipitation in **D** climate zones

II. The polar (E) climates
  A. Located beyond the Arctic and Antarctic Circles (66 ½° N & S)
  B. Six months of light in summer, six months of darkness in winter
    1. extensive ice fields in winter months
  C. Average temperature for warmest month is less than 10° C (50° F)
  D. The tundra (**ET**) climate
    1. warmest average monthly temperature between 0° C (32° F) and 10° C (50° F)
    2. stunted trees, mosses, lichens
  E. The ice cap (**EF**) climate
    1. lowest annual temperatures on Earth
    2. warmest monthly average temperatures are not above freezing

II. High-altitude (H) climates
  A. Vertical zonation with altitude
    1. climates become progressively colder with increasing altitude, mimic the pattern as climates progress from the equator to higher latitudes

a. tropical or desert climate, surface-1200m [4,000 feet])
b. subtropical climate, 1200m [4,000 feet] - 2400m [8,000 feet]
c. mesothermal climate, 2400m[8,000feet]-3600m[12,000 feet]
d. microthermal climate, 3600m[12,000feet]-4800m [16,000 feet]
e. permanent ice and snow, above 4800m [16,000 feet]

REVIEW QUESTIONS

1. Compare and contrast the tundra (**ET**) and icecap (**EF**) climates.

2. Describe the vertical zonation scheme of **H** climates.

SELF-TEST

Multiple-Choice Questions

1. **D** climates are characterized by:

   (a) harsh summers and mild winters (b) harsh winters and mild summers (c) drought (d) only maritime climate regions (e) lack of precipitation

2. The taiga climate is:

   (a) a humid continental climate (b) dry year-round (c) home to vast population centers (d) a generally warm climate (e) associated with rainforest vegetation

3. Acid precipitation results from high levels of oxides of :

   (a) oxygen and nitrogen (b) selenium (c) selenium and nitrogen (d) sulfur and oxygen (e) sulfur and nitrogen

4. The climate in which the warmest monthly temperature averages do not rise above freezing is:

   (a) taiga (b) humid continental (c) tundra (d) ice cap (e) polar savanna

5. Tundra vegetation includes:

   (a) mosses and lichens (b) dense forest (c) thick prairie grasses (d) palm trees (e) there is no vegetation supported

6. Highland climates below 1200 m (4,000 feet) are:

    (a) tropical (b) subtropical (c) mesothermal (d) microthermal (e) polar

True-False Questions

__ 1. Highland climates exhibit vertical zonation.
__ 2. Almost all of the tundra climates are found in the Northern Hemisphere.
__ 3. Microthermal climates cover approximately 20 percent of the Earth's land area.
__ 4. Permafrost extends only a few feet below the surface.
__ 5. The lowest temperatures on Earth are found in the tundra climate.
__ 6. Highland climates shift with vertical, rather than horizontal distance.

UNIT SUMMARY

Earth's environmental history is marked by constant climatic change. The evidence exists in various forms, including surface landforms, soils, fossils, and the contents of sediments obtained by coring the floors of seas and lakes as well as ice sheets. The recent climatic history of the Earth is surveyed within five nested time periods, respectively extending back for 150, 1500, 15,000, 150,000, and 1,500,000 years. Alternating cold (glaciation) and warm (interglacial) periods have prevailed as the Late Cenozoic Ice Age unfolded. Mechanisms of climate change are interpreted within the atmosphere-ocean-ice-Earth system. External processes include variations in the receipt of solar radiation and shifts in the configurations of continents and oceans. Internal processes drive change in the distribution of heat and moisture flows within the atmosphere. Predicting future climate change is a hugely difficult challenge, which may now be further complicated by the as-yet-unknown impacts of human interference in the operation of atmospheric systems.

UNIT OBJECTIVES

1. To examine various lines of evidence for climate change.

2. To give a brief history of climate change over the past 1.5 million years.

3. To discuss mechanisms that cause variations in climatic conditions.

GLOSSARY OF KEY TERMS

Glaciation   A period of global cooling during which continental ice sheets and mountain glaciers expand.

Interglacial   A period of warmer global temperatures between the most recent deglaciation and the onset of the next glaciation.

Teleconnections   Relationships involving long-distance linkages between weather patterns that occur in widely separated parts of the world; El Niño is a classic example.

UNIT OUTLINE

I. Earth's environmental history
      A. Formation of the atmosphere
      B. *Snowball Earth* hypothesis
      C. Cambrian explosion of life
      D. Climate change

II. Evidence of climate change
    A. Landforms and soils
    B. Animal and plant fossils
    C. Oceanic and lake sediment
    D. Assembling the record of recent climatic variation
        1. written records of direct observations
        2. seafloor and ice sheet cores
        3. tree rings
        4. fossil pollen
        5. glacial varves

IV. Mechanisms of climate change
    A. Challenging complexities
        1. climate change analysis involves all five Earth spheres
        2. focus on the interlinked atmosphere-ocean-ice-Earth system
    B. External processes
        1. variations in solar radiation
            a. sunspots (short-term)
            b. orbital cycles involving stretch, roll, and wobble (longer-term)
        2. volcanism
        3. uplifting and wearing away of land surface
        4. plate tectonics (shifting distribution of landmasses and oceans)
        5. greenhouse effect
    C. Internal processes
        1. circulation of heat and moisture by atmosphere
        2. positive feedback effects
        3. negative feedback effects
        4. teleconnections

IV. The climatic future
    A. Speculation taking into account human interference

REVIEW QUESTIONS

1. Briefly describe the climate changes that have occurred from 1940 to the present.

2. Chart the general climate trends for the past 1.5 million years, citing major episodes of glaciations and interglacials.

3. Define the concepts of positive and negative feedback as they apply to internal processes of climate change, illustrating each with an example.

SELF-TEST

Multiple-Choice Questions

1. Earth has been relatively warm for _____ years, accompanied by only minor changes in the global distribution of climates.

    (a) 1 million (b) 100,000 (c) 65,000 (d) 11,000 (e) 140

2. From 1940 to 1975, the Earth experienced a:

    (a) worldwide drought (b) cooling trend (c) warming trend (d) climatic reversal (e) deglaciation

3. Fifteen thousand years ago, the Earth was experiencing:

    (a) a glaciation (b) an interglacial (c) the Holocene (d) the Eemian interglacial (e) the Medieval Optimum

4. Which of the following is a short-term external climate change factor:

    (a) change in the Earth's orbit (b) change in the tilt of the Earth's axis (c) sunspots (d) an eclipse (e) a teleconnection

5. Long-distance linkages between weather patterns that occur in distant locations are called:

    (a) positive feedbacks (b) negative feedbacks (c) greenhouse effects (d) teleconnections (e) Cambrian explosions

6. The Little Ice Age began:

    (a) prior to A.D. 1000 (b) around A.D. 1200 (c) around A.D. 1800 (d) in the 20th century (e) prior to the Holocene

True-False Questions

____ 1. The Holocene interglacial was a warming period.
____ 2. Ocean floor sediments can yield climatic data.
____ 3. Earth has been experiencing a cooling trend from 1940 to the present.
____ 4. The Late Cenozoic Ice Age included approximately 20 advances and retreats of continental ice sheets.
____ 5. During the past 1.5 million years, the general trend has been one of extended interglacials separated by brief glaciations.
____ 6. The Late Cenozoic Ice Age occurred long before the Pleistocene.

UNIT 21: HUMAN-CLIMATE INTERACTIONS AND IMPACTS

UNIT SUMMARY

Four types of heat flows can be observed in the human body – radiant, metabolic, evaporative, and convectional. Climate is seen to significantly influence the types of shelter built in a given location. Urban areas are great producers of mass and energy. Urban areas exhibit greater temperatures due to the burning of fossil fuels, multiple reflections off of vertical surfaces, and entrapment of polluted air by dust domes. Urban heat islands can form at any time over large cities, and the maximum difference in temperature between neighboring urban and rural environments is called the heat-island intensity. The peculiarities of metropolitan climates include increased runoff leading to lower relative humidities; slower than average wind speeds because of the cityscape; wind circulation cells of dust domes; and increased levels of fog due to the greater number of particles in the air. Primary pollutants can be gaseous or solid, while secondary pollutants are produced in the atmosphere by the interaction of two or more primary pollutants. The problem of air pollution is a large-scale one, and pollution plumes can form when domes over urban areas detach from a metropolis due to increased prevailing wind speed, and spread airborne contaminants far from their source location.

UNIT OBJECTIVES

1. To relate our understanding of atmospheric processes to the human environment.

2. To illustrate the utility of using energy balance concepts to characterize systems of the human environment.

3. To focus on several of the impacts human have had, and may come to have, on our climatic environment.

GLOSSARY OF KEY TERMS

Dust dome The characteristic shape taken by the large quantities of dust and gaseous pollutants in a city's atmosphere.

Heat-island intensity The maximum difference in temperature between neighboring urban and rural environments.

Microclimate Climate region on a localized scale.

Pollution plume When prevailing winds exceed 13 kph (8mph), dust domes begin to detach themselves from the cities they are centered over; the polluted air streams out as a plume above the downwind countryside.

Primary pollutants Gaseous or solid pollutants that come from an industrial or domestic source or the internal combustion engine of a motor vehicle.

Secondary pollutants Produced in the air by the interaction of two or more primary pollutants or from reactions with normal atmospheric constituents.

UNIT OUTLINE

I. The heat balance of the human body
  A. Average body temperature fluctuates 3 to 6 degrees; body has very limited temperature range for survival
    1. humans receive shortwave radiation and emit longwave radiation
    2. human body converts chemical (food) energy to heat energy (metabolic energy)
    3. perspiration provides heat loss
    4. convectional flow can heat or cool body

II. Shelter, houses and climate
  A. Climate plays a large role in the design of dwellings

III. Urban microclimates
  A. About 50 percent of the world's population resides in metropolitan areas
  B. Mass, energy, and heat in the city
    1. cities have their own metabolism; including consumption of food, water, and fossil fuels, and production of sewage, refuse, and pollution
    2. heat values produced by a city in winter equal or exceed heat available from Sun
    3. greater heat produced due to burning of fossil fuels, reflection from objects, and entrapment by dust domes
  C. Urban heat islands
    1. can form at any time in large cities
    2. microscale variations often seen
  D. Peculiarities of metropolitan climates
    1. more runoff from precipitation because most areas impenetrable by water
    2. winds slowed by friction from tall buildings; less efficient
    3. occasional high-velocity channeled air between skyscrapers
    4. dust dome provides a lot of condensation nuclei, more clouds and fog form
    5. more precipitation in urban areas due to heat rising from built-up surface

IV. Air Pollution
  A. Primary pollutants
    1. primary gaseous pollutants
      a. carbon dioxide

     b. water vapor
     c. hydrocarbons
     d. carbon monoxide
     e. oxides of sulfur and nitrogen
    2. primary solid pollutants
     a. iron
     b. manganese
     c. titanium
     d. lead
     e. benzene
     f. nickel
     g. copper
     h. coal or smoke particles
  B. Secondary pollutants
    1. produced by interactions of primary pollutants with each other or the atmosphere
    2. secondary reducing pollutants
     a. sulfur dioxide $\rightarrow$ sulfur trioxide $\rightarrow$ sulfuric acid
    3. secondary oxidizing pollutants
     a. 1 : nitrogen dioxide + sunlight = nitrogen monoxide + O
      2 : $O_2 + 0 = O_3$ (ozone)
  C. Larger-scale air pollution
    1.   pollution plume

V. Human activities and the global climate machine
  A. Human activities can interfere with the atmosphere

REVIEW QUESTIONS

1. How does an urban heat island develop, and what are the consequences of this phenomenon?

2. List several of the primary pollutants and secondary pollutants.

SELF-TEST

Multiple-Choice Questions

1. The human body converts chemical energy to:
  (a) heat energy (b) potential energy (c) kinetic energy (d) solar energy (e) light energy

2. Which of the following is not a factor that increases urban temperatures?

   (a) reflections off vertical surfaces (b) dust domes (c) burning of fossil fuels (d) winds (e) all of these

3. When isotherms on a map give the impression of a city being an area of increased elevation this phenomenon is known as a(n):

   (a) highland climate (b) urban heat island (c)dust dome (d) conurbation (e) conversion

3. Peculiarities of a city climate include:

   (a) wind eddies on corners (b) very low temperatures (c) overall decreased wind speed (d) increased solar radiation levels (e) very low air pressure

4. All of the following are primary air pollutants except:

   (a) water vapor (b) carbon dioxide (c) sulfuric acid (d) hydrocarbons (e) iron

5. When prevailing winds from a dust dome detach themselves from a city, they produce a:

   (a) dome remnant (b) pollution dome (c) pollution cell (d) duststorm
   (e) pollution plume

True-False Questions

___ 1. Heat-island intensity measures the average maximum temperatures felt on islands in the western Pacific Ocean.
___ 2. Secondary pollutants can be reducing or oxidizing.
___ 3. Primary pollutants are strictly gaseous.
___ 4. There is often high-velocity channeled windflow within cities.
___ 5. A city produces huge amounts of mass and energy.
___ 6. The types of heat flows that can be altered in humans include radiant, metabolic, evaporative, and convectional.

UNIT SUMMARY

Natural geography is introduced as an umbrella term that encompasses the major geographic components of the biosphere: *soil geography* (a part of the science of pedology) and *biogeography*, divided into the geographic study of plants (phytogeography) and animals (zoogeography). Soil represents the interface between the lithosphere and atmosphere, and is not only the key to plant life but is also a living entity itself. The contents of biogeography are noted, and the evolution of this field is briefly traced and emphasizes some key advances in knowledge. The Perspective box focuses on biodiversity, and underscores the importance of this concept. The unit concludes with a brief survey of conservation, its connection to physical geography, and the importance of good environmental management and sustainable development strategies.

UNIT OBJECTIVES

1. To expand our concept of physical geography by including biotic systems operating at the Earth's surface.

2. To relate biotic systems to our understanding of global climates.

3. To link physical geography to the more general topic of conservation.

GLOSSARY OF KEY TERMS

Biodiversity Shorthand for *biological diversity*; the variety of the Earth's life forms and the ecological roles they play.

Biogeography The geography of plants (*pytogeography*) and animals (*zoogeography*).

Conservation The careful management and use of natural resources, the achievement of significant social benefits from them, and the preservation of the natural environment.

Pedology Soil science; the study of soils.

Phytogeography The geography of flora or plant life; where botany and physical geography overlap.

Species A population of physically and chemically similar organisms within which free gene flow takes place.

Sustainable development Conservation movement which the World Commission on Environment and Development defines as "development that meets the needs of the present without compromising the ability of future generations to meet their own needs."

Zoogeography The geography of animal life or fauna; where zoology and physical geography overlap.

UNIT OUTLINE

I. Natural geography
    A. Constituents
        1. soil geography (spatial pedology [soil science])
        2. biogeography
            a. phytogeography (geography of plants)
            b. zoogeography (geography of animals)
    B. Geography of soils
        1. interface between atmosphere and lithosphere
        2. key to plant life
        3. soil as a living entity
        4. human use and misuse of soils
    C. Biogeography
        1. species: about 30 million worldwide
        2. biodiversity (Perspective box, pp. 282-283)
        3. von Humboldt's pioneering work on vegetation systems
        4. Wallace's pathbreaking analysis of zoogeographical regions

II. Conservation and the biosphere
    A. Human destruction of plant and animal life
    B. The movement to develop careful management of environmental resources
    C. Case study: the Dust Bowl of the 1930s in the U.S. Great Plains
    D. Case study: the Tennessee Valley Authority as a government policy response
    E. Conservation in the twenty-first century
    F. Sustainable development

REVIEW QUESTIONS

---

1. What is *natural geography*, and what are its constituent subjects?

2. What is *biodiversity* and how does it relate to biogeography?

3. How do the Dust Bowl and the Tennessee Valley Authority, respectively, reflect human misuse and enlightened management of the natural environment?

SELF-TEST

Multiple-Choice Questions

1. The geography of flora is largely concerned with:

    (a) vegetation (b) animals (c) wildlife (d) soils (e) zoogeography

2. The science that studies soils is called:

    (a) zoology (b) zoogeography (c) conservation (d) pedology (e) phytology

3. Wallace's Line is an important concept in the field known as:

    (a) phytogeography (b) plant science (c) pedology (d) sustainable development
      (e) zoogeography

4. Which of the following states was most heavily affected by the Dust Bowl?

    (a) California (b) Nebraska (c) New York (d) Florida (e) Tennessee

5. The river most closely associated with the TVA is the:

    (a) Amazon (b) Mississippi (c) Tennessee (d) Thames (e) Tigris

6. The Environmental Protection Agency was created by the federal government in:

    (a) 1801 (b) 1868 (c) 1904 (d) 1936 (e) 1970

True-False Questions

___ 1. Biodiversity is heavily concerned with the number of species residing in a given
      area.
___ 2. Phytogeography is concerned with plants and flora in general.
___ 3. The TVA was created just after the Civil War.
___ 4. Less than one million of Earth's 30 million species have been identified and
      classified.
___ 5. Soils represent the interface between the lithosphere and hydrosphere.
___ 6. Alexander von Humboldt was a pioneer in identifying faunal regions near Australia.

UNIT SUMMARY

Soil is defined, its major characteristics as a renewable resource are specified, and te stage is set for a survey of soil formation. The four components of soil are minerals, organic matter, water, and air. The five factors of soil formation are parent material (underlying deposits of broken-down rocks), climate, biological agents, topography, and time. Four fundamental processes shape the actual formation of soil: (1) addition; (2) transformation; (3) depletion; and (4) translocation. The soil profile is constituted by a number of layers called horizons. The concept of soil regimes is useful to soil geographers for understanding regional variations in soil formation across the Earth's mosaic of natural environments.

UNIT OBJECTIVES

1. To understand the components of soil.

2. To outline the factors affecting soil formation.

3. To describe and explain a typical soil profile and the processes responsible for the formation of soil horizons.

GLOSSARY OF KEY TERMS

Addition The soil-layer formation process involving the gains made by the soil through the adding of organic matter from plant growth, or sometimes when loose surface material moves downslope and comes to rest on the soil; expressed as a dark-colored upper layer, whose appearance is attributable to that added organic matter.

Depletion The soil-layer formation process involving the loss of soil components as they are carried downward by water, plus the loss of other material in suspension as the water percolates through the soil from upper to lower layers; while the upper layers are depleted accordingly, the dissolved and suspended materials are redeposited lower down in the soil.

Eluviation Means "washed out," and refers to the soil process that involves the removal from the **A** horizon and downward transportation of soluble minerals and microscopic, colloid-sized particles of organic matter, clay, and oxides of aluminum and iron.

Humus Decomposed and partially decomposed organic matter that forms a dark layer at the top of the soil; contributes importantly to a soil's fertility.

Illuviation The soil process in which downward-percolating water carries soluble minerals and colloid-sized particles of organic matter and minerals into the **B** horizon, where these materials are deposited in pore spaces and against the surfaces of soil grains.

Leaching The soil process in which downward-percolating water dissolves and washes away many of the soil's mineral substances and other ingredients.

Nonrenewable resources One that when used at a certain rate will ultimately be exhausted (metallic ores and petroleum being good examples).

Parent material The rocks of the Earth, and the deposits formed from them, from which the overlying soil is formed.

Renewable resources Resources that can regenerate as they are exploited.

Residual soil The simplest kind of soil formation in which a soil forms directly from underlying rock; when this occurs, the dominant soil minerals bear a direct relationship to that original rock.

Soil A mixture of fragmented and weathered grains of minerals and rocks with variable proportions of air and water; the mixture has a fairly distinct layering, and its development is influenced by climate and living organisms.

Soil horizon Soil layer; the differentiation of soils into layers is called *horizonation*.

Soil profile The entire array of soil horizons (layers) from top to bottom.

Soil regime The variations in behavior of changeable elements in the soil-formation environment; the term implies there is some regularity in the (spatial) pattern, but recognizes changes within it. Thus, even if their parent material remained constant all over the world, soils would differ because they would form under varying temperature, moisture, biogeographic, and other conditions.

Transformation The soil-layer formation process involving the weathering of rocks and minerals and the continuing decomposition of organic material in the soil; weathering is most advanced in the upper soil layers.

Translocation The soil-layer formation process involving the introduction of dissolved and suspended particles from the upper layers into the lower ones.

Transported soil When a soil is totally independent of the underlying solid rock because the parent material has been transported and deposited by one or more of the gradational agents, often far from its source area.

UNIT OUTLINE

I. Introduction to soil
    A. Definitions of soil
    B. Soil as a renewable resource, capable of regeneration

II. The formation of soil
    A. Soil components
        1. minerals
        2. organic matter
        3. water
        4. air
    B. Factors in the formation of soil
        1. parent material
            a. residual soils
            b. transported soils
        2. climate
            a. atmospheric temperature
            b. soil moisture
            c. wind
        3. biological agents
            a. organic matter, including humus
            b. plant nutrients
            c. earthworms and other macroorganisms
        4. topography
            a. slope steepness
            b. drainage conditions
        5. time
            a. natural stability of soil environment
            b. human abuses and soil degradation

III. Processes in the soil
    A. Addition (of organic matter, especially vegetational)
    B. Transformation (rock weathering and decomposition of organic material)
    C. Depletion (leaching of soil components by downward-percolating water)
    D. Translocation (redeposition by downward movement of soil particles)

IV. Soil profiles
    A. Horizonation (layering)
    B. Master Horizons: **O, A, E, B, C, R**

V. Soil regimes
    A. Spatial patterns of soil formation
    B. Soil development in different environmental regions

REVIEW QUESTIONS

1. How do the five major factors of soil formation relate to the four processes of soil formation?

2. What is leaching and what role does it play in soil formation?

3. Draw a model soil profile containing each of the six master horizons.

SELF-TEST

Multiple-Choice Questions

1. Which of the following is not a process of soil formation?

    (a) translocation (b) transpiration (c) transformation (d) depletion (e) edition

2. Which of the following is a master horizon?

    (a) **R** (b) **D** (c) **Oa** (d) **Ob** (e) **Oc**

3. Downward percolation of soil water is most closely associated with:

    (a) transformation (b) addition (c) illuviation (d) horizonation (e) regolith weathering

4. The soil horizon most closely identified with eluviation is designated by the letter:

    (a) **A** (b) **O** (c) **E** (d) **R** (e) **F**

5. Oxisols are most closely associated with:

    (a) illuviation in steep-sloped zones (b) moist tropical soil regimes (c) translocated **D** horizons (d) humus-controlled leaching in pine-needle-dominated desert environments (e) a and c

6.   Which of the following is not a soil component?

(a) air (b) water (c) bedrock (d) minerals (e) organic matter

True-False Questions

___ 1. Spodosols are never found in tropical rainforest soil regimes.
___ 2. Eluviation refers to the upward movement of dissolved soil materials.
___ 3. A residual soil is composed of parent material transported in from another area.
___ 4. Soil is a good example of a nonrenewable resource.
___ 5. The **O** horizon is the uppermost of the soil profile's master horizons.
___ 6. The process of transformation occurs only in the soil's lowest layer.

UNIT 24: PHYSICAL PROPERTIES
OF SOIL

UNIT SUMMARY

The study of the physical properties of soil begins with a discussion of the notions of *sol* and *ped*. Soil texture is then elaborated and categories based on sand-silt-clay percentages are introduced. The four basic structures of soil are categorized as platy, prismatic, blocky (angular), and spheroidal (granular). Soil color is considered, and the basic notions of soil chemistry introduced in Unit 23 are expanded in a brief discussion of soil acidity and alkalinity. Soils of hills and valleys are treated in the context of soil catenas. The unit concludes with an overview of the soil-development system.

UNIT OBJECTIVES

1. To introduce terminology used to describe soil characteristics.

2. To define some important properties that arise out of a soil's physical characteristics.

3. To illustrate the likely arrangement of soil characteristics in a hypothetical landscape.

GLOSSARY OF KEY TERMS

Blocky (angular) structure Involves irregularly shaped peds with straight sides that fit against the flat surfaces of adjacent peds, thereby giving a soil considerable strength.

Field capacity The ability of a soil to hold water against the downward pull of gravity; also the maximum amount of water a soil can contain before becoming waterlogged.

Loam A soil containing grains of all three texture size categories– sand, silt, and clay; however, refers not to a size category, but to a certain combination of variously sized particles.

Pedon A column of soil drawn from a specific location, extending from the **O** horizon (if present) all the way down to the level where the bedrock shows signs of being transformed into **C**-horizon material.

Platy structure Involves layered peds that look like flakes stacked horizontally.

Prismatic structure Involves peds arranged in columns, giving a soil vertical strength.

Soil catena Derived from a Latin word meaning chain or series, refers to a sequence of soil profiles appearing in regular succession on landform features of uniform rock type; most frequently associated with hillsides where the same parent material has produced an arrangement of different soil types.

Solum Consists of the **A** and **B** horizons of a soil. that part of the soil in which plant roots are active and play a role in the soil's development.

Spheroidal (granular) structure Involves peds that are usually very small and often nearly round in shape, so that the soil looks like a layer of bread crumbs.

UNIT OUTLINE

I. *Sol* and *ped*
    A. *Sol*
        1. Russian word for soil
        2. *solum*: the **A** and **B** horizons where plant roots are active
    B. *Ped*
        1. Greek word for ground
        2. *pedon*: column of soil, extending from the **O** horizon to the bedrock

II. Soil texture
    A. Aspects of soil-particle size
    B. Sand-silt-clay size hierarchy
    C. Particle-size combinations: loam
    D. Soil porosity
    E. Soil permeability
    F. Field capacity

III. Soil structure
    A. Structural typology
        1. platy
        2. prismatic
        3. blocky (angular)
        4. spheroidal (granular)
    B. Soil consistence

IV. Soil Color

V. Soil acidity and alkalinity
    A. Acid-alkaline pH scale
    B. Moisture conditions
        1. acidic soils—moist climates
        2. alkalinic soils—drier climates
    C. Soil fertility implications

VI. Soils of hills and valleys
    A. Topography and soil formation
    B. Slope and soil horizion

C. Soil catenas

VII. The soil-development system
   A. Diagrammed and discussed on pp. 306-307

REVIEW QUESTIONS

1. What are the major size categories of soil particles and how do they impact a soil's overall physical properties?

2. What are the four basic types of soil structure, and how are they distinguished form each other?

3. What generalizations can you make about slopes and soil formation?

SELF-TEST

Multiple-Choice Questions

1. A sequence of soil profiles that appears in regular succession on landforms of uniform rock type is called a:

   (a) resistant residue (b) nonresistant residue (c) soil catena (d) soil consistence (e) loam

2. The peds associated with platy soil structure most closely resemble:

   (a) flakes (b) columns (c) bread crumbs (d) clay cubes (e) small ropes

3. The peds associated with prismatic soil structure most closely resemble:

   (a) flakes (b) columns (c) bread crumbs (d) clay cubes (e) small ropes

4. The peds associated with spheroidal soil structure most closely resemble:

   (a) flakes (b) columns (c) bread crumbs (d) clay cubes (e) small ropes

5. The soil-particle size with the greatest field capacity is:

    (a) sand (b) alluvium (c) silt (d) colluvium (e) clay

6. Which country's pedology was so prominently developed that its word for soil is now part of the name of every major soil type?

    (a) Germany (b) Great Britain (c) the United States (d) Russia (e) Israel

True-False Questions

___ 1. Alluvial soils are mostly found on valley floors.
___ 2. The particles of a sandy soil are smaller than those of a silty soil.
___ 3. A soil's pedon is vertically longer than its solum.
___ 4. Spheroidal and granular are terms that both apply to the same basic type of soil
      structure.
___ 5. A soil with a pH of 7 is neither acidic nor alkalinic.
___ 6. A loam soil cannot contain sand-sized soil particles.

UNIT SUMMARY

Soil classification has been in progress for over a century and continues to evolve. Today's Soil Taxonomy represents the latest advances, and the first half of this unit systematically traces the 12 largest soil categories, which are known as Soil Orders. For the moment, the geographic framework for this survey is the model, hypothetical continent displayed on p. 311. The 12 Soil Orders discussed in turn are entisols; histosols; vertisols; inceptisols; gelisols; andisols; aridisols; mollisols; alfisols; spodosols; ultisols; and oxisols. The second half of the unit moves beyond the hypothetical continent and examines the actual spatial distribution of soils--and the soil regions they produce--across the conterminous United States (see Fig. 25.14) and then the world as a whole (see Fig. 25.15).

UNIT OBJECTIVES

1. To present a brief history of pedology and highlight problems in achieving a universal soil classification scheme.

2. To outline the current system of soil classification, the Soil Taxonomy.

3. To survey the 12 Soil Orders in the Soil Taxonomy and examine their regional patterns on both the U.S. and the world map.

GLOSSARY OF KEY TERMS

Alfisol One of the 11 Soil Orders of the Soil Taxonomy, found in moister, less continental climate zones than the mollisols; characterized by high mineral content, moistness, and sizeable clay accumulation in the **B** horizon.

Andisol One of the 11 Soil Orders of the Soil Taxonomy; established to include certain weakly developed, parent-material-controlled soils, notably those developed on volcanic ash that are very finely distributed throughout the Pacific Ring of Fire, Hawaii, and the world's other volcanic zones.

Aridisol One of the 11 Soil Orders of the Soil Taxonomy, and the most widespread on the world's landmasses; dry soil (unless irrigated) associated with arid climates, light in color, and often contains horizons rich in calcium, clay, or salt minerals.

Entisol One of the 11 Soil Orders of the Soil Taxonomy, which contains all the soils that do not fit into the other 10 Soil Orders; is of recent origin, evinces little or modest development, and is found in many different environments.

Gelisol The newest of the 11 Soil Orders of the Soil Taxonomy, added in 1998, defined as high-latitude or high-altitude soils that have permafrost within 100 cm of the soil surface, or gelic materials within 100 cm of the surface and permafrost within 200 cm.

Histosol One of the 11 Orders of the Soil Taxonomy; organic soil associated with poorly drained, flat-lying areas that, when drained, can become quite productive in root-crop agriculture.

Inceptisol One of the 11 Soil Orders of the Soil Taxonomy; forms quickly, is relatively young (though older than an entisol), has the beginnings of a **B** horizon, and contains significant organic matter.

Mollisol One of the 11 Soil Orders of the Soil Taxonomy, found in the world's semiarid climate zones; characterized by a thick, dark surface layer and high alkaline content.

Oxisol One of the 11 Soil Orders of the Soil Taxonomy, found in tropical areas with high rainfall; heavily leached and usually characterized by a pronounced oxic horizon, red or orange in color.

Soil Order In the Soil Taxonomy, the broadest possible classification of the Earth's soils into one of the 11 major categories; a very general grouping of soils with broadly similar composition, the presence or absence of certain diagnostic horizons, and similar degrees of horizon development, weathering, and leaching.

Soil Taxonomy The soil classification scheme used by contemporary pedologists and soil geographers; evolved from the Comprehensive Soil Classification Scheme (CSCS) that was derived during the 1950s.

Spodosol One of the 11 Soil Orders of the Soil Taxonomy, which develops where organic soil acids associated with pine needle decay cause the depletion of most **A** horizon minerals; that **A** horizon is characterized by an ash-gray color, the signature of silica that is resistant to dissolving by organic acids.

Ultisol One of the 11 Soil Orders of the Soil Taxonomy; usually quite old, not especially fertile, and located in warm subtropical environments with pronounced wet seasons.

Vertisol One of the 11 Soil Orders of the Soil Taxonomy, found in tropical as well as mesothermal wet-and-dry climates; this soil type is heavy in clay composition, cracking during the dry season and swelling with moisture when the rains return.

UNIT OUTLINE

I. Classifying soils
    A. Russian beginnings
    B. The Marbut System
    C. Comprehensive Soil Classification System (CSCS)
    D. Soil Taxonomy used today

II. The Soil Taxonomy
    A. Hierarchical organization (Table 25.1)
    B. Soil Orders, their properties, and their components (Table 25.2)
    C. Soil distribution on a hypothetical continent
    D. The 12 Soil Orders (see **GLOSSARY** section above for major features of each)
        1. entisols
        2. histosols
        3. vertisols
        4. inceptisols
        5. gelisols
        6. andisols
        7. aridisols
        8. mollisols
        9. alfisols
        10. spodosols
        11. ultisols
        12. oxisols

III. Spatial distribution of soils
    A. U.S. regional patterns (map, p. 321)
    B. The global soil map (pp. 322-323)

REVIEW QUESTIONS
---

1. Trace the development of the Soil Taxonomy.

2. List and briefly describe the major features of each Soil Order.

3. Compare and contrast the regional distribution of soils across the hypothetical continent, the conterminous United States, and the Earth's landmasses.

SELF-TEST

Multiple-Choice Questions

1. Which of the following is not a Soil Order?

   (a) andisols (b) antisols (c) aridisols (d) alfisols (e) entisols

2. Permafrost environments are most likely to exhibit soils of the Order known as:

   (a) histosols (b) icisols (c) glacisols (d) gelisols (e) mollisols

3. The Soil Order associated with volcanic-ash-derived soils is called:

   (a) lavasols (b) ultisols (c) alfisols (d) pyrosols (e) andisols

4. Oxisols are most widespread in:

   (a) deserts (b) polar areas (c) semiarid grasslands (d) the rainy tropics (e) high-mountain environments

5. Which of the following pedologists devised the Soil Taxonomy?

   (a) Charles Marbut (b) Vasily Dokuchayev (c) Konstantin Glinka (d) Mikhail Solstoy (e) none of these

6. The "ent" in *entisol* derives from the word:

   (a) recent (b) patient (c) parent (d) enter (e) invent

True-False Questions

__ 1. Gelisols comprise the newest Soil Order added to the Soil Taxonomy.
__ 2. Andisols cover a larger area of the global land surface than any other Soil Order.
__ 3. In the Soil Taxonomy there are more Great Groups than Suborders.
__ 4. The conterminous United States does not contain soils of the oxisol Order.
__ 5. The Seventh Approximation refers to the soil classification scheme developed directly after the Soil Taxonomy.
__ 6. Vertisols can often be identified by large cracks that open during the dry season.

UNIT 26: BIOGEOGRAPHIC PROCESSES

UNIT SUMMARY

This is the first of three units on biogeography, and the first of two units on natural vegetation. The dynamics of the biosphere are introduced via the process of photosynthesis, its limitations, and the related concept of phytomass. This overview then expands to include the topics of ecosystems, energy flows, ecological efficiency, and plant successions. The unit concludes with an extended discussion of the geographic dispersal of plant (and animal) species, focusing on physical (temperature, water availability, soils, landforms) and biotic factors (competition, amensalism, predation, mutualism, endemism). The Perspective box treats the species-richness gradient and the various theories that purport to explain it.

UNIT OBJECTIVES

1. To discuss the process of photosynthesis and relate it to climatic controls.

2. To introduce the concept of ecosystems and highlight the important energy flows within ecosystems.

3. To outline the factors influencing the geographic dispersal of plant and animal species within the biosphere.

GLOSSARY OF KEY TERMS

Allogenic succession Plan succession in which vegetation change is brought about by some external environmental factor, such as disease.

Amensalism Biological interaction in which one species is inhibited by another.

Biomass The total living organic matter, encompassing all plants and animals, produced in a particular geographic area.

Carnivores Animals that eat herbivores and other animals.

Climax community Achieved at the end of a plant succession; the vegetation and its ecosystem are in complete harmony (dynamic equilibrium) with the soil, the climate, and other parts of the environment.

Cyclic autogenic succession Plant succession in which one type of vegetation is replaced by another, which in turn is replaced by the first, with other series possibly intermixed.

Dispersal Ancestral species from which modern species evolved arrived in a given area by movement over land, swimming, rafting, or flying.

Ecosystem A linkage of plants or animals to their environment in an open system as far as energy is concerned.

Endemism Tendency of an isolated region to contain significant percentages of species of plants, animals, and other life forms that exist nowhere else on Earth.

Food chain The stages that energy in the form of food goes through within an ecosystem.

Herbivores Animals that live on plants, or more generally the first consumer stage of a food chain.

Linear autogenic succession A plant succession that occurs when the plants themselves initiate changes in the environment that consequently cause vegetation changes.

Mutualism Biological interaction in which there is a coexistence of two or more species because one or more is essential to the survival of the other(s); also called *symbiosis*.

Photosynthesis The process in which plants convert carbon dioxide and water into carbohydrates and oxygen through the addition of solar energy; carbohydrates are a significant component of the food and tissue of both plants and animals.

Phytomass The total living organic plant matter produced in a given geographic area; often used synonymously with biomass, because biomass is measured by weight (plants overwhelmingly dominate over animals in total weight per unit area).

Plant succession The process in which one type of vegetation is replaced by another.

Species-richness gradient The phenomenon involving the general decline over distance in the number of species per unit area as one proceeds from the equatorial to higher latitudes.

Trophic level Each of the stages along the food chain in which food energy is passed through the ecosystem.

Vicariance Ancestral species from which modern species evolved arrived in a given area by being carried along as landmasses drifted apart over tens of millions of years.

UNIT OUTLINE

I. Dynamics of the biosphere
    A. Photosynthesis
        1. a process rooted in the Earth's evolution
        2. chlorophyll and light absorption
        3. chemical foundations and environmental implications
        4. limitations
            a. variations in solar-energy receipt
            b. variations in water availability
        5. phytomass productivity
            a. regional variations in total plant matter produced (see Fig. 26.3)
            b. greatest in moist tropical lowlands
            c. at its least in desert, upland, and high-latitude zones
    B. Ecosystems and energy flows
        1. *ecosystem*: a linkage of plants or animals to their environment in an open system as far as energy is concerned
        2. exemplified through food chains
    C. Ecological efficiency
        1. trophic levels within food chains (see Fig. 26.5)
        2. variation in ecosystem efficiencies

II. Plant successions
    A. Linear autogenic succession
    B. Cyclic autogenic succession
    C. Allogenic succession
    D. Climax communities

III. Geographic dispersal
    A. Physical factors
        1. temperature
        2. availability of water
        3. other climatic factors
            a. daylight duration
            b. wind action
            c. duration of snow cover
        4. distribution of soils
        5. landform (especially slope) variations
    B. Biotic factors
        1. competition
        2. amensalism (inhibition of one species by another)
        3. predation
        4. mutualism (symbiosis)

REVIEW QUESTIONS

1. Discuss the connections between photosynthesis and the broad distribution of plant life across the Earth's landmasses.

2. What are ecosystems and how energy-efficient are they at different trophic levels?

3. List the biotic and physical factors that shape the distribution of natural vegetation.

SELF-TEST

Multiple-Choice Questions

1. *Symbiosis* is identical to the term:

   (a) vicariance (b) climax community (c) mutualism (d) amensalism (e) allogenic succession

2. Which of the following is not a biotic factor that affects the geographic dispersal of plants?

   (a) photosynthesis (b) mutualism (c) competition (d) amensalism (e) endemism

3. The green pigment of plants that assures the absorption of sunlight is called:

   (a) the respiration effect (b) the biomass gradient (c) the vicariant level (d) chlorophyll (e) verdantium

4. The total living organic plant matter of a given area is known as its:

   (a) highest trophic level (b) first trophic level (c) megatherm (d) hygrophytic quotient (e) biomass

5. Animals that eat herbivores are known as:

   (a) carnivores (b) allosauruses (c) autotrophic predators (d) mesotherms (e) there are no animals that eat herbivores

6. Which of the following is one of the types of plant succession:

   (a) autocyclogenic (b) linear autogenic (c) ecogenic (d) phytogenic (e) trophic herbogenic

True-False Questions

___ 1. The term *allogenic* applies to one of the three types of plant succession.
___ 2. Vicariance refers to the substitution of one plant type for another.
___ 3. Plants adapted to low heating levels of the atmosphere are called microtherms.
___ 4. Trees that drop their leaves seasonally are known as deciduous.
___ 5. The inhibition of one species in the geographic dispersal of another is called amensalism.
___ 6. A climax community can never be the first stage in a cyclic autogenic plant succession.

UNIT SUMMARY

Mapping vegetation at the global scale is a formidable challenge, similar to those faced by geographers working with worldwide distributions of climates and soils. They key is to identify the largest spatial units of plant association: *biomes*. A biome is the broadest possible subdivision of the plant and animal world, an assemblage of vegetation and wildlife that forms a regional ecological unit of subcontinental dimensions. Following an elaboration of the biome concept, the eight principal terrestrial biomes are introduced and briefly surveyed. These biomes are the (1) tropical rainforest, (2) tropical savanna, (3) desert, (4) temperate grassland, (5) temperate forest, (6) Mediterranean scrub, (7) northern coniferous forest, and (8) tundra. Each biome is discussed in context of the world map (see Fig. 27.1), and those of North America are examined in greater detail (see Fig. 27.2). In addition to horizontal spatial patterns, vertical relationships are covered as well (see Fig. 27.3).

UNIT OBJECTIVES

1. To briefly survey the principal terrestrial biomes.

2. To examine other aspects of the biome concept, including its altitudinal zonation.

GLOSSARY OF KEY TERMS

Biome The broadest justifiable subdivision of the plant and animal world, an assemblage and association of plants and animals that forms a regional ecological unit of subcontinental dimensions.

Desert biome Characterized by sparse, xerophytic vegetation or even the complete absence of plant life.

Mediterranean scrub biome Consists of widely spaced evergreen or deciduous trees and often dense, hard-leaf evergreen scrub; thick waxy leaves are well adapted to the long dry summers, Sometimes referred to as chaparral or maquis.

Northern coniferous forest biome The upper-midlatitude boreal forest (known in Russia as the snowforest or *taiga*); dominated by dense stands of slender, cone-bearing, needleleaf trees.

Savanna biome The transitional vegetation of the environment between the tropical rainforest and the subtropical desert; consists of tropical grasslands with widely spaced trees.

Temperate deciduous biome Dominated by broadleaf trees; herbaceous plants are also abundant, especially in spring before the trees grow new leaves.

Temperate evergreen forest biome Dominated by needleleaf trees; especially common along western midlatitude coasts where precipitation is abundant.

Temperate grassland biome Occurs over large midlatitude areas of continental interiors; perennial and sod-forming grasses are dominant.

Tropical rainforest biome Vegetation is dominated by tall, closely spaced evergreen trees; a teeming arena of life that is home to a greater number and diversity of plant and animal species than any other biome.

Tundra biome Microtherm plant assemblage of the coldest environments; dominated by perennial mosses, lichens, and sedges.

UNIT OUTLINE

I. Biomes
    A. The challenges of mapping plant and animal regions on the global scale
    B. Biomes represent the broadest possible spatial units of plant association
    C. Terrestrial vs. marine biomes
    D. Factors that determine the distribution of biome regions
        1. climate
        2. topography (see vertical sequencing in Fig. 27.3)

II. Principle terrestrial biomes
    A. Tropical rainforest biome
        1. contains the greatest number of species
        2. dense canopies of tall trees admit minimal light to the forest floor
        3. human abuses abound, especially deforestation (see Perspective box, p. 212)
        4. monsoon rainforest subtype
    B. Tropical savanna biome
        1. transitional environment between tropical rainforest and desert
        2. tropical grassland with widely-spaced trees
        3. associated with pronounced wet and dry seasons of the **Aw** climate
        4. large herds of grazing animals common, and grass burnings are frequent
    C. Desert biome
        1. Earth's driest environments (**BW** climate prevails)
        2. sparse xerophytic vegetation where plants exist at all
            a. perennials (e.g. cactuses) store water and are mostly dormant
            b. ephemerals grow quickly after short seasonal rains and soon die off
        3. Animal life limited and must also be adapted to extreme aridity

113

D. Temperate grassland biome
    1. common in continental interiors, especially in Eurasia and North America.
    2. range from short-grass (steppe) to tall-grass prairies
    3. highly susceptible to human influence—and environmental degradation
E. Temperate forest biome
    1. major subtypes
        a. temperate deciduous forest
        b. temperate evergreen forest
    2. human influences widespread, especially clearing for agriculture
F. Mediterranean scrub
    1. **Csa** and **Csb** climates produce hot dry summers and cool dry winters
    2. widely-spaced evergreen or deciduous trees
    3. trees interspersed with often dense, hard-leaf evergreen scrub with waxy leaves adapted to survive long arid summers
        a. chaparral (coastal California)
        b. maquis/macchia (Mediterranean Europe)
    4. densely populated, intensively farmed, and environments greatly modified by long-term human activity
G. Northern coniferous forest biome
    1. upper-midlatitude boreal forest (taiga)
    2. dominated by needle-leaf trees well adapted to harsh winters and drought
H. Tundra
    1. most continuous biome, occurring throughout the poleward margins of the Northern Hemisphere continents
    2. only cold-tolerant plants survive, such as mosses, lichens, and sedges
    3. poor drainage due to widespread permafrost in subsoil
    4. surprisingly varied fauna, with huge bird and insect populations during the short summer
    5. extremely fragile environment from human standpoint

REVIEW QUESTIONS

1. Discuss the challenges for mapping plant and animal assemblages at the global scale, and compare them to those faced by physical geographers who map climates and soils at this level of generalization.

2. Prepare a brief profile of each terrestrial biome, highlighting its major vegetational features, climatic constraints, and human impacts.

SELF-TEST

Multiple-Choice Questions

1. The number of principal terrestrial biomes that can be identified is:

    (a) 3 (b) 6 (c) 8 (d) 37 (e) more than 150

2. The biome associated most strongly with the semiarid **BS** climate is the:

    (a) tundra (b) desert (c) steppe (d) northern coniferous forest (e) temperate grassland

3. Which of the following vegetation types is not found in the Mediterranean scrub biome?

    (a) epiphytes (b) chaparral (c) maquis (d) macchia (e) mattoral

4. Which of the following biomes contains muskegs?

    (a) desert (b) tropical rainforest (c) tropical savanna (d) temperate deciduous forest (e) northern coniferous forest

5. The biome most likely to contain ephemeral vegetation is the:

    (a) tundra (b) tropical rainforest (c) desert (d) temperate evergreen forest (e) northern coniferous forest

6. Which of the following biomes has been profoundly modified by humans through the long-term combination of burning, grazing, and intensive cultivation?

    (a) tropical savanna (b) temperate grassland (c) tropical rainforest (d) Mediterranean scrub (e) temperate deciduous forest

True-False Questions

___ 1. It is possible to identify marine as well as terrestrial biomes.
___ 2. Lianas and epiphytes are signature plant types of the tropical savanna biome.
___ 3. Leathery and waxy plant leaves represent adaptations to environments that exhibit long periods of dryness.
___ 4. The U.S. Great Plains are mainly located in a temperate forest biome.
___ 5. The Mediterranean scrub biome is largely associated with the Mediterranean climate.
___ 6. The biome characterized by vegetation dominated by mosses and lichens is the tundra.

UNIT 28: ZOOGEOGRAPHY:
SPATIAL ASPECTS OF ANIMAL POPULATION

UNIT SUMMARY

The geography of fauna is introduced by a brief review of the processes that drive animal evolution. The notions of ecological niche and habitat adaptation are elaborated using the example of East Africa's Serengeti Plain. The development of the field of zoogeography is traced, highlighting the contributions of Alexander von Humboldt, Charles Darwin, and Alfred Russel Wallace. The focus then shifts to a survey of the Earth's zoogeographic realms. Next comes an overview of recent work in zoogeography, and the unit concludes with a discussion of wildlife conservation issues that highlights the human impact on animal habitats. The Perspective box offers a vignette on the human role in the spread of insects from one region to another, a reminder of the devastating impacts that people can inflict on ecosystems in our ever-shrinking world.

UNIT OBJECTIVES

1. To briefly outline the theory of evolution and related principles such as natural selection, which led to the present-day spatial distribution of animals.

2. To give a brief history of zoogeography.

3. To relate zoogeography to the larger context of environmental conservation.

GLOSSARY OF KEY TERMS

Animal ranges The area of natural occurrence of a given animal species; often changes over time, and in some cases even seasonally.

Convergent evolution Theory that holds that organisms in widely separated biogeographic realms, although descended from diverse ancestors, develop similar adaptations to measurably similar habitats.

Ecological niche The way a group of organisms makes its living in nature, or the environmental space within which an organism operates most efficiently.

Ecological zoogeography The study of animals as they relate to their total environment.

Habitat The environment a species normally occupies within its geographical range.

Mutation Variation in reproduction in which the message of heredity (DNA) contained in the genes is imperfectly passed on and from which new species may originate.

Wallace's Line Zoogeographer Alfred Russel Wallace's controversial boundary line that purportedly separates the unique faunal assemblage of Australia from the very different animal assemblage of neighboring Southeast Asia; Wallace's famous line, introduced over a century ago, is still the subject of debate today.

UNIT OUTLINE

I. Processes of evolution
  A. Natural selection
    1. genetic combination
    2. mutations
  B. Ecological niche
    1. environmental spaces in which a species operates most efficiently
    2. habitats: larger, more complex ecological niches
    3. animal adaptations to their habitats
      a. changing natural environments
      b. Serengeti Plains example of complex adaptations

II. Emergence of zoogeography
  A. von Humboldt's path-breaking studies
  B. Darwin and the theory of evolution
  C. Wallace's pioneering work on faunal assemblages in Southeast Asia
    1. Wallace's Line
    2. Weber's Line
    3. the continuing debate about zoogeographical boundaries

III. The Earth's zoogeographic realms
  A. Paleotropic (Ethiopian) realm
  B. Indomalayan (Oriental) realm
  C. Madagascan realm
  D. Australian realm
  E. New Zealand realm
  F. Neotropic realm
  G. Nearctic realm
  H. Palearctic realm
  I. Pacific realm
  J. Antarctic realm

IV. Further studies in zoogeography
  A. Darlington's updating of Wallace's approach
  B. Emergence of ecological zoogeography
    1. Simpson's incorporation of evolution
    2. Maurer's work on biodiversity
    3. Jarvis's emphasis on plant and animal introductions
  C. Island zoogeography
    1. pioneering work of MacArthur and Wilson
    2. subsequent studies

V. Zoogeography and conservation
   A. Animal ranges
   B. Human impacts on animal habitats
   C. Preservation efforts

REVIEW QUESTIONS

1. Discuss the concept of faunal niches and link it to the notion of animal ranges.

2. Describe the global distribution of zoogeographic realms and list the main features of the realms that span the Americas, Eurasia, and Africa.

3. What was the significance of Wallace's Line? Trace the evolution of this controversy since that boundary was first drawn.

SELF-TEST

Multiple-Choice Questions

1. Wallace's Line was drawn to separate Australia's unique faunal assemblage from that of:

   (a) Southeast Asia (b) South America (c) New Zealand (d) the Pacific realm
   (e) Ethiopia

2. Convergent evolution is particularly evident in the zoogeographic realm called the:

   (a) Nearctic (b) Neotropic (c) Palearctic (d) Paleotropic (e) Australian

3. The Galapagos Islands were first used as a laboratory for biogeographical studies by:

   (a) von Humboldt (b) Wallace (c) Darlington (d) Darwin (e) the ancient
   Indomalayans

4. The zoogeographic realm that blankets North America is called the:

   (a) Paleotropic (b) Palearctic (c) Pacific (d) Neotropic (e) Nearctic

5. The lengthening of the evolving giraffe's neck to better feed on the higher branches of trees demonstrates the concept of:

    (a) convergent evolution (b) adaptation (c) animal ranges (d) all of these (e) none of these

6. Prolonged isolation and the effects of separate evolution mark the zoogeographic realm known as the:

    (a) Palearctic (b) Indomalayan (c) Australian (d) Neotropic (e) Pacific

True-False Questions

__ 1. Australia and New Zealand share the same zoogeographic realm.
__ 2. Marsupials are unique to the Australian zoogeographic realm.
__ 3. The Paleotropic zoogeographic realm blankets most of Africa south of the Sahara.
__ 4. North America and South America belong to the same zoogeographic realm.
__ 5. Zoogeographic regions are spatially embedded within larger zoogeographic realms.
__ 6. The lessons learned by those studying island biogeography can apply to other isolated and/or inaccessible places, such as the tops of steep-sided hills.

UNIT 29: PLANET EARTH IN PROFILE: THE LAYERED INTERIOR

UNIT SUMMARY

Information about the internal structure of the Earth can be obtained from samples of crustal material, as well as measurement of wavelengths of received sunlight, magnetic fields, internal temperatures and pressures, and most importantly, from earthquake analysis. Seismographs record shocks and tremors in the surface, with seismic waves being proportional to the density of the material through which they are propagating. There are several types of seismic waves, including **P** (compressional) waves, which move material parallel to the direction of movement, **S** (shear) waves, which move objects at right angles to the wave, and **L** (surface) waves which travel along the crustal surface. The internal structure of Earth below its crust includes a partially molten upper mantle, a solid lower mantle, a liquid outer core, and a solid inner core. The Mohorovičić discontinuity (Moho) is a plane of contact between Earth's crust and the upper mantle. Continental and oceanic crust are noticeably different – continents are composed of less-dense sial, whereas oceanic crust is largely denser sima. The lithospheric (tectonic) plates float on the soft plastic upper mantle. Topographic relief refers to the vertical difference between the highest and lowest relief in a particular location. The continental shields (cratons) are low-relief expanses of old rock, while orogenic belts consist of high-relief mountain chains. Gradational processes include physical, chemical, and biological weathering, as well as mass movements and erosion.

UNIT OBJECTIVES

1. To outline the relevant properties of the Earth's five internal layers and to discuss some of the evidence leading to their discovery.

2. To introduce the salient properties of the Earth's lithosphere, the nature of the crust, and the underlying mantle.

3. To provide an outline of the gradational processes responsible for continually creating and removing relief elements of the Earth's crust.

GLOSSARY OF KEY TERMS

Asthenosphere The soft plastic layer of the upper mantle that underlies the lithosphere, which is able to move over it.

Body waves A seismic wave that travels through the interior of the Earth; consists of two kinds – **P** waves and **S** waves.

Continental shield A large, stable, relatively flat expanse of very old rocks that may constitute one of the earliest "slabs" of solidification of the primeval Earth's molten crust into hard rocks; forms the geologic core of a continental landmass.

Earthquake A shaking and trembling of the Earth's surface; caused by sudden releases of stresses that have been building slowly within the planetary crust.

Gradational processes A process that works to wear down the geologic materials that are built up on the Earth's landmasses.

Inner core The solid, most inner portion of the Earth, consisting mainly of nickel and iron.

Lithosphere The outermost shell of the solid Earth, lying immediately below the land surface and ocean floor (*lithos* means rock); composed of the Earth's thin crust together with the solid uppermost portion of the upper mantle that lies just below.

Lithospheric plate One of the fragmented, rigid segments of the lithosphere (also called a *tectonic plate*, which denotes its active mobile character); these segments or plates move in response to the plastic flow in the hot asthenosphere that lies just below the lithosphere.

Lower mantle The solid interior shell of the Earth that encloses the liquid outer core.

Mohorovičić discontinuity (Moho) The contact plane between the Earth's crust and the mantle that lies directly below it.

Orogenic belt A chain of linear mountain ranges.

Outer core The liquid shell that encloses the Earth's interior core, whose composition involves similar materials.

Relief The vertical distance between the highest and lowest elevations in a given area.

Seismic wave The pulses of energy generated by earthquakes that can pass through the entire planet.

Sial Derived from the chemical symbols for the minerals **si**licon and **al**uminum; refers to generally lighter-colored rocks of the continents, which are dominated by granite.

Sima Derived from the chemical symbols for the minerals **si**licon and **ma**gnesium; refers to the generally-darker rocks of the ocean floors, which are dominated by basalt.

Upper mantle The viscous (syrup-like) interior shell of the Earth that encloses the solid lower mantle; the uppermost part of the upper mantle, however, is solid, and this zone, together with the crust that lies directly above it, is called the lithosphere.

UNIT OUTLINE

I. Evidence of the Earth's internal structure
   A. Analysis of rocks, crust, magnetic fields, temperatures, and pressures
   B. Earthquakes are the shaking and trembling of Earth's crust by releases of stress within the crust
   1. seismic waves are pulses of energy generated by earthquakes
   2. seismographs measure earthquake intensity
   3. seismic reflection when waves bounce back off of a surface
   4. seismic refraction when waves are bent by a surface
   C. Types of seismic waves
   1. surface (**L**) waves travel along Earth's crust
   2. there are two types of body waves
       a. **P** waves are compressional, or push waves: move objects parallel to their direction of movement
       b. **S** waves are shear, or shake waves: move objects at right angles to their direction of movement

II. The earth's internal layers
   A. **P** and **S** waves are measured up to 103 degrees from the earthquake's origin
   B. Neither **P** nor **S** waves are measured from 103 to 142 degrees from the origin
   C. From 142 to 180 degrees from the origin **P** waves are recorded
   D. Evidence that there is a solid core that refracts seismic waves
   E. Solid inner core
   1. radius of only 1220 km (760 mi)
   2. lies 5150 km (3200 mi) below sea level
   F. Liquid outer core
   1. lies 2900 km (1800 mi) below sea level
   G. Solid lower mantle
   1. believed to be composed of oxides of iron, magnesium, and silicon
   H. Upper mantle
   1. extends from base of crust to lower mantle
   2. part of upper mantle is solid
   3. solid upper mantle and crust together form the lithosphere

III. Earth's outer layer
   A. Structural properties of the crust
   1. Mohorovičić (Moho) discontinuity is a contact plane between the continental (or oceanic) crust and the mantle
   2. continental crust contains lighter sial
   3. oceanic crust contains the denser sima
   B. The lithosphere
   1. comprised of crust and uppermost solid mantle
   2. the asthenosphere is the plastic-like transition zone between the lithosphere and the molten mantle; the lithosphere floats on it

C. Lithospheric plates
    1. usually called tectonic plates
    2. plates move in response to movement of asthenosphere

IV. The crustal surface
  A. Topographic relief
    1. relief is vertical difference between the highest and lowest elevations in an area
    2. low relief
      a. continental shields – Laurentian (Canadian), Guyana (Venezuelan), Brazilian, Scandanavian, Siberian, Indian, African, Australian, and Antarctic Shield
  B. Gradational processes
    1. weathering includes the physical, chemical, and biological processes that break down rock
      a. mass movements are generated by gravity
      b. erosion is long-distance removal of weathered materials

REVIEW QUESTIONS

1. What are seismographs and what type of data do they record?

2. List the differences between the different types of seismic waves (**P**, **S**, and **L**).

3. Beginning with the innermost layer, describe each of the principal layers of the inner Earth, using Fig. 29.5 as a reference.

SELF-TEST

Multiple-Choice Questions

1. Which type of seismic waves travel along Earth's crust?

    (a) **L** waves (b) **P** waves (c) **S** waves (d) **E** waves (e) **Z** waves

2. Which internal layer of Earth has the smallest diameter?

    (a) upper mantle (b) inner core (c) outer core (d) lower mantle (e) upper core

3. The Mohorovičić discontinuity is a contact plane between the crust and the:

    (a) core (b) lower mantle (c) upper mantle (d) asthenosphere (e) lithosphere

4. The crust and the upper mantle together form the:

    (a) asthenosphere (b) cryosphere (c) troposphere (d) outer core (e) lithosphere

5. Which of the following is not an orogenic belt?

    (a) the Alps (b) the Andes (c) the Himalayas (d) the African Shield
      (e) the Great Dividing Range

6. Which of the following is a gradational process?

    (a) weathering (b) a volcano (c) deposition (d) mountain-building (e) sublimation

True-False Questions

__ 1. The asthenosphere is a solid, rigid zone.
__ 2. Lithospheric plates are the same thing as tectonic plates.
__ 3. **P** waves (compressional waves) move objects at right angles to their direction of
      movement.
__ 4. **S** waves (shear or shake waves) move objects at right angles to their direction of
      movement.
__ 5. Erosion refers to longer-distance removal of weathered materials than that
      associated with weathering.
__ 6. The Mohorovičić discontinuity marks the base of the earth's crust.

UNIT 30: MINERALS AND IGNEOUS ROCKS

UNIT SUMMARY

An element is a naturally occurring substance that cannot be broken down further, and 92 of them are arranged by increasing atomic number on the periodic table. Minerals may contain a single element or a combination of elements, and are crystalline in structure. Rocks are composed of mineral assemblages. Minerals are identified by several key properties, including chemical composition, hardness, cleavage/fracture, color/streak, and luster. Minerals can be grouped as silicates (containing sulfur and oxygen) and nonsilicates. When rocks are classified by their origins, they are categorized as igneous, sedimentary, and metamorphic. Igneous rocks are called primary rocks, because they solidified first from Earth's primeval molten crust. Sedimentary rocks form from the deposition and compression of rock and mineral fragments. Metamorphic rocks are formed when heat and/or pressure transforms existing rock. Cooled magma forms intrusive igneous rocks when it remains below the surface, and extrusive igneous rocks when the magma spills onto the Earth's surface. Intrusions are termed discordant when they cut across existing strata, and concordant when they do not disrupt previously formed strata. Discordant forms include batholiths and stocks, whereas laccoliths and sills are concordant forms. The tendency of rocks to form parallel fractures without obvious faulting is called jointing. Exfoliation is a special type of jointing in which the outer layers of rock peel away when pressure is released, to expose lower rock layers. Igneous rocks form several noticeable forms in the landscape, including mesas, dikes, and volcanoes.

UNIT OBJECTIVES

1. To understand the relationship between rocks and their constituent minerals.

2. To briefly investigate the important properties of minerals and to provide an elementary scheme for their classification.

3. To discuss some important aspects of igneous rocks and their influence on landscape forms.

GLOSSARY OF KEY TERMS

Batholith A massive, discordant body of intrusive igneous rock (pluton) that has destroyed and melted most of the existing geologic structures it has invaded.

Concordant (intrusion) Intrusive magma that did not disrupt or destroy surrounding, existing geologic structures but conformed to them.

Crystalline Atoms arranged in a regular, repeating pattern.

Dike A discordant intrusive igneous form in which magma has cut vertically across preexisting strata , forming a kind of barrier wall.

Discordant (intrusion) Intrusive magma that did not conform to but cut across or otherwise disrupted surrounding, existing geologic structures.

Exfoliation A special kind of jointing that produces a joint pattern resembling a series of concentric shells, much like the layers of an onion; caused by the release of confining pressure, the outer layers progressively peel away and expose the lower layers.

Extrusive igneous rock Rocks formed from magma that cooled and solidified, as lava or ash, on the Earth's surface.

Igneous rock The (primary) rocks that formed directly from the cooling of molten magma; igneous is Latin for "formed from fire."

Jointing The tendency of rocks to develop parallel sets of fractures without any obvious movement such as faulting.

Laccolith A concordant intrusive igneous from in which a magma pipe led to a subterranean chamber that grew, dome-like, pushing up the overlying strata into a gentle bulge without destroying them.

Lava Magma that reaches the Earth's surface.

Magma The liquid molten mass from which igneous rocks are formed.

Metamorphic rock The (secondary) rocks that were created from the transformation , by heat and/or pressure, of existing rocks.

Mineral Naturally occurring inorganic element or compound having a definite chemical composition, physical properties, and usually, a crystalline structure.

Rock Any naturally formed, firm, and consolidated aggregate mass of mineral matter, of organic or inorganic origin, that constitutes part of the planetary crust.

Sedimentary rock The (secondary) rocks that formed from the deposition and compression of rock and mineral fragments.

Sill A concordant intrusive igneous form in which magma has inserted itself as a thin layer between strata of preexisting rocks without disturbing those layers to any great extent.

Stock A discordant pluton that is smaller than a batholith.

UNIT OUTLINE

I. Minerals and rocks

A. Elements are the most basic substances—they cannot be broken down further

B. A mineral is a crystalline, naturally occurring inorganic element or compound with a definite chemical composition, physical properties, and structure

C. Rocks are composed of assemblages of minerals

D. Mineral properties
1. chemical composition identified by a one or two-lettered symbol
2. hardness
3. cleavage/fracture – tendency to break
4. color/streak – streak is mineral's color when it is rubbed on porcelain in powdered form
5. luster (sheen)

E. Mineral types
1. silicates – contain silicon and oxygen
2. nonsilicates – carbonates, sulfates, sulfides, halides

II. Classification of rock types

A. Igneous rocks formed by the cooling and solidifying of magma

B. Sedimentary rocks are produced by the deposition and compression of rock fragments

C. Metamorphic rocks are formed when existing rocks are modified by heat or pressure

D. Sedimentary and metamorphic rocks are secondary rocks

III. Igneous rocks

A. Formed by cooling of lava (magma)

B. Igneous rocks are a complex mix of many minerals and gases
1. intrusive igneous rocks form from magma that never reached Earth's surface
2. extrusive igneous rocks form from magma that spilled out onto Earth's surface

C. Intrusive forms
1. intrusions are discordant if they disrupt existing structures
   a. batholith
   b. stock
   c. dike
2. intrusions are concordant if they do not cut across existing rock
   a. sill
   b. laccolith

D. Jointing and exfoliation
1. jointing is the tendency of rock to form parallel fractures without any obvious movement
2. joint planes are planes of weakness and separation

      3. exfoliation is a special kind of jointing that forms concentric circles, caused by release of overlying pressure on rock, and subsequent expansion

   E. Igneous rocks in the landscape
      1. resist weathering and erosion
      2. mesa
      3. dike
      4. volcanoes

REVIEW QUESTIONS

1. List five of the properties of minerals which aid in their classificiation.

2. What is the difference between igneous and sedimentary rocks?

3. List and describe a few of the intrusive forms in the landscape, using Fig. 30.4.

SELF-TEST

Multiple-Choice Questions

1. The most basic substances, which cannot be broken down further, are:

    (a) compounds (b) minerals (c) elements (d) rocks (e) primary chemicals

2. Rocks are composed of:

    (a) minerals (b) graphite (c) gases (d) silicates only (e) laccoliths

3. Which of the following is not an identifying property of a mineral?

    (a) chemical composition (b) hardness (c) fracture (d) exfoliation (e) luster

4. All of the following landforms result from igneous rock except:

    (a) mesa (b) dike (c) Mount St. Helens (d) volcano (e) river bed

5. Which of the following is not a discordant intrusion?

    (a) batholith (b) laccolith (c) dike (d) stock (e) pluton

6. Which rock type is the result of deposition and compression of rock and mineral fragments?

    (a) sedimentary rock (b) igneous rock (c) metamorphic rock (d) magma (e) granite

True-False Questions

__ 1. Metamorphic rocks are existing rocks that have been modified by heat and pressure.
__ 2. The sulfate minerals all contain sulfur and oxygen.
__ 3. A mineral is a naturally occurring organic compound.
__ 4. The hardest mineral is quartz.
__ 5. The natural elements include gold and carbon.
__ 6. Igneous rocks are highly resistant to weathering and erosion.

UNIT SUMMARY

Igneous rocks are the primary rocks on Earth, formed from the cooling of the molten primeval crust. Sedimentary and metamorphic rocks are termed secondary rocks because they are derived from preexisting rock. Sedimentary rocks are formed by the deposition and compaction (lithification) of rock fragments and mineral grains. Compaction is accompanied by cementation, where mineral matter is laid down in thin films on grain surfaces, and effectively glues sedimentary rock together. Clastic sedimentary rocks are formed from particles of other rocks, whereas nonclastic rocks are created by deposition of chemical solution or organic materials. Clastic rock includes conglomerate, sandstone, shale, and limestone. The formation sequence of sedimentary rock can be seen in the landscape when rock strata, or bedding planes are examined. Disruption of the stratigraphy is known as an unconformity. Crossbedding occurs when successive sedimentary rock layers are deposited at varying inclines. Metamorphic rocks are formed when existing rock is subjected to additional heat and/or pressure. Contact metamorphism is seen where intrusive action by magma is taking place. Sandstone metamorphoses into quartzite, limestone is converted to marble, shale becomes slate, and schist is formed when the preexisting rock is so altered, it impossible to determine what its previous identity was.

UNIT OBJECTIVES

1. To discuss the circumstances under which sedimentary and metamorphic rocks form.

2. To identify common sedimentary and metamorphic rock types.

3. To discuss some observable structure within sedimentary and metamorphic rock masses.

GLOSSARY OF KEY TERMS

Breccia In clastic sedimentary rocks when pebble-sized fragments in a conglomerate are not rounded but angular and jagged.

Cementation During the lithification process of compaction as the grains of sediments are tightly squeezed together, water in the intervening pore spaces, which contains dissolved minerals, is deposited on the grain surfaces and acts as a glue to further bond the grains together.

Clastic sedimentary rocks Sedimentary rocks made from particles of other rocks.

Compaction The lithification process whereby deposited sediments are compressed by the weight of newer, overlying sediments; this pressure will compact and consolidate lower strata, squeezing their grained sediments tightly together. Usually occurs in conjunction with cementation.

Conglomerate A composite sedimentary rock composed of gravels, pebbles, and sometimes boulders.

Contact metamorphism Metamorphic changes in rocks induce by their local contact with molten magma or lava.

Crossbedding Consists of successive rock strata deposited not horizontally but at varying inclines; like ripple marks on sand, this usually forms on beaches and in dunes.

Foliation The unmistakable banded appearance of certain metamorphic rocks, such as gneiss and schist; bands formed by minerals realigned into parallel strips during metamorphism.

Gneiss Metamorphic rock derived from granite that usually exhibits pronounced foliation.

Limestone A nonclastic sedimentary rock mainly formed from the respiration and photosynthesis of marine organisms in which calcium carbonate is distilled from seawater; finely textured and therefore resistant to weathering when exposed on the surface, it is susceptible to solution that can produce karst landscapes both above and below the ground.

Marble Metamorphosed limestone; the hardness and density of this rock is preferred by sculptors for statues that can withstand exposure to the agents of erosion for millennia.

Nonclastic sedimentary rocks Derived not from particles of other rocks, but from chemical solution by deposition and evaporation or from organic deposition.

Quartzite A very hard metamorphic rock that resists weathering; formed by the metamorphosis of sandstone (made of quartz grains and a silica cement).

Rocks Any naturally formed, firm, and consolidated aggregate mass of mineral matter, of organic or inorganic origin, that constitutes part of the planetary crust.

Rock cycle Cycle of transformation that affects all rocks and involves all parts of the Earth's crust: plutons form deep in the crust, uplift pushes them to the surface, erosion wears them down, and the sediments they produce become new mountains.

Sandstone A common sedimentary rock possessing sand-sized grains.

Schist A common metamorphic rock so altered that its previous form is impossible to determine; fine-grained, exhibits wavy bands, and breaks along parallel planes (but unevenly, inlike slate).

Shale The soft, finest-grained of the sedimentary rocks; formed from compacted mud.

Slate Metamorphosed shale; a popular building material, it retains shale's quality of breaking along parallel planes.

Strata Layers.

Stratification Layering.

Stratigraphy The order and arrangement of rock strata.

Unconformity A gap in the geologic history of an area as found in the rock record, owing to a hiatus in deposition, followed by erosion of the surface, with further deposition continuing later; more specifically, can also refer to the contact between the eroded strata and the strata of resumed deposition.

UNIT OUTLINE

I. Sedimentary rocks
    A. Formed by deposition and compaction of rock and mineral grains from other rocks
        1. pressure of overlying rock removes water in the process of compaction
        2. silica or calcite cements the rock together
    B. Clastic and nonclastic sedimentary rocks
        1. clastic rocks are formed from particles of other rocks
        2. nonclastic rocks form from chemical solution or organic deposition
        3. conglomerate is the coarsest type of sedimentary rock
            a. if pebbles in conglomerate are jagged, called breccia
        4. sandstone is usually composed from grains of quartz, highly resistant
        5. shale is softer than sandstone, formed from compacted mud
        6. limestone can be formed from
            a. marine shell fragments
            b. calcium carbonate from respiration and photosynthesis of marine life
    C. Sedimentary rocks in the landscape
        1. stratification or layering of rock beds
        2. unconformity where stratification interrupted
    D. Features of sedimentary strata
        1. most strata horizontally layered
        2. cross-bedding where layers deposited on varying inclines
        3. folds, faults, deformations

II. Metamorphic rocks
    A. Existing rocks that have been changed by heat and pressure
    B. Tectonic or volcanic action
    C. Metamorphic rock types
        1. quartzite
        2. marble
        3. slate
        4. schist
        5. gneiss
    D. Metamorphic rocks in the landscape
        1. weakest along foliation points

III. The rock cycle
    A. Plutons of molten magma form in crust, pushed upward eroded – no beginning or end to this cycle
    B. See Fig. 31.12 to trace each of the stages of cycle

REVIEW QUESTIONS

1. Describe the processes of compaction and cementation.

2. What is an unconformity and how is it formed?

3. How does crossbedding occur?

SELF-TEST

Multiple-Choice Questions

1. Which of the following is a process of sedimentary rock formation?

    (a) compaction (b) exfoliation (c) metamorphism (d) cooling (e) rippling

2. Which of these rocks is not a sedimentary rock?

    (a) shale (b) marble (c) sandstone (d) limestone (e) breccia

3. Which of these rocks is not a metamorphic rock?

    (a) limestone (b) marble (c) slate (d) quartzite (e) schist

4. A rock that exhibits exfoliation is:

   (a) marble (b) granite (c) slate (d) gneiss (e) limestone

5. When intrusive action occurs, rocks nearby are affected. This is called:

   (a) contact abrasion (b) jointing (c) exfoliation (d) shear (e) contact metamorphism

6. Shale can be metamorphosed into:

   (a) granite (b) marble (c) slate (d) limestone (e) breccia

True-False Questions

__ 1. The process of compaction alone forms sedimentary rocks.
__ 2. There is a definite beginning and end to the rock cycle.
__ 3. Shale is a softer rock than most sandstones.
__ 4. Limestone can form from calcium carbonate.
__ 5. The Earth's first rocks were sedimentary rocks.
__ 6. When sedimentary rock is deposited at varying inclines, this process is called cross-bedding.

UNIT 32: PLATES OF THE LITHOSPHERE

UNIT SUMMARY

The theory of continental drift was proposed by Alfred Wegener in 1915, and described a primeval supercontinent named Pangaea, subdivided into Laurasia in the north and Gondwana in the south. Wegener hypothesized that this huge landmass broke apart, forming the continents and oceans, and that the continents continued to move away from their origin. Geologists and physical geographers later proposed the mechanism for this movement as lithospheric plates moving on top of heated convection cells. Evidence of seafloor spreading later confirmed this theory. The Earth's surface is divided into eight major plates, and a number of smaller plates. Plate boundaries are marked by increased volcanic and seismic activity, as in the Pacific Ring of Fire. The movement of the tectonic plates creates widespread landscapes and landforms. There are three major types of plate boundaries: divergent, convergent, and transform. Plate divergence results in rift and rift valley formation. Convergent plate boundaries are subduction zones, where there can be oceanic-oceanic, oceanic-continental, or continental-continental plate convergence. Lateral plate contacts, where plates are sliding past one another, are called transform faults. The San Andreas Fault in California is a classic example of a transform fault.

UNIT OBJECTIVES

1. To introduce the concepts of continental drift and plate tectonics.

2. To identify the major plates of the lithosphere.

3. To discuss the important boundary zones between lithospheric plates in which rifting, subduction, and transform faulting occur.

GLOSSARY OF KEY TERMS

Continental drift The notion hypothesized by Alfred Wegener concerning the fragmentation of Pangaea and the slow movement of the modern continents away from this core supercontinent.

Crustal spreading The geographic term for seafloor spreading; not all crustal spreading occurs on the ocean floor.

Gondwana The southern portion of the primeval supercontinent, Pangaea.

Island arc A volcanic island chain produced in a zone where two oceanic plates are converging; one plate will subduct the other, forming deep trenches as well as spawning volcanoes that may protrude above sea level in an island-arc formation.

Laurasia The northern portion of the primeval supercontinent, Pangaea.

Lithospheric plates One of the fragmented, rigid segments of the lithosphere (also called a tectonic plate, which denotes its active mobile character); these segments or plates move in response to the plastic flow in the hot asthenosphere that lies just below the lithosphere.

Pacific Ring of Fire The Circum-Pacific belt of high volcanic and seismic activity, stretching around the entire Pacific Basin counterclockwise through western South America, western North America, and Asia's island archipelagoes (from Japan to Indonesia) as far as New Zealand.

Pangaea The primeval supercontinent, hypothesized by Alfred Wegner, that broke apart and formed the continents and oceans as w know them today; consisted of two parts – a northern Laurasia and a southern Gondwana.

Rift An opening of the crust, normally into a trough or trench, that occurs in a zone of plate divergence.

Rift valley Develops in a continental zone of plate divergence where tensional forces pull the crustally thinning surface apart; the rift valley is the trough that forms when the land sinks between parallel faults in strips.

Seafloor spreading The process wherein new crust is formed by upwelling magma at the midoceanic ridges, and then continuously moves away from its source toward the margins of the ocean basin.

Subduction The process that takes place when an oceanic plate converges head-on with a plate carrying a continental landmass at its leading edge; the lighter continental plate overrides the denser oceanic plate and pushes it downward.

Transform fault A special case of transcurrent faulting in which the transverse fault marks the boundary between two lithospheric plates that are sliding past each other.

UNIT OUTLINE

I. Continental drift
    A. Proposed by Alfred Wegener, 1915, *The Origin of Continents*
    B. All continents were formerly part of the Pangaea supercontinent
        1. Laurasia in the north
        2. Gondwana in the south
    C. Continental drift is the fragmenting of Pangaea and slow movement of continents away from it
        1. fossil evidence of plants and animals
        2. jigsaw-like fit of continents

II. Continents and seafloors
   A. Arthur Holmes (1939) proposed existence of convection cells deep inside Earth that dragged the continents
   B. Midoceanic ridges discovered to be formed by seafloor spreading: the continuous creation and upward deposition of new crust, and its subsequent movement away from its source
      1. Earth divided into lithospheric (tectonic) plates
      2. if ocean floor is created and spreads in one area, must be crushed and destroyed in another location
         a. volcanoes
         b. earthquakes
         c. mountain building

III. Distribution of plates
   A. Pacific Plate
   B. North American Plate
   C. Eurasian Plate
   D. African Plate
   E. South American Plate
   F. Australian Plate
   G. Indian Plate
   H. Antarctic Plate
   I. Many smaller plates associated with the eight major plates
   J. Location of plate boundaries
      1. represented by linear earthquake zones
      2. continental and submarine volcanism
         a. Pacific Ring of Fire

IV. Movement of plates
   A. Plates maintain their direction of movement for millions of years
   B. Movement of plate directly creates earth's landscapes
   C. Plate divergence
      1. midoceanic ridges spread apart by rising magma, rifts in seafloor created
      2. rift valley occurs when tensional forces are underneath a landmass
      3. seafloor spreading now called crustal spreading because it is not confined to just the oceans
   D. Plate convergence
      1. oceanic-continental plate convergence: subduction occurs when an oceanic plate and a continental plat collide; the lighter continental plate overrides the oceanic plate, and pushes it downward
      2. oceanic-oceanic plate convergence: convergent plate densities are the same, when collision occurs, huge contortions formed, deep trenches and huge volcanoes result

3. continental-continental plate convergence: convergent plate densities are the same, huge distortions made, lower plate not forced downward, earthquakes
E. Lateral plate contact
   1. boundary where two plates are sliding past one another
   2. create transform faults
   3. earthquakes and crustal deformation
   4. San Andreas Fault

REVIEW QUESTIONS

1. What is the Pacific Ring of Fire?

2. Describe generally the formation of a rift valley, using Fig. 32.6 as a guide.

3. Contrast oceanic-oceanic plate convergence with oceanic-continental plate convergence.

SELF-TEST

Multiple-Choice Questions

1. Pangaea's northern portion is called:

   (a) Gondwana (b) Laurasia (c) Eurasia (d) Norda (e) Lorentia

2. Seafloor spreading causes the formation of:

   (a) new crust (b) magma (c) the asthenosphere (d) convection cells (e) subterranean caves

3. The Pacific Ring of Fire is a zone of:

   (a) burning lithospheric crust (b) no plate boundaries (c) volcanic activity (d) lateral plate contact (e) little plate contact

4. Which of the following is not one of the eight major lithospheric plates?

   (a) North American Plate (b) Indian Plate (c) Pacific Plate (d) Caribbean Plate (e) African Plate

5.   Plate divergence results in:

(a) no change in the landscape (b) island arcs (c) volcanoes (d) mountain building (e) rift valleys

6.   The San Andreas Fault is a(n):

(a) oceanic-continental plate boundary (b) lateral plate boundary (c) oceanic-oceanic plate boundary (d) subduction zone (e) geologically dormant zone

True-False Questions

___ 1. The North American and Pacific Plates meet at the San Andreas Fault.
___ 2. In subduction, the heavier continental plate overrides the lighter oceanic plate.
___ 3. Laurasia and Pangaea were components of Gondwana.
___ 4. Many of Earth's landscapes are created by seafloor (crustal) spreading.
___ 5. The midoceanic ridge is linear and unbroken.
___ 6. Oceanic-oceanic plate convergence creates massive contortions in landscapes.

UNIT 33: PLATE MOVEMENT: CAUSES AND EFFECTS

UNIT SUMMARY

The movement of Earth's lithospheric plates and location of the midoceanic ridges is evidenced by a drop in temperature of the oceanic crust with increasing proximity to the continental margins. The process by which Earth's continents formed remains debatable, but the fact that certain areas of rock were removed from their plates of origin and joined to others by accretion is seen in the field. Terranes are regions of rock that are consistent in age, type, and structure. Suspect terranes are mismatched areas of rock in comparison with their surroundings. Isostasy refers to a condition of equilibrium between the landmasses and the asthenosphere. This phenomenon balances the effects of erosion, and contributes to both dramatic and smaller types of topographic relief.

UNIT OBJECTIVES

1. To outline briefly the mechanisms and processes the move lithospheric plates.

2. To discuss the evolution of the Earth's continental landmasses.

3. To discuss the concept of isostasy and relate it to the topography of the continents.

GLOSSARY OF KEY TERMS

Accretion Process in which bodies of rock from another plate are attached to a given landmass.

Isostasy Derived from an ancient Greek term (*iso* the same; *stasy* to stand), the condition of vertical equilibrium between floating landmasses and the asthenosphere beneath them; this situation of sustained adjustment is maintained despite the forces that constantly operate to change the landmasses.

Suspect terrane A subregion of rocks possessing properties that sharply distinguish it from surrounding regional rocks; a terrane consisting of a "foreign" rock mass that is mismatched to its large-scale geologic setting.

Terrane A geological region of "consistent" rocks in terms of age, type, and structure; mismatched subregions can occur and are known as suspect terranes.

UNIT OUTLINE

I. Mechanism of crustal spreading
    A. Sublithospheric magma continuously spreads out of ridges, keeping them open
    B. Some material subducted and reabsorbed by asthenosphere
    C. Entire mantle may be in motion

II. Evolution of continents
    A. Crustal formation
        1. landmasses appear to have about same volume as 2.5 billion years ago, crust has been recycled since then
        2. continental shields relatively stable, margins more active with plate boundaries
    B. Terranes and suspect terranes
        1. a terrane is a region of consistent (similar) rocks
        2. when there is a subregion of different rocks, they form a suspect terrane such as Wrangellia

III. Isostasy
    A. A condition of equilibrium between floating landmasses and the asthenosphere below
    B. Isotasy and erosion
        1. as erosion removes load from a landmass, isostatic adjustment raises the rocks to compensate
        2. as material is deposited (such as in a river delta) isostatic adjustment constantly lowers the level of the material
    C. Isostasy and drifting plates
        1. when plates collide, deformations occur
        2. where mountains are built, trenches also exist to maintain isostatic equilibrium
    D. Isostasy and regional landscapes
        1. isostasy also active on continental plains – erosion by wind, water, ice removes material, and adjustment is required
        2. plains and uplands affected by isostasy in phases – when erosion first takes place and sialic root is deep, more isostatic uplift; as more material eroded and root shorter, uplift slower
        3. ice sheets cause isostatic sinking of crust, when glaciers retreat rapidly, it takes isostatic rebound a long time to fully raise the land back up to its original level
        4. dams and crustal equilibrium
           a. the weight of damned up water can cause isostatic sinking of the crust below it

REVIEW QUESTIONS

1. How does isostasy affect regional landscapes?

2. Contrast terranes and suspect terranes.

3. Draw a sketch of Airy's mountain root hypothesis, labeling sial and sima, using Fig. 33.5 as a guide.

SELF-TEST

Multiple-Choice Questions

1. Temperatures of oceanic crust are highest near:

   (a) midoceanic ridges (b) continental margins (c) tropical latitudes (d) continental shelves (e) the Southern Hemisphere

2. An "exotic" rock mass among a region of consistent rocks is known as a(n):

   (a) ridge (b) mineral (c) suspect terrane (d) artificial terrane (e) conglomerate

3. The condition of equilibrium between landmasses and the asthenosphere is:

   (a) continental drift (b) isostasy (c) uplift (d) crustal spreading (e) rebound

4. When erosion first begins and the sialic root is deep, isostatic adjustment occurs:

   (a) very slowly (b) in sporadic bursts with gaps of inactivity in-between (c) not at all (d) only if the landmass is a volcano (e) almost continuously

5. Isostatic rebound after the rapid retreat of glaciers occurs:

   (a) very rapidly (b) in abrupt phases (c) slowly (d) not at all (e) too quickly for equilibrium to exist

6. In a comparison of sial and sima, which substance would "float" (is less dense)?

   (a) sial (b) sima (c) neither would float (d) both would float (e) sial would float only in Arctic latitudes

True-False Questions

___ 1. Crust of ocean floors drops in temperature as it reaches continental margins.
___ 2. Wrangellia, in North America, is an example of a suspect terrane.
___ 3. Isostasy is a condition of disequilibrium.
___ 4. As erosion occurs, isostatic uplift compensates for it.
___ 5. The weight of water behind a dam can stimulate isostatic uplift.
___ 6. The Earth's crust is permanent, unchanging, and solid.

UNIT SUMMARY

Volcanism is defined as the eruption of molten rock at the Earth's surface, with approximately 75 percent of the planet's volcanoes existing on the seafloor. Volcanism is located in areas of seafloor spreading and subduction zones of convergent plate boundaries. Volcanoes are categorized as active when they have erupted in recorded history; dormant when there is evidence of recent activity but no record; and extinct when it shows signs of activity and is weathered/eroded. Lava and magma composition varies, as do their viscosity and gas percentages. Pyroclastics are the solidified fragments that have been erupted from a volcano. The four types of volcanic landforms are composite volcanoes, lava domes, cinder cones, and shield volcanoes. Composite volcanoes are large in size and form over subduction zones; lava domes are created when acidic lava oozes onto the surface; cinder cones are formed from pyroclastics that volcanoes eject during explosive activity; shield volcanoes are formed from fluid basaltic lava flows. Hot spots are plumes of extraordinary heat that remain at a fixed location, over which the tectonic plates pass, forming shield volcanoes in the process. When the walls of a volcano sometimes collapse, a caldera is formed. Phreatic eruptions occur when water enters into the magma chamber below a volcano, and are extremely violent explosions. Krakatau, Tambora, and Santorini are examples of such eruptions. Volcanoes create unique landscapes, and can be imposing both physically and mentally for those who settle near them. Mount Vesuvius and Mount Etna are two examples of this phenomenon.

UNIT OBJECTIVES

1. To relate volcanic activity to plate boundary types.

2. To discuss typical landforms produced by volcanic eruptions.

3. To cite some dramatic examples of human interaction with volcanic environments.

GLOSSARY OF KEY TERMS

Aa Angular, jagged, blocky-shaped lava formed from the hardening of not especially fluid lavas.

Caldera A steep-walled, circular volcanic basin usually formed by the collapse of a volcano whose magma chamber emptied out; can also result from a particularly powerful eruption that blows off the peak and crater of a volcano.

Cinder cone Volcanic landform consisting mainly of pyroclastics; often formed during brief periods of explosive activity, they normally remain quite small.

Composite volcano Volcano formed, usually above a subduction zone, by the eruption of a succession of lavas and pyroclastics that accumulate as a series of alternating layers; the larger and more durable composite volcanoes are called *stratovolcanoes*.

Hot spot A place of very high temperatures in the upper mantle that reaches the surface as a "plume" of extraordinarily high heat; a linear series of shield volcanoes can form on lithospheric plates moving over this plume, as happened in the case of the Hawaiian island chain.

Lahar A mudflow largely comprised of volcanic debris. Triggered high on a snowcapped volcano by an eruption, such a mudflow can advance downslope at high speed and destroy everything in its path; frequently solidifies where it comes to rest.

Lava dome A small volcanic mound produced when acidic lava penetrates and oozes out onto the surface.

Nuée ardente A cloud of high-temperature volcanic gas that races downslope following a spectacular explosion associated with unusually high pressures inside the erupting volcano; incinerates everything in its path.

Pahoehoe Ropy-patterned lava; forms where very fluid lavas develop a "smooth" skin upon hardening that wrinkles as movement continues.

Phreatic eruption An extraordinarily explosive volcanic eruption involving the penetration of water into a superheated magma chamber; such explosions of composite volcanoes standing in water can reach far beyond a volcano's immediate area.

Pyroclastics The collective name for the solid lava fragments that are erupted explosively from a volcano.

Shield volcano Formed from fluid basaltic lavas that flow in sheets that are gradually built up by successive eruptions; in profile their long horizontal dimensions peak in a gently rounded manner rounded manner that resembles a shield. The main island of Hawaii has some of the world's most active shield volcanoes.

Vent An opening through the Earth's crust from which lava erupts; most eruptions occur through pipe-shaped vents that build volcanic mountains, but fissure eruptions also occur through lengthy cracks that exude horizontal sheets of lava.

UNIT OUTLINE

I. Distribution of volcanic activity
    A. Most volcanism is related to seafloor spreading or subduction zones
    B. Active, dormant, and extinct volcanoes

      1. active volcano has erupted in recorded history

      2. dormant volcano has not been seen erupting, but shows evidence that it has

      3. extinct volcanoes show no signs of eruption, and are weathered and eroded

  C. Lava and landforms

      1. viscosity of lava and magma varies

          a. basaltic lavas quite fluid

          b. silica-rich lava and magma are viscous

      2. volcanic bombs are globs of lava thrown into the air that solidify in mid-air

      3. pyroclastics (volcanic cinders, ash, and dust) are formed from smaller fragments of lava

      4. fissure eruptions do not create mountains, make plateaus

II. Volcanic mountains

  A. Composite volcanoes

      1. large mountains formed in subduction zones

          a. stratovolcanoes of great height

      2. extremely dangerous, erupt with little or no warning

  B. Lahars are deposits of hot ash on snowcapped volcanoes, creating mudslides

  C. Nuée ardente is a cloud of hot gas and dust associated with a volcanic eruption; can descend rapidly downslope, incinerating all in its path

  D. Risk prediction of volcanic eruption is improving, but is by no means error-free

  E. Volcanic domes are produced by oozing lava

  F. Cinder cones are composed mainly of pyroclastics (fragments), generally small in size

  G. Shield volcanoes are formed from fluid basaltic lavas

      1. peaks are unimpressive, horizontal dimensions greater

      2. pahoehoe is the slightly hardened lava, which is still moving

  H. Hot spots are unusually hot "plumes" in a fixed location; as plates move over it, shield volcanoes then form

      1. can calculate speed and direction of plate movement from observing hot spots

III. Calderas

  A. Formed when a volcano is no longer supported by a source of magma, and it crumbles

      1. earthquakes can contribute to caldera formation

      2. Crater Lake, Oregon

      3. Ngorongoro Crater, Tanzania

  B. Phreatic eruption

      1. when water enters a magma chamber, can blow top off of volcano, creating huge craters

a. Krakatau (1883), phreatic eruption created tsunamis (seismic sea waves)
b. Tambora (1815), phreatic eruption created so much dust, that solar radiation interfered with; temperatures plunged, crops ruined
c. Santorini (around 1645 B.C.E.), seawater may have entered magma chamber, cataclysmic explosion, sky dark with dust for days, huge caldera created

IV. Landscapes of volcanism
A. Volcanic features dominate an area's physical and mental landscapes

REVIEW QUESTIONS

1. What is pahoehoe, and how does it differ from aa?

2. List the four types of volcanic landforms.

3. How does lava flow during a fissure eruption? Use Fig. 34.2 as a reference.

SELF-TEST

Multiple-Choice Questions

1. Which of the following sites did not experience a recorded phreatic eruption?

   (a) Tambora (b) Santorini (c) Krakatau (d) Mt. St. Helens (e) all experience phreatic eruptions

2. What is the term for a dangerous cloud of gas and dust expelled from a volcano?

   (a) nuée ardente (b) lahar (c) pahoehoe (d) hot spot (e) aa

3. When the walls of a volcano collapse, what landform is created?

   (a) a cordillera (b) a shield (c) a plate (d) a dome (e) a caldera

4. Landforms resulting from oozing, acidic lava are:

   (a) cinder cones (b) lava domes (c) pahoehoes (d) lahars (e) volcanic shields

5. The type of eruption in which water enters the magma chamber is:

    (a) pyroclastic (b) phreatic (c) composite (d) dormant (e) hydrologic

6. An example of a caldera in the landscape is:

    (a) the Alps (b) the Andes (c) Crater Lake (d) San Andreas Fault (e) the Appalachians

True-False Questions

___ 1. About seventy-five percent of all the world's volcanoes are under the sea.
___ 2. A dormant volcano shows no signs of life and is weathered and eroded.
___ 3. A cinder cone contains no pyroclastics.
___ 4. Angular, jagged blocks of solidified lava are called aa.
___ 5. The largest volcanoes, formed over subduction zones, are composite volcanoes.
___ 6. A plume of intense heat that constantly migrates along plate boundaries is termed a hot spot.

UNIT 35: EARTHQUAKES AND LANDSCAPES

UNIT SUMMARY

An earthquake releases energy (as seismic waves) that was slowly built up as rocks were increasingly deformed. The focus of an earthquake is its point of origin, and the epicenter is the point on the Earth's surface directly above the focus. Magnitude of an earthquake refers to the amount of shaking of the ground that it produces, and is measured by the logarithmic *Richter Scale*. Earthquake intensity measures the impact on the cultural landscape, and is recorded on the more qualitative *Modified Mercalli Scale*. The global distribution of earthquakes is greatest in the *Circum-Pacific belt*, and is also significant in the *Trans-Eurasian belt*, as well as along the *midoceanic ridges*. Intraplate earthquakes occur in areas other than those marking tectonic plate boundaries, and India's Bhuj earthquake of 2001 is a classic example. One landform created by seismic action is called a fault scarp, bearing an exposed cliff-like face known as the fault plane. Tsunamis are seismic sea waves, and occur when an earthquake's epicenter is located on the ocean floor or near a coastline.

UNIT OBJECTIVES

1. To describe and quantify the magnitude and intensity of earthquakes.

2. To relate the spatial pattern of earthquakes to plate tectonics.

3. To discuss landscapes and landforms that bear the signature of earthquake activity.

GLOSSARY OF KEY TERMS

Earthquake A shaking and trembling of the Earth's surface; caused by sudden releases of stresses that have been building slowly within the planetary crust.

Epicenter The point on the Earth's surface directly above the focus (place of origin) of an earthquake.

Fault A fracture in crustal rock involving the displacement of rock on one side of the fracture with respect to rock on the other side.

Fault plane The surface of contact along which blocks on either side of a fault move.

Fault scarp The exposed cliff-like face of a fault plane created by geologic action without significant erosional change.

Fault trace The lower edge of a fault scarp; the line on the surface where a fault scarp intersects the surface.

Focus The place of origin of an earthquake, which can be near the surface or deep inside the crust or upper mantle.

Intensity (earthquake) The size and damage of an earthquake as measured – on the Modified Mercalli Scale – by the impact on structures and human activities on the cultural landscape.

Intraplate earthquake Earthquakes occurring in areas other than tectonic plate contact zones.

Magnitude (earthquake) The amount of shaking of the ground during an earthquake as measured by a seismograph.

Tsunami A seismic sea wave, set off by a crustal disturbance, that can reach gigantic proportions.

UNIT OUTLINE

I. Earthquake terminology
    A. A fault is a fracture in the crust that displaces rock on one side of the fault as compared to the other side.
    B. An earthquake is a release of energy that has slowly built up during deformation of rock
        1. an earthquake's origin is the focus, and the point above the focus on Earth's surface is the epicenter
        2. magnitude is the amount of shaking of the ground during a quake
            a. Richter Scale for measurement
            b. Moment Magnitude Scale
        3. intensity reflects the impact of an earthquake on a given landscape
            a. Modified Mercalli Scale

II. Earthquake distribution
    A. Heaviest concentration in Circum-Pacific belt
    B. Trans-Eurasian belt
    C. Midoceanic ridges
    D. Intraplate earthquakes can also occur
        1. New Madrid, Missouri

III. Earthquakes and Landscapes
    A. Physical and cultural landscapes modified by earthquakes
        1. fault scarp is the result of rock deformation, with one block raised with respect to the other
        2. fault plane is the exposed cliff-like face of the scarp
        3. fault trace is the lower edge of the fault scarp
            a. fault breccia often in fault trace
        4. landslides and mudslides can occur with a lot of rain in these areas

IV. Tsunamis
A. Seismic sea wave that occurs when an earthquake's epicenter is on the ocean floor

REVIEW QUESTIONS

1. Discuss the geographic distribution of recent earthquake activity with the aid of Fig. 35.5.

2. Define fault; fault plane; fault scarp; and fault trace.

3. Describe what an intraplate earthquake is, and give an example of where a famous one occurred.

SELF-TEST

Multiple-Choice Questions

1. The place of origin of an earthquake is its:

   (a) epicenter (b) focus (c) fault (d) fracture (e) locus

2. The amount of shaking of the ground associated with an earthquake is its:

   (a) magnitude (b) intensity (c) density factor (d) focal factor (e) force factor

3. The amount of impact that an earthquake has on the physical and cultural landscape is its:

   (a) magnitude (b) force factor (c) density factor (d) focal factor (e) intensity

4. A visible landform resulting from an earthquake is a:

   (a) cliff (b) caldera (c) fault scarp (d) seamount (e) phreatic depression

5. A seismic sea wave is known as a:

   (a) tidal wave (b) hurricane (c) typhoon (d) tsunami (e) monsoon

6. The most widely used measure of earthquake magnitude used at present is the:

    (a) Saffir-Simpson scale (b) Richter Scale (c) Modified Mercalli Scale
        (d) Moment Magnitude Scale (e) Mercalli Force Factor scale

True-False Questions

___ 1. An earthquake releases energy that has accumulated from the increasing
        deformation of rocks.
___ 2. A tsunami and a tidal wave are two different names for the same thing.
___ 3. The point on Earth's surface directly above the epicenter is the focus.
___ 4. Earthquakes only occur at plate boundaries.
___ 5. A fault scarp is the exposed face of a fault plane.
___ 6. The Circum-Pacific belt contains the highest number of earthquakes on Earth.

UNIT 36: SURFACE EXPRESSIONS
OF SUBSURFACE STRUCTURES

UNIT SUMMARY

The many types of stresses imposed on rock are evidenced by a variety of surface landforms. In order to describe the orientation of structures, the term strike is used to define the compass direction of the line of intersection between a layer of rock and the horizontal, whereas the word dip describes the angle at which a rock layer tilts from the horizontal. A fault is a fracture in crustal rock, where there is displacement on one side of that fracture compared to the other. There are three types of faults: normal, reverse, and transcurrent. A fracture with no displacement is called a joint. Compressional forces create parallel (echelon) faults, and when the angle of a fault plane is very low, thrust faults are formed. Tensional forces form normal faults, with sunken blocks known as grabens wedged between parallel normal faults. Horsts are raised blocks in-between reverse faults. Transcurrent faults occur when blocks of crustal rock move laterally, and motion along the fault plane is horizontal. Transcurrent faults are also known as strike-slip faults because movement is taking place along the strike of the fault. Transform faults are special cases of transcurrent faulting, and mark the contact boundary between two tectonic plates. Folds are primarily compressional features, and folding and faulting generally occur together. Folding produces arching upfolds called anticlines, and troughlike downfolds called synclines. Folds at extreme angles can become recumbent or overturned. Primary landforms are formed by tectonic activity, whereas secondary landforms are produced by weathering and erosion. Earth's crust can also undergo slight deformation in areas of stable lithosphere. Diastrophism, or crustal warping, was the term given to this type of motion; epeirogeny refers to the vertical movement of the crust over very large areas.

UNIT OBJECTIVES

1. To introduce basic terminology used in describing rock structure.

2. To distinguish between types of fault movements and the landforms they produce.

3. To discuss the folding of rocks and relate it to the landforms produced.

GLOSSARY OF KEY TERMS

Anticline An arch-like upfold with the limbs dipping away from its axis.

Dip The angle at which a rock layer tilts from the horizontal.

Fault A fracture in crustal rock involving the displacement of rock on one side of the fracture with respect to rock on the other side.

Folding Bending or warping in layered rock.

Graben A crustal block that has sunk down between two fairly parallel normal faults in response to tensional forces.

Horst A crustal block that has been raised between two reverse faults by compressional forces.

Normal fault A tensional fault exhibiting a moderately inclined fault plane that separates a block that has remained fairly stationary from one that has been significantly down-thrown.

Overturned fold An extremely compressed fold that doubles back on itself with an axial plane that is oriented beyond the horizontal.

Primary landform A structure created by tectonic activity.

Recumbent fold A highly compressed fold that doubles back on itself with an axial plane that is near horizontal.

Reverse fault The result of one crustal block overriding another along a steep fault plane between them; caused by compression of the crust into a smaller horizontal space.

Secondary landform A landform that is the product of weathering and erosion.

Strike The compass direction of the line of intersection between a rock layer and a horizontal plane.

Strike-slip fault (see transcurrent fault)

Syncline A trough-like downfold with its limbs dipping toward its axial plane.

Thrust fault A compressional fault in which the angle of the fault plane is very low; sometimes called an *overthrust fault*.

Transcurrent fault A transverse fault in which crustal blocks move horizontally in the direction of the fault; also known as a *strike-slip fault* because movement at a transcurrent fault occurs along the strike of a fault.

Transform fault A special case of transcurrent faulting in which the transverse fault marks the boundary between two lithospheric plates that are sliding past each other; California's San Andreas Fault is a classic example.

UNIT OUTLINE

I. Terminology of structure
    A. Strike is the compass direction of the line of intersection between a rock and a horizontal plane

B. Dip is the angle at which a rock tilts from the horizontal
    1. direction of dip
C. An outcrop is a prominently exposed area of rock

II. Fault structures

A. A fracture in the crust involving displacement of rock on one side as opposed to the other
B. A joint is a fracture with no displacement
C. Where plates converge, there are compressional stresses
D. Where plates diverge, there are tensional stresses
E. Where plates slide past one another horizontally, there are transverse stresses
F. Compressional faults
    1. one block rides over the other where rock collides, forming a reverse fault
    2. upthrown and downthrown blocks
    3. parallel echelon faults
    4. a thrust fault is formed when the angle of a fault plane is very low
    5. horsts are raised blocks between reversed faults
G. Tensional faults
    1. normal faults are produced when one block remains fairly stationary, and the other block is downthrown as the plates pull apart
        a. rift-valley topography
    2. grabens are sunken blocks raised between two reverse faults
H. Transverse faults
    1. movement of blocks is lateral, no upthrown or downthrown blocks
    2. fault is transcurrent, movement is in the direction of the fault
    3. transform faults are unique because it marks a plate boundary, movement occurs at the strike of the fault; called strike-slip faults as well
I. Field evidence of faulting
    1. examine erosion, weathering of faults
    2. slickensides are smooth, glass-like areas on a scarp that suggest faulting

III. Fold structures

A. Rocks also respond to stress by folding
B. Characteristic of sedimentary layered rock
C. Folding and faulting usually occur together
D. Anticlines and synclines
    1. anticlines are upfolds
    2. synclines are downfolds
    3. core of synclines has younger rock
E. Plunging folds and landscapes
    1. a plunge is a dip in the axis of an anticline or syncline
    2. many anticlines and synclines overturned or recumbent
    3. primary landforms created by tectonic action

4. secondary landforms made by weathering and erosion

IV. Regional deformation
    A. Crust often deformed in a minor way
        1. called diastrophism or crustal warping
        2. epeirogeny refers to vertical movement of crust with little or no bending or breaking of crust

---

REVIEW QUESTIONS

1. What is a horst? A graben? How are they formed?

2. Define the terms diastrophism, crustal warping, and epeirogeny.

3. Draw a sketch of an anticline and a syncline.

SELF-TEST

Multiple-Choice Questions

1. The compass line of direction between a rock layer and a horizontal plane is the ridge's:

    (a) strike (b) angle of dip (c) direction of dip (d) echelon (e) line of thrust

2. Compressional forces produce which type of fault?

    (a) normal (b) reverse (c) transverse (d) tensional (e) stacked

3. Tensional forces produce which type of fault?

    (a) angled (b) reverse (c) transverse (d) thrust (e) normal

4. A sunken block between two parallel normal faults is a(n):

    (a) horst (b) echelon (c) graben (de) anticline (e) caldera

5. All of the following are associated with horizontal plate movement except:

    (a) transcurrent faults (b) transform faults (c) strike-slip faults (d) reverse faults (e) all are associated with horizontal plate movement

6. A fracture in the crust without displacement is a:

    (a) joint (b) fault (c) transform fault (d) recumbent fold (e) crease

True-False Questions

___ 1. A transcurrent fault is the same thing as a strike-slip fault.
___ 2. Anticlines are downfolds and synclines are upfolds.
___ 3. Primary landforms are those created by tectonic activity.
___ 4. Epeirogeny refers to the horizontal movement of crust involving no bending or breaking of rock.
___ 5. Slight crustal deformation without folding or faulting is known as diastrophism or crustal warping.
___ 6. When the angle of a fault plane in a compressional fault is very high, a thrust fault occurs.

UNIT 37: THE FORMATION
OF LANDSCAPES AND LANDFORMS

UNIT SUMMARY

Primary landforms are the result of tectonic activity, whereas secondary landforms are created by weathering and erosion. A landform is a single and typical unit forming part of the Earth's surface. An aggregation of (often similar) landforms creates a landscape. The term degradation refers to the lowering, reducing, and smoothing of landmasses; and is accompanied by aggradational processes, which deposit materials removed by degradation. Degradational processes include weathering, mass movements, and erosion. Weathering is the breakdown of rocks in situ, and includes mass movement, the spontaneous downslope movement of materials under the force of gravity. Erosion involves the longer-distance removal of materials, and some effective erosional agents include running water, glaciers, wind, and coastal waves. The field of regional physiography brings together the topics of climate, soil, vegetation, topography, terrain, and relief.

UNIT OBJECTIVES

1. To introduce three primary degradational processes: weathering, mass movements, and erosion.

2. To focus attention on the aggradational processes that produce secondary landforms.

3. To recognize the roles of degradation and aggradation in the formation and evolution of landscapes.

GLOSSARY OF KEY TERMS

Aggradation The combination of processes that builds up the surface through the deposition of material that was removed from elsewhere by degradation; contributes to the lowering of relief by reducing the height differences between the high and low places in an area.

Degradation The combination of processes that wear down the landmasses; implies the lowering, reducing, and smoothing of those surfaces.

Erosion The long-distance carrying away of weathered rock material, and the associated processes whereby the Earth's surface is worn down.

Geologic time scale The standard timetable or chronicle of Earth history used by scientists; the sequential organization of geologic time units, whose dates continue to be refined.

Landform   A single and typical unit that forms parts of the overall shape of the Earth's surface; also refers to a discrete product of a set of geomorphic processes.

Landscape   An aggregation of landforms, often of the same type; also refers to the spatial expression of the processes that shaped those landforms.

Mass movement   The spontaneous downslope movement of Earth materials under the force of gravity; materials involved move *en masse* – in bulk.

Primary landform   A structure created by tectonic activity.

Secondary landform   A landform that is the product of weathering and erosion.

Weathering   The chemical alteration and physical disintegration of Earth materials by the action of air, water, and organisms; more specifically, the breakdown of rocks in situ, their disintegration and decomposition without distant removal of the products.

UNIT OUTLINE

I. Landscapes and landforms
   A. Primary landforms are created by horizontal and vertical tectonic plate movement
   B. Secondary landforms are created by erosion
   C. A landform is a single unit, such as a mountain, a sinkhole, or a sand dune
   D. A landscape is an aggregation of landforms

II. Gradation
   A. Forces that work to flatten, or grade the landscape
      1. erosion
      2. weathering
      3. gravity (avalanches, mudslides, landslides)
   B. Degradation is the collective term for processes that wear down landmasses
   C. Aggradation is the deposition of material, which can lower relief by filling in differences of high and low points in a landscape
   D. Degradational processes and landscapes
      1. weathering is the in situ breakdown of rocks
      2. mass movement is the spontaneous downslope shift of material due to gravity
      3. erosion involves long distance transport of the products of weathering and mass movement
         a. water is the most effective erosional agent
         b. glaciers are also erosional agents
         c. wind is effective only in some areas as an erosional agent (sandy areas)
         d. coastal waves have enormous impact on continental margin landscapes

      e. chemical solution, such as when limestone is subjected to humid conditions and dissolves

  E. Aggradational processes and landforms
     1. streams, glaciers, wind, and waves also deposit materials

III. Erosion and tectonics

  A. Downward erosion is compensated for by upward rebound of crust (isostatic principle)

IV. Regional landscapes

  A. Use criteria of regional physiography to map regional landscapes
     1. climate
     2. soil
     3. vegetation
     4. terrain

REVIEW QUESTIONS

1. Define the term degradation and give an example of this process.

2. Name the three categories of degradational processes.

3. List five of the most effective erosional agents.

SELF-TEST

Multiple-Choice Questions

1. Gradational processes include all of the following except:

   (a) weathering (b) erosion (c) mass movement (d) mountain building (e) all are gradational processes

2. All of the following are erosional agents except:

   (a) running water (b) wind (c) plant roots (d) glaciers (e) coastal waves

3. Regional physiography is not concerned with:

   (a) soil (b) terrain (c) climate (d) vegetation (e) population density

4. An aggregation of landforms is a:

    (a) landscape (b) region (c) landmass (d) platform (e) landform cluster

5. The spontaneous downslope shift of materials due to gravity is:

    (a) erosion (b) mass movement (c) weathering (d) aggradation (e) slumping

6. In which degradational process do particles remain closest to their origin?

    (a) erosion (b) mass movement (c) weathering (d) deposition (e) sublimation

True-False Questions

___ 1. Secondary landforms are created by weathering and erosion.
___ 2. Mountain ranges and horizontal lava flows are good examples of primary
   landforms.
___ 3. A key force in gradational processes is gravity.
___ 4. Degradational processes are never accompanied by aggradational processes.
___ 5. Weathering usually removes its products to greater distances than erosion does.
___ 6. Glaciers are effective agents of erosion and deposition.

UNIT SUMMARY

The major types of weathering processes include mechanical, chemical, and biological weathering. Mechanical weathering is also called physical weathering, and involves destruction of rocks from physical stresses. Frost action is a powerful destroyer of rocks, creating rock seas (also known as *blockfields* or *felsenmeers*) when large fragments remain close to their original location; or talus cones (also known as *scree slopes*) when small fragments roll downslope and accumulate vast piles of rock debris. Another formation prevalent in Arctic regions is the stone net, created when ice forms on the underside of rocks, wedging them upwards and sideways. Salt crystals in arid areas perform the same function as ice, forming salt wedges in the landscape. Chemical weathering encompasses several processes, including hydrolysis and subsequent spheroidal weathering; oxidation which forms the products iron and aluminum; and carbonation, leading to deeply pitted and grooved limestone and dolomite landforms. Biological weathering comes from a number of sources, including burrowing animals and worms that contribute to the mixing and formation of soil (bioturbation); from lichens that remove minerals from rock by ion exchange; and from humans who pollute the air, quarry and mine rock, and farm and fertilize the soil. Weathering processes are more intense in the lower latitudes, which experience greater heat, humidity, and copious rainfall – all of which are conditions conducive to weathering processes.

UNIT OBJECTIVES

1. To differentiate the major categories of weathering – mechanical, chemical, and biological.

2. To introduce and briefly discuss common weathering processes.

3. To note the general environmental controls over weathering processes.

GLOSSARY OF KEY TERMS

Biological weathering The disintegration of rock minerals via biological means; earthworms and plant roots are important in the development of soil, lichens contribute to the breakdown of rocks, and humans, of course, play various roles in the disintegration of rocks and the operation of soil-formation processes.

Carbonation The reaction of weak carbonic acid (formed from water and carbon dioxide) with minerals; carbonic acid, in turn, reacts with carbonate minerals such as limestone in a form of chemical weathering that can be quite vigorous in certain humid areas, where solution and decay lead to the formation of karst landscapes.

Chemical weathering The disintegration of rock minerals via chemical means; in any rock made up of a combination of minerals, the chemical breakdown of one set of mineral grains leads to the decomposition of the whole mass.

Frost action A form of mechanical weathering in which water penetrates the joints and cracks of rocks, expands and contracts through alternate freezing and thawing, and eventually shatters the rocks.

Hydrolysis A form of chemical weathering that involves moistening and the transformation of rock minerals into other mineral compounds; expansion in volume often occurs in the process, which contributes to the breakdown of rocks.

Mechanical weathering Involves the destruction of rocks by physical means through the imposition of certain stresses, such as freezing and thawing or the expansion of salt crystals; also known as *physical weathering*.

Oxidation The chemical combination of oxygen and other materials to create new products (biologists call this process *respiration*).

Rock sea The area of blocky rock fragments formed when weathered rocks – particularly from frost wedging – remain near their original location; also known as a *blockfield* or *felsenmeer*, and a *boulder field* when the rock fragments are dominated by large boulders.

Spheroidal weathering A product of the chemical weathering process of hydrolysis; in certain igneous rocks such as granite, hydrolysis combines with other processes to cause the outer shells of the rock to flake off in what looks like a small-scale version of *exfoliation*.

Talus cone A steep accumulation of weathered rock fragments and loose boulders that rolled downslope in free fall; particularly common at the bases of cliffs in the drier climates of the western United States (also called a *scree slope*).

UNIT OUTLINE

I. The heat balance of the human body
    A. Destruction of rocks through stress
        1. frost action
    B. Rock seas are produced when large pieces of rock accumulate near their origin
        1. also known as a blockfield or felsenmeer
    C. Talus cones form when small rock fragments roll downslope
        1. also known as scree slope
    D. Stone nets are created when ice forms under rocks and wedges them together
    E. Salt wedging in arid regions

II. Chemical weathering
    A. Rocks vary in their ability to resist weathering

B. Hydrolysis occurs when minerals are moistened, changed chemically, and expand in volume
    1. spheroidal weathering is hydrolysis and other processes combining to flake off outer layers of rock

C. Oxidation
    1. minerals react with oxygen in the air, producing iron and aluminum

D. Carbonation
    1. water is converted to a mild acid, which is the weathering agent
        a. carbonic acid

III. Biological weathering

A. Soil mixed by burrowing animals and worms

B. Action of lichens (a combination of algae and fungi)

C. Action of humans
    1. pollution
    2. quarrying, mining
    3. farming and fertilization

IV. Geography of weathering

A. More intense weathering in lower latitudes with higher heat, rainfall, and humidity

B. Stone nets only form under certain conditions, particularly in Arctic areas

C. Wedging effect of frost action only in higher latitudes

REVIEW QUESTIONS

1. List some of the factors that make weathering processes more intense in the lower latitudes.

2. What is a talus cone? A rock sea? A salt wedge?

3. In what ways do humans contribute to the process of biological weathering?

SELF-TEST

Multiple-Choice Questions

1. When pieces of rock accumulate near their origin after weathering they from a:

    (a) talus cone (b) rock sea (c) scree slope (d) salt wedge (e) mineral slope

2. When minerals are moistened, expand, and are chemically altered, this process is known as:

    (a) hydrolysis (b) oxidation (c) carbonation (d) biological weathering (e) mechanical weathering

3. In carbonation, water is altered into a weak:

    (a) base (b) acid (c) solid (d) salt (e) volatile gas

4. A talus cone is formed from:

    (a) soil (b) dust particles (c) mud (d) ice crystals (e) rock fragments

5. Burrowing animals and worms mix soil in a process called:

    (a) biopredation (b) mechanical weathering (c) biologic turnover (d) bioturbation (e) chemical weathering

6. Which of the following is not a major type of weathering process:

    (a) mechanical weathering (b) chemical weathering (c) biological weathering (d) hydrologic weathering (e) all are types of weathering processes

True-False Questions

__ 1. A scree slope is another name for a talus cone.
__ 2. Frost action can shatter even the strongest igneous rocks.
__ 3. Carbonation is a particularly vigorous process in arid regions.
__ 4. Lower latitudes are associated with greater intensities of weathering.
__ 5. Humans are not agents of biological weathering.
__ 6. Spheroidal weathering involves the process of hydrolysis.

UNIT SUMMARY

The force of gravity plays a major role in shaping Earth's landscapes, and mass movement is the process by which these surface materials are moved. There are four types of mass movements: creep, flow, slide, and fall. Creep movements are the slowest type of mass movement, with soil creep and rock creep resulting from the alternate freezing/thawing or wetting/drying of soil particles. Solifluction is a special category of soil creep, where rock and soil debris are saturated with water, and flow together as one mass. Flow movements have a stronger effect than creep movements, and earth flows involve a section of soil or weak rock being saturated and lubricated by water until a flow occurs. Slumping is an associated feature of hillside flow, as are mudflows. When high angles and steep slopes are involved, slide movements can occur. When a portion of the material breaks away from its origin, a high-speed landslide or rockslide results. Fall movements are the most dramatic type of mass movement, evidenced by the downslope rolling of pieces of loosened rock. Rock fragments that remain near their origin are called talus cones or scree slopes. Knowledge of mass movements is vitally important for both planning and public policy, as it relates to the building of infrastructures and private dwellings.

UNIT OBJECTIVES

1. To demonstrate the role of gravity in promoting mass movements in weathered materials.

2. To discuss the various types of mass movements and the circumstances under which they usually occur.

GLOSSARY OF KEY TERMS

Creep The slowest form of mass movement; involves the slow, imperceptible motion of a soil layer downslope, as revealed in the slight downhill tilt of trees and other stationary objects.

Earth flow A form of mass movement in which a section of soil or weathered bedrock, lying on a rather steep slope, becomes saturated by heavy rains until it is lubricated enough to flow.

Fall The fastest form of mass movement that involves the free fall or downslope rolling of rock pieces loosened by weathering; these boulders form a talus cone or scree slope at the base of the cliff from which they broke away.

Landslide A slide form of mass movement that travels downslope more rapidly than flow movements; in effect; it is a collapse of a slope and does not need water as a lubricant (can also be triggered by an earthquake as well as human activities).

Mass movement The spontaneous downslope movement of earth materials under the force of gravity; materials involved move *en masse* – in bulk.

Mudflow A flow form of mass movement involving a stream of fluid, lubricated mud; most common where heavy rains strike an area that has long been dry and where weathering has loosened ample quantities of fine-grained material.

Rockslide A landslide-type of mass movement consisting mainly of rock materials.

Slumping A flow type of mass movement in which a major section of regolith, soil, or weakened bedrock comes down a steep slope as a backward-rotating slump block.

Solifluction A special kind of soil creep in which soil and rock debris are saturated with water and flow in bulk as a single mass; most common in periglacial zones.

UNIT OUTLINE

I. Gravitational forces
  A. Gravity plays a major role in shaping landscapes
    1. angle of repose is the maximum angle at which granular substances can resist the pull of gravity (Fig. 39.2)
    2. the steeper the slope, the greater the shearing stress (downslope pull)
    3. friction counteracts shearing stress
    4. water on a slope adds weight and reduces friction

II. Mass movement
  A. The movement of materials by gravitational force
    1. the term mass wasting is sometimes used
    2. important process for breaking down rock
  B. Creep movements (Fig. 39.5)
    1. the slowest type of mass movement, involving the movement of the soil layer downslope
    2. soil creep created by alternate freeze/thaw or wet/dry cycles
      a. particles expand or rise when wet or frozen, then resettle slightly downslope when dry or thawed
      b. solifluction is a kind of soil creep in which soil and rock debris flows downslope with water
  C. Flow movements (Figs. 39.6, 39.7)
    1. in an earth flow, a mass of soil or weathered rock at a steep angle is saturated and starts to flow downsope
    2. slumping is a type of earth flow that involves a large section of soil or rock that stands in a vertical position

3. a mudflow is caused by heavy rains, and carries fine material in a thin, fluid, stream of mud
D. Slide movements (Fig. 39.9)
   1. when a segment of rock or soil at a very steep angle suddenly breaks away, a landslide or rockslide occurs
   2. much faster than a flow, a collapse; can be very destructive
   3. bedrock also removed, unlike creep and flow movements

E. Fall movements (Fig. 39.11)
   1. in a free fall, pieces of rock that have become loosened by weathering roll downslope
   2. material generally not carried far from its origins, forms a talus cone at the base of the slope

III. The importance of mass movements
   A. All streams are constantly being shaped by mass movements, although is not always visible
   B. Location and effects of mass movements needs to be considered in planning and policymaking
   C. Mass movements expose new bedrock to weathering and eventual removal

---

REVIEW QUESTIONS

1. Compare and contrast slide movements and fall movements.

2. Describe the process that occurs during an earth flow.

SELF-TEST

Multiple-Choice Questions

1. The steeper a slope is, the greater the:

   (a) shearing stress (b) friction (c) angle of repose (d) pressure (e) distance material falls

2. Which is the slowest type of mass movement?

   (a) landslide (b) soil creep (c) mudflow (d) avalanche (e) slumping

3. Which type of landform is produced by the fastest type of mass movement?

    (a) lobe-shaped mass (b) slump block (c) talus cone (d) canyon (e) caldera

4. Which type of movement occurs when a section of soil or weak rock at a steep angle becomes saturated by heavy rains?

    (a) earth slump (b) a free fall (c) solifluction (d) shearing (e) an earth flow

5. All of the following are types of mass movements except:

    (a) flow movements (b) fall movements (c) creep movements (d) stress movements (e) slide movements

6. Cycles of alternate freezing/thawing and wetting/drying directly leads to:

    (a) soil creep (b) landslides (c) avalanches (d) shearing stress (e) talus cones

True-False Questions

__ 1. The angle of repose is the maximum angle at which liquid material remains at rest.
__ 2. Mass wasting is another term sometimes used for mass movement.
__ 3. Mass movements are extremely important in the breakdown of rocks.
__ 4. Fluids are less important in slide movements than in flow movements.
__ 5. Slide movements are faster than free falls.
__ 6. Slumping is associated with earth flows.

UNIT 40: WATER IN THE LITHOSPHERE

UNIT SUMMARY

Water arriving at the Earth's surface may be intercepted by vegetation and evaporate before it reaches the ground, in a process called interception. Infiltration refers to the process by which water reaching the ground enters the pores, or openings in soil. If the volume of water received at the surface exceeds the infiltration rate, surface detention occurs, and runoff can follow when the detention hollow capacity is exceeded. River channels are characterized by their gradient, or slope, which is the difference in elevation between two points along the stream course. The velocity of a river is greatest at the center of its channel, and the river's discharge is defined as the volume of water passing a given cross-section of its channel in a given time. A hydrograph plots a river's discharge over time. Groundwater is the water below ground within the lithosphere, and contains two zones. The zone of aeration (vadose zone) is the upper layer, whereas the zone of saturation (phreatic zone) is the lower layer. In the zone of aeration, water moves downward by percolation and/or upward by capillary action. Field capacity is the maximum amount that soil can hold by capillary tension against gravity's force. The water table is located at the top of the phreatic zone. Aquifers are porous and permeable layers that can be at least partially saturated. There are two general types of wells— traditional wells, which are simply a hole in the ground that taps the water table; or artesian wells, whose water emerges from the surface under its own pressure, and are associated with confined aquifers. Springs are surface streams of flowing water that emerge from the ground. Hot springs are often located above buried magma chambers, and are used for energy production, therapeutic, and recreational purposes.

UNIT OBJECTIVES

1. To discuss the various paths water may take on and within the surface of the lithosphere.

2. To introduce fundamental aspects of river flow.

3. To outline basic concepts related to groundwater hydrology.

GLOSSARY OF KEY TERMS

Aquiclude Impermeable rock layer that resists the infiltration of groundwater; consists of tightly packed or interlocking particles, such as in shale.

Aquifer A porous and permeable rock layer that can at least be partially saturated with groundwater.

Artesian well One that flows under its own natural pressure to the surface; usually associated with a confined aquifer that is recharged from a remote location where that aquifer reaches the surface.

Discharge The volume of water passing a given cross-section of a river channel within a given amount of time; measured as average water velocity multiplied by the cross-sectional area.

Field capacity The ability of a soil to hold water against the downward pull of gravity; also the maximum amount of water a soil can contain before becoming waterlogged.

Gradient (slope) The slope of a river channel as measured by the difference in elevation between two points along the stream course.

Groundwater Water contained within the lithosphere; this water hidden below the ground accounts for about 25 percent of the world's fresh water.

Hydrograph A graph of a river's discharge over time.

Infiltration The flow of water into the Earth's surface through the pores and larger openings in the soil mass.

Interception The blocking of rainwater from reaching the ground by vegetation; raindrops land on leaves and other plant parts and evaporate before they can penetrate the soil below.

Perched water table A separate local water table that forms at a higher elevation than the nearby main water table; caused by the effects of a local aquiclude.

Runoff The removal – as overland flow via the network of streams and rivers – of the surplus precipitation at the land surface that does not infiltrate the soil or accumulate on the ground through surface detention.

Slope See **gradient (slope)**.

Spring A surface stream of flowing water that emerges through the ground.

Velocity The rate of speed at which water moves in at a river channel; this rate varies within the stream.

Water table The top of the (phreatic) zone of saturation; does not lie horizontally but follows the general profile of the land surface above.

Zone of aeration The upper of the two subterranean zones that contains groundwater; lies above the water table and is normally unsaturated, except during heavy rainfall (also known as the *vadose zone*).

Zone of saturation The lower of the two subterranean zones that contains groundwater; lies below the water table and is also known as the *phreatic zone*).

UNIT OUTLINE

I. Water at the surface
    A. Interception occurs when water falls on vegetation and evaporates before it reaches the soil

    B. Impermeable surfaces do not allow water to pass through them, permeable surfaces do

    C. Infiltration is the flow of water into the surface through pores in the soil
        1. infiltration rate depends upon
            a. characteristics of the soil
            b. how moist the soil is
            c. type and amount of overlying vegetation
            d. slope of the surface
            e. type of rainfall (intensity)
        2. water accumulates in any hollows on surface (known as surface detention
        3. runoff (overland flow) occurs when there is more rainfall than the soil can hold

II. Water flow in rivers (Fig. 40.4)
    A. A river's gradient (slope) is the difference in elevation between two points along its course
        1. when the gradient is high, flow is more turbulent

    B. Movement is not uniform in a river channel, water at the center moves faster where resistance is lowest

    C. The discharge of a river is the amount of water flowing in a given cross-section of it
        1. calculated by multiplying average velocity by cross-sectional area

    D. River flow
        1. eddies have almost as much backward as forward movment
        2. discharge of a river varies with season, year, etc.
        3. hydrograph is a graph of a river's discharge over time
        4. rivers contain about 0.03% of total fresh water supply

III. Water beneath the surface (Fig. 40.7)
    A. Groundwater is water underneath the Earth's surface
        1. about 25% of total fresh water supply is groundwater
        2. zone of aeration (vadose zone) is the upper zone
        3. zone of saturation (phreatic zone) is the lower zone
    B. Soil moisture in the zone of aeration

1. rainwater enters soil by infiltration, and is called soil moisture
2. water continues to move downward by percolation
3. water can move upward by capillary action
4. moisture can also move by evaporation, water vapor movement, and recondensation
5. field capacity is the maximum amount of water that can be held by soil without it becoming saturated
6. hygroscopic water is a thin film of moisture that clings to soil particles, and is unavailable to plant roots
7. the wilting point is the lower limit to soil moisture, below which plants will be damaged
8. the total soil storage capacity is the product of average depth of roots and the water storage per cm for that type of soil

C. Groundwater in the zone of saturation (Fig. 40.8)
1. the water table is the upper surface of the phreatic zone
2. aquifers are porous, permeable layers that can be saturated
   a. sandstone
   b. limestone
3. aquicludes (aquitards) are zones of impermeable rock layers
   a. mudstone
   b. shale
4. unconfined aquifers get water from local infiltration
5. confined aquifers lie in-between aquicludes, and get water from more distant sources by gravity flow

D. Wells and springs (Figs. 40.9 & 40.10)
1. a traditional well is a hole that penetrates the water table
2. artesian wells are dug into confined aquifers that are constantly recharged by a distant water source
3. a cone of depression may form when water is drawn out of a well faster than it is replaced, causing the local water table around it to drop
   a. drawdown is the amount that the water table drops when a cone of depression form
4. springs are surface streams that emerge above the surface, commonly when an aquiclude halts the percolation of water, and is forced upwards
   a. a perched water table often forms higher than the regular water table to feed the spring
5. hot springs usually occur where the spring lies over a buried magma chamber
   a. geothermal steam can be used as an energy source
   b. mineral springs are a form of hot springs, used for medicinal or recreational purposes

REVIEW QUESTIONS

1. How does an artesian well differ from a traditional well?

2. What are the conditions necessary for spring formation? Use Fig. 40.10 as a reference.

3. How does water velocity vary within a river channel? Refer to Fig. 40.4.

SELF-TEST

Multiple-Choice Questions

1. The infiltration rate depends upon all of the following except:

    (a) soil characteristics (b) type of vegetation cover (c) slope of surface (d) air temperature (e) the rate depends on all of these factors

2. The water velocity in the center of a river's channel is _____ than the velocity at the edges of the channel.

    (a) faster (b) slower (c) no different (d) more measurable (e) less measurable

3. The volume of water passing through a cross-section of a river's channel is its:

    (a) runoff (b) velocity (c) discharge (d) infiltration rate (e) flow rate

4. The lower zone of groundwater is known as the:

    (a) zone of aeration (b) zone of saturation (c) vadose zone (d) hydroscopic zone (e) zone of hydration

5. Which type of rock would form a permeable aquifer?

    (a) mudstone (b) shale (c) granite (d) basalt (e) limestone

6. The water table is located at the top of the:

    (a) zone of aeration (b) vadose zone (c) phreatic zone (d) lower aquiclude (e) upper hydration zone

173

True-False Questions

__ 1. Springs are usually formed when the downward percolation of water is stopped by an aquiclude.

__ 2. An artesian well is simply a hole dug in the ground that penetrates the water table.

__ 3. A surface stream that emerges above the surface is called an aquifer.

__ 4. A confined aquifer usually lies in-between two aquicludes.

__ 5. Hot springs are generally located above buried magma chambers.

__ 6. If rain is able to reach the ground through surface vegetation, this is known as interception.

UNIT SUMMARY

Fluvial processes are geomorphic processes that are associated with running water – the Latin word *fluvius* means river. The hydrologic cycle results in constant fluvial erosion of the Earth's surface. The infiltration capacity of a soil is the rate at which it is able to absorb water from the surface. If the rate of erosion on a steep slope exceeds the rate of soil formation, denudation will occur. Rain that is not absorbed by soil is lost as sheet flow, with this thin film of water removing fine-grained materials as sheet erosion. Surface runoff creates rills, brooks, creeks, and often larger, more permanent streams. A river and its tributaries constitute a drainage basin, sometimes called a watershed. To assess a river's erosional activity, sediment yield and alluvium deposits are measured; and the major factors influencing the erosion rate are precipitation, vegetation, relief, lithology, and the impact of humans. The three functions of streams include erosion, transportation, and deposition. Stream erosion takes place by hydraulic action, abrasion, and corrosion. Erosion and transportation are coupled processes, and four mechanisms work together as a stream carries its load of sediment: traction, saltation, suspension, and solution. Stream capacity refers to the maximum load that a stream can carry, while stream competence depends on velocity, which determines the size of rocks removed by the stream. A flood occurs when abnormally high rainfall or a snowmelt causes a stream to overflow its channel. Floodplains are the low-lying areas adjacent to a stream channel. The base level of a river or stream is the level below which a stream cannot erode its bed, and absolute base level lies no deeper than a few meters below sea level. Rivers can be characterized as open systems, with both energy and matter flowing through them. The potential energy of the stream due to elevation is converted to kinetic energy as the water flows. A river is considered graded once a longitudinal profile has been established, with no degradation or aggradation along its course.

UNIT OBJECTIVES

1. To discuss the processes associated with the erosion of hillslopes.

2. To outline the factors influencing the erosional activity of rivers and to discuss the mechanisms of stream erosion and sediment transport.

3. To characterize the river as a system and to identify the processes associated with this system.

GLOSSARY OF KEY TERMS

Abrasion The erosive action of boulders, pebbles, and smaller grains of sediment as they are carried along a river valley; these fragments dislodge other particles along the stream bed and banks, thereby enhancing the deepening and widening process.

Absolute base level The elevational level lying a few meters below sea level.

Alluvium Sediment laid down by a stream on its valley floor; deposition occurs when the stream's velocity decreases and the valley fills with a veneer of unconsolidated material. Since soil particles washed from slopes in the drainage basin form a large part of these deposits, alluvial soils are usually fertile and productive.

Base level The elevational level below which a stream cannot erode its base.

Corrosion The process of stream erosion whereby certain rocks and minerals are dissolved by water; can also affect coastal bedrock that is susceptible to such chemical action.

Delta The often major sedimentary deposit surrounding and extending beyond the mouth of a river where it empties into the sea or a lake; frequently assumes a triangular configuration; hence its naming after the Greek letter of that shape.

Denudation The combined processes of weathering, mass movement, and erosion that over time strip a slope of its soil cover unless the local rate of soil formation is greater.

Drainage basin The region occupied by a complete stream system formed by the trunk river and all its tributaries (also known as a *watershed*).

Flood An episode of abnormally high stream discharge; water overflows from the stream channel and temporarily covers its floodplain (which continues to build from the alluvium that is deposited by the floodwaters).

Floodplain The flat, low-lying ground adjacent to a stream channel built by successive floods as sediment is deposited as alluvium.

Fluvial processes Flow processes involving running water; the Latin word for river is *fluvius*.

Graded river The slope of a river channel as measured by the difference in elevation between two points along the stream course.

Headward erosion The upslope extension, over time, of the "head" or source of a river valley, which lengthens the entire stream network.

Hydraulic action The erosional work of running water in a stream or in the form of waves along a coast. In a river, rock material is dislodged and dragged away from the valley floor and sides; where waves strike a shoreline, the speed and weight of the water, especially when air is compressed into rock cracks by the power of the waves, can fracture and erode coastal rocks quite rapidly.

Infiltration capacity The rate at which a soil is able to absorb water percolating downward from the surface.

Local base level The base level for a river that flows into a lake at whatever altitude it may lie.

Saltation The transportation process that entails the downstream bouncing of sand- and gravel- sized fragments along the bed of a moving stream.

Sheet erosion The erosion produced by sheet flow as it moves fine-grained surface materials.

Solution The transportation process by whereby rock material dissolved by corrosion is carried within a moving stream.

Stream capacity The maximum load of sediment that a stream can carry within a given discharge.

Suspension The transportation process whereby very fine clay- and silt- sized sediment is carried within a moving stream.

Temporary base level Base level of a stream formed of especially hard, resistant rock, limits further upstream channel incision for a time.

Traction Transportation process that involves the sliding or rolling of particles along a riverbed.

UNIT OUTLINE

I. Erosion and the hydrologic cycle
    A. Infiltration capacity of a soil is the rate at which it is able to absorb surface water
    B. Runoff results when the infiltration capacity is exceeded
    C. Splash erosion occurs when large raindrops dislodge soil
        1. splash erosion on a slope can result in loss of soil cover, or denudation, in time
        2. vegetation cover lessens the effects of splash erosion

II. Streams and basins
    A. Sheet flow is rain that is not absorbed by soil
        1. sheet flow (sheet wash) results in sheet erosion
        2. continued runoff can form rills, brooks, creeks, and streams
    B. A river system has several parts
        1. trunk river
        2. tributary streams
    C. A river system as a whole forms a drainage basin (watershed)
        1. drainage basins are separated by divides, or topographic barriers

      2. sediment yield is the total amount of sediment leaving a basin, but some remains as deposited alluvium

   D. Conditions that affect erosion rates in drainage basins

      1. precipitation

      2. vegetation

      3. relief

      4. underlying lithography

      5. human impact

III. Stream functions and valley properties (Fig. 41.4)

   A. Rivers are not static, they are constantly changing

      1. organic model describes a river's life cycle with stages of youth, maturity, and old age

   B. A river's course lengthens over time in several ways

      1. headward erosion

      2. building of deposits in delta

      3. valley lengthening

   C. Valley deepening occurs when water in V-shaped cross-section rushes downslope

   D. Erosion by rivers

      1. hydraulic action is the physical removal of rock and debris by the water itself

      2. abrasion is the further removal of materials by rock and sediment that have already been dislodged, and are being carried downstream

      3. corrosion is the process by which certain types of rock are dissolved by water

         a. limestone

         b. sandstone

   E. Transportation by rivers (Fig. 41.6)

      1. traction is sliding or rolling of particles in the river bed by hydraulic action

      2. saltation is traction and suspension, particles bounce along the river bed

      3. suspension carries very fine sediment, does not contact the river bed

      4. solution carries dissolved particles, does not contact the river bed

   F. Deposition by rivers

      1. as distance increases from source, particle size decreases, as does erosional power

IV. Factors in stream erosion

   A. Stream power

      1. stream capacity is the maximum load that a stream can carry with a given discharge

      2. stream competence refers to the effectiveness of erosion

         a. the faster the stream, the more effective it is at eroding materials

B. Stream floods
   1. a flood occurs when a river overflows its channel
   2. floods occur infrequently, effects are very limited over long time periods
   3. floodplains, the low-lying areas adjacent to the channel, are built up by the alluvial deposits of floodwaters
C. Base levels
   1. the level below which a stream cannot erode its bed
   2. absolute base level lies no more than a few meters below sea level
   3. the lake level is the local base level of a river
   4. temporary base level is reached when stream erosion reaches a particularly resistant or hard layer of rock, limiting upstream channel incision for a time

V. The river as a system
   A. Energy and the work in a river system (Fig. 41.11)
      1. water generates kinetic energy as it flows downstream, powered by Sun
      2. potential energy is transformed into kinetic energy
      3. a river is a steady-state system, water and energy are input and output equally
         a. tendency for the least work to be done
         b. tendency for work to be uniformly distributed
         c. graded river profile is a compromise between these two principles
   B. A graded river system
      1. a river is considered graded if its load is transported with no degradation or aggradation to its profile
   C. Factors that influence a river's tendency to be graded
      1. independent factors (not under river's control)
         a. discharge
         b. sediment load
         c. ultimate base level
      2. semidependent factors (somewhat under river's control)
         a. channel width
         b. channel depth
         c. bed roughness
         d. grain size of sediment
         e. velocity
         f. meander/braid tendency
      3. dependent factor (under river's control)
         a. slope
   D. Not all rivers are graded, and not all graded rivers have a smooth profile

REVIEW QUESTIONS

1. Define the terms flood and floodplain.

2. Diagram the river as an open system, using Fig. 41.11 as a guide.

3. What are the four major processes at work when a stream is transporting its load?

SELF-TEST

Multiple-Choice Questions

1. The complete system of a river's trunk and tributaries forms a:

   (a) fluvial area (b) drainage basin (c) lithology (d) divide (e) base level

2. Streams perform all of the following functions except:

   (a) transportation (b) degradation (c) pressure gradation (d) aggradation (e) streams perform all of these functions

3. Which of the following is an erosive process of rivers?

   (a) abrasion (b) corrosion (c) hydraulic action (d) infiltration (e) a, b, and c

4. The sliding of particles along a river bed by hydraulic action is called?

   (a) traction (b) saltation (c) suspension (d) solution (e) extrusion

5. The process which alternately uses traction and suspension to move particles is called:

   (a) traction (b) saltation (c) suspension (d) solution (e) scouring

6. The level below which a stream cannot erode its bed is its:

   (a) base level (b) floodplain (c) water table (d) channel (e) crust level

True-False Questions

__ 1. Water generates potential energy as it flows downstream.
__ 2. If a stream's load can be transported with no aggradation or degradation, it is graded.
__ 3. A river is not usually a steady-state system, its input and output levels are variable.
__ 4. When suspension is the dominant form of particle transportation, the water is muddy.
__ 5. Splash erosion on an incline can lead to denudation of the slope.
__ 6. The term *fluvial* denotes soils that are deposited in a river's delta.

UNIT 42: DEGRADATIONAL LANDFORMS OF STREAM EROSION

UNIT SUMMARY

There are four major factors influencing fluvial erosion, including geologic structure, bedrock type (lithology), tectonic activity, and climate. Prominent landforms created and/or modified by stream erosion are hogbacks, cuestas, circular cuestas, ridges, valleys, domes, faults, mesas, and buttes. The effectiveness of a drainage system can vary, and is directly related to drainage density, the total length of the stream's channels in a unit area of the basin. The five characteristic drainage patterns are radial, annular, trellis, rectangular, and dendritic. Superimposed streams maintain their original courses despite changing lithologies and rock bodies in their path. Antecedent streams predate the surrounding lithology, and usually have kept pace with ridge formation around them. William Morris Davis proposed that a cycle of erosion affects all landscapes. The three facets of this theory were geologic structure, geographic process, and time (or stage). Davis argued that every landscape has an underlying peneplain, or flat surface. He felt that erosion lowered the landscape in a convex fashion, forming intermediate structures termed interfluves and monadnocks. Fenneman and Gilbert later suggested that some landscapes did not fit Davis' model; they proposed that erosion wore them down in a concave manner, eventually forming pediplanes.

UNIT OBJECTIVES

1. To outline the roles of geologic structure, lithology, tectonics, and climate in influencing fluvial erosion.

2. To introduce terminology to characterize drainage networks and controls on fluvial erosion.

3. To briefly consider how landscapes might change or evolve through time in response to river erosion.

GLOSSARY OF KEY TERMS

Annular drainage A concentric stream pattern that drains the interior of an excavated geologic dome.

Antecedent stream A river exhibiting transverse drainage across a structural feature that would normally impede its flow because the river predates the structure and kept cutting downward as the structure was uplifted around it.

Butte Small, steep-sided, caprock-protected hill, usually found in dry environments; an erosional remnant of a plateau.

Cuesta A long ridge with a steep escarpment on one side and a gently dipping slope and rockbeds on the other.

Cycle of erosion The evolutionary cycle proposed by William Morris Davis that purportedly affects all landscapes.

Dendritic drainage A tree-limb-like stream pattern that is the most commonly observed; indicates surface of relatively uniform hardness or one of flat-lying sedimentary rocks.

Drainage density The total length of the stream channels that exist in a unit area of a drainage basin.

Geologic structure Refers to landscape features originally formed by geologic processes, which are sculpted by streams and other erosional agents into characteristic landforms.

Hogback A prominent steep-sided ridge whose rockbeds dip sharply.

Interfluve The ridge that separates two adjacent stream valleys.

Mesa Flat-topped, steep-sided upland capped by a resistant rock layer; normally found in dry environments.

Monadnock A prominent, not-yet-eroded remnant of an upland on a peneplain.

Pediplane A surface formed by the coalescence of numerous pediments after a long period of erosion has led to parallel slope retreat.

Peneplain The concept of a "near plane" developed by William Morris Davis to describe the nearly flat landscape formed by extensive erosion over long periods of time.

Radial drainage A stream pattern that emanates outward in many directions from a central mountain.

Rectangular drainage A stream pattern dominated by right-angle contacts between rivers and tributaries, but not as pronounced as in trellis drainage.

Stream piracy The capture of a segment of a stream by another river.

Superimposed stream A river exhibiting transverse drainage across a structural feature that would normally impede its flow because the feature was at some point buried beneath the surface on which the river developed; as the feature became exposed, the river kept cutting through it.

Trellis drainage A stream pattern that resembles a garden trellis; flows only in two orientations, more or less at right angles to each other; often develops on parallel-folded sedimentary rocks.

Water gap A pass in a ridge or mountain range through which a stream flows.

UNIT OUTLINE

I. Factors affecting stream degradation
    A. Geologic structure
        1. hogbacks are dikes that become steep-sided ridges (Fig. 42.1)
        2. cuestas are less prominent ridges of sedimentary strata at a low-angle dip (Fig. 42.1)
        3. parallel ridges and valleys produced by erosion of synclines and anticlines
        4. domes are eroded to form circular cuestas (Fig. 42.2)
        5. fault-line scarps are fault scarps that have been eroded (Fig. 42.3 & 42.4)
        6. volcanic landforms eroded to plateau-like mesas or smaller buttes (Fig. 42.6)
        7. metamorphic rock may show regional foliation
    B. Bedrock type
        1. rocks have varying hardness and tendencies to form vertical slopes
    C. Tectonic activity
        1. rivers are altered and even rejuvenated by slight tilting produced by shifting lithospheric plates
            a. uplifting results in increased velocity and erosional capacity
    D. Climate
        1. landscapes in humid areas thought to be more rounded and eroded than arid regions, may be a misperception
        2. must account for long-term climate change
        3. climate does play a role in shaping the overall landscape in the long run

II. Drainage patterns (Fig. 42-10)
    A. Drainage density is the erosional effectiveness of a drainage system
    B. Radial drainage pattern shows drainage of conical mountains, often volcanic cones
    C. Annular drainage occurs on domes, forms a concentric circular pattern
    D. Trellis pattern often found on parallel folded or dipping rocks, flow in two directions
    E. Rectangular drainage tends to occur in small areas with joint and/or faults
    F. Dendritic drainage is a tree-limb pattern, found on batholiths or flat-rock areas; slopes toward trunk river

III. Overcoming geologic structure
    A. Superimposed and antecedent streams (Figs. 42.11 & 42.12)

1. as streams erode downward across mountain peaks, a water gap is produced, the river becomes a superimposed stream
2. if a river predates a ridge that is pushed up tectonically, and is able to keep pace by erosion, it is called an antecedent stream
B. Stream capture (stream piracy)
   1. one river captures a segment of another river
   2. one river strengthened at the expense of another

IV. Regional Geomorphology

A. Slopes and plains
1. cycle of erosion proposed by William Morris Davis
2. three elements of cycle are structure, geographic process, and time
3. high mountains eventually leveled to nearly flat peneplain
4. flat areas then transformed into mountains, highlands, hilly interfluves, and flat areas once again
5. most prominent not-yet-eroded remains called monadnocks
6. other geomorphologists proposed that flat areas reduced to pediplanes
7. humid areas may exhibit more convex slopes, with higher drainage densities than arid areas, which have more concave structures

REVIEW QUESTIONS

1. Describe the formation of a hogback and a cuesta.

2. Explain how lithology (bedrock type) influences landscape evolution.

3. List the five characteristic drainage patterns, using Fig. 42.10 as a guide.

SELF-TEST

Multiple-Choice Questions

1. Which of the following factors does not affect fluvial erosion?

   (a) climate (b) geologic structure (c) bedrock type (lithology) (d) pressure gradients (e) all of these factors affect fluvial erosion

2. A fault scarp that has been modified by erosion is called:

   (a) a fault-line scarp (b) a fault trace (c) a cuesta (d) a hogback (e) a talus cone

3. Erosion of upthrown blocks can form:

    (a) mesas (b) cuestas (c) domes (d) hogbacks (e) plateaus

4. Which of the following is not a drainage pattern?

    (a) annular (b) dendritic (c) trellis (d) radial (e) circumflected

5. A peneplain is a flattened area that is:

    (a) concave (b) convex (c) superimposed (d) antecedent (e) uplifted

6. In Davis' theory of erosion, the most prominent, not-yet eroded remnants are termed:

    (a) peneplains (b) monadnocks (c) interfluves (d) pediplanes (e) hogbacks

True-False Questions

__ 1. In the formation of a superimposed stream, a water gap is produced.
__ 2. Trellis drainage often occurs on parallel folded or dipping sedimentary rocks.
__ 3. Pediplanes are concave features.
__ 4. Radial drainage is typical of flat-lying sedimentary rocks.
__ 5. An antecedent river forms after the ridge it cuts through.
__ 6. Stream capture refers to one river capturing a portion of another stream.

UNIT 43: AGGRADATIONAL LANDFORMS OF STREAM EROSION

UNIT SUMMARY

Alluvial fans contain sediment deposited by both permanent and ephemeral (intermittently flowing) streams. The process of alluvial fan formation begins with the creation of a midstream bar. After continued deposition, the stream becomes divided into smaller, intertwined channels, and is termed a braided stream. Under these conditions, the stream's ability to erode downward is greatly reduced, and the alluvial fan grows in size. When several alluvial fans coalesce, an alluvial apron, or bajada is formed. Meanders occur in a stream when its depositional function increases, as the channel is eroded laterally. Meanders grow in width over time, as well as shifting downstream, creating floodplains adjacent to the channel. Oxbow lakes occur when a meander completely detaches from is stream channel. Flooding onto river banks and its associated sediment deposition forms natural levees over time. Artificial levees have also been constructed in order to direct streamflow. Terraces are the remnants of older floodplains that stand above newer bluffs, and may be paired or unpaired. Paired terraces exist at the same elevation on either side of a rejuvenated stream. A triangular shaped deposit at the mouth of a river is called a delta. Channels at the apex of a delta that carry water in several directions are known as distributaries. A trunk river receives tributaries in its drainage basin and develops distributaries where its delta is formed. Delta formation is influenced by three major factors, including the volume of the stream and the amount of sediment that it carries; the configuration of the offshore continental shelf near the river mouth; and the strength of currents and waves. As a delta grows toward the sea, its deltaic plain is stabilized. A birdfoot delta is created when distributaries that would have naturally become clogged are kept open by artificial means. The profile of a delta is characterized by bottomset beds containing the finest grained sediment, topset beds that are constantly modified by continuous deposition, and foreset beds that are built from the leading edge of the topset beds as the delta grows outward.

UNIT OBJECTIVES

1. To identify the types of landforms built by rivers.

2. To examine the formation and development of the stream floodplain.

3. To investigate the evolution of river deposits.

GLOSSARY OF KEY TERMS

Alluvial fan   A fan-shaped deposit consisting of alluvial material located where a
   mountain stream emerges onto a plain; primarily a desert landform.

Arroyo Gullies cut into alluvial fans due to increased streamflow.

Artificial levee An artificially constructed levee built to reinforce a natural levee, most often along the lowest course of a river.

Bajada A coalesced assemblage of alluvial fans that lines a highland front (also known as an *alluvial apron*); primarily a desert feature.

Braided stream One carrying a high sediment load that subdivides into many intertwined channels that reunite some distance downstream; as these channels shift position, stretches of deposited alluvium become divided between them, giving the "braided" appearance.

Delta The often major sedimentary deposit surrounding and extending beyond the mouth of a river where it empties into the sea or a lake; frequently assumes a triangular configuration, hence its naming after the Greek letter of that shape.

Distributaries The several channels a river subdivides into when it reaches its delta; caused by the clogging of the river mouth by deposition of fine-grained sediment as the stream reaches base level and water velocity declines markedly.

Entrenched meander Meanders of a rejuvenated stream incised into hard bedrock from overlying floodplain topography; caused by the uplifting of the land surface above the stream's base level.

Ephemeral stream An intermittently flowing stream in an arid environment; precipitation (and subsequent stream flow) is periodic, and when the rains end the stream soon runs dry again.

Floodplain The flat, low-lying ground adjacent to a stream channel built by successive floods as sediment is deposited as alluvium.

Meander The smooth, rounded curves or bends of rivers that can become quite pronounced as floodplain development proceeds; also characteristic of many ocean currents, which, after the passage of storms, can produce such extreme loops that many detach and form localized eddies.

Midstream bar A midchannel sandbar that is deposited where sediment-clogged water of a stream significantly slows in velocity.

Natural levee A river-lining ridge of alluvium deposited when a stream overflows its banks during a periodic flood; when the river contracts after the flood, it stays within these self-generated "dikes" or levees.

Oxbow lake A lake formed when two adjacent meanders link up and one of the bends in the channel, shaped like a bow, is cut off.

Terrace The higher-lying remnant of an old floodplain that stands above the bluffs lining the newer floodplain of a rejuvenated river; when two terraces lie at the same elevation, they are called paired terraces.

UNIT OUTLINE

I. Alluvial fans (Fig. 43.2)

    A. An ephemeral stream (one that flows intermittently) deposit alluvial material where it emerges onto a plain

        1. alluvial fans are best developed in arid areas

    B. Formation of alluvial fans includes two stages

        1. formation of a midstream bar

        2. formation of a braided stream

    C. An alluvial apron (bajada) forms when alluvial fans coalesce

        1. over time, can weather into desert pavement

II. Rivers to the sea (Fig. 43.4)

    A. Major rivers eventually drain into the sea, forming deltas

    B. As a river begins to deposit material, it erodes laterally and forms meanders (bends)

    C. The floodplain (Fig. 43.5)

        1. the flat, low-lying area on either side of a river's channel, created as meanders erode laterally and downstream

        2. oxbow lakes form when a meander is cut off (Fig. 43.6)

        3. bluffs are created by meandering streams (Fig. 43.5)

        4. a meander scar often remains on the landscape where a meander once existed

        5. natural levees are broad ridges of deposited material along both sides of a river

            a. artificial levees can also be constructed

    D. Terraces (Fig. 43.10)

        1. when a stream is rejuvenated, it cuts downward, and the remains of the old higher floodplain level are visible as terraces

            a. terraces are sometimes paired on either side of a river at the same elevation

            b. terraces can be constructed of rock or alluvial material

            c. if land is uplifted, whole meander belts produce entrenched meanders

III.. Deltas (Fig. 43.12)

    A. Large fan-shaped areas of alluvial deposits at the mouths of rivers

    B. Distributaries develop where the mouth of the river becomes clogged with sediment, carrying water in several directions

    C. Factors influencing delta formation

        1. stream volume

        2. configuration of offshore continental shelf

3. strength of currents and waves
D. Deltaic plain is the flat land portion of a delta
E. Birdfoot delta can develop if distributaries are kept open by dredging
F. The delta profile (Fig. 43.14)
    1. finest sediment is deposited in bottomset beds where water is quiet
    2. topset beds lie under deltaic plain, constantly added to
    3. foreset beds are built from leading edge of topset beds
        a. Mississippi River

REVIEW QUESTIONS

1. Draw a general diagram of a delta profile, using Fig. 43.14 as a reference.

2. What are terraces? Paired terraces?

3. List the three major factors that influence delta formation.

SELF-TEST

Multiple-Choice Questions

1. The first step in alluvial fan formation is:

    (a) formation of a braided stream (b) formation of a midstream bar
    (c) formation of an apex (d) formation of a bajada (e) formation of a terrace

2. When several alluvial fans coalesce, the result is a(n):

    (a) arroyo (b) meander (c) ephemeral stream (d) oxbow lake (e) bajada

3. When a meander is cut off permanently from a river, it forms a(n):

    (a) bluff (b) oxbow lake (c) bajada (d) floodplain (e) gully

4. Remnants of older floodplains lying above a new floodplain is called:

    (a) a shelf (b) a delta (c) a terrace (d) a distributary (e) an oxbow

5. When distributaries are kept open by dredging, what type of delta is formed?

    (a) birdfoot (b) foreset (c) topset (d) bottomset (e) midset

6. The finest sediments from a river are deposited on which type of bed?

    (a) topset (b) foreset (c) birdfoot (d) bottomset (e) midset

True-False Questions

___ 1. A trunk river receives distributaries in its drainage basin and develops tributaries in its delta.
___ 2. Floodplains develop when meanders widen and shift downstream.
___ 3. Floods deposit material that add to a river's natural levee.
___ 4. An ephemeral stream is different from a permanent stream only in terms of overall size.
___ 5. After the formation of a midstream bar, a stream becomes braided.
___ 6. A river may have paired or unpaired terraces.

UNIT SUMMARY

When conditions are right water can dissolve soluble rocks and minerals, carrying them away in solution. This occurs both on the surface, where unique landforms are sculpted, and below ground, where caves and associated features are produced. The most common soluble rock is limestone, and its dissolution sculpts the distinctive terrain that is known as a *karst* landscape. Karst processes are reviewed in terms of their geochemistry, the physical properties of varieties of limestone, and the roles of surface-, soil-, and groundwater as well as relief. Three types of karst landscapes are introduced: temperate, tropical, and Caribbean. Karst landforms are then discussed, highlighting those associated with disappearing streams, sinkholes, and towers. The unit concludes with a brief survey of caves, which emphasizes their formation and the wondrous features they often produce.

UNIT OBJECTIVES

1. To discuss the general environmental conditions that favor the formation of karst landscapes.

2. To analyze the landforms that characterize karst landscapes.

3. To relate karst processes to the development of extensive underground cave systems.

GLOSSARY OF KEY TERMS

Caribbean karst The rarest karst topography, associated with nearly flat-lying limestones; underground erosion dominated by the collapse of roofs of subsurface conduits, producing characteristic sinkhole terrain.

Cave Any substantial opening in bedrock , large enough for an adult person to enter, that leads to an interior open space.

Cockpit karst In tropical karst areas, the sharply contrasted landscape of prominent karst towers and the irregular, steep-sided depressions lying between them; *cockpit* refers to the depressions.

Collapse sinkhole In karst terrain, a surface hollow created by the collapse or failure of the roof or overlying material of a cave, cavern, or underground solution cavity.

Column The coalescence of a stalactite and a stalagmite that forms a continuous column from the floor to the roof of a cave.

Karst The distinctive landscape associated with the underground chemical erosion of particularly soluble limestone bedrock.

Solution sinkhole In karst terrain, a funnel-shaped surface hollow (with the shaft draining the center) created by solution; ranges in size from a bathtub to a stadium.

Stalactite An icicle-like rock formation hanging from the roof of a cave.

Stalagmite An upward-tapering, pillar-like rock formation standing on the floor of a cave.

Temperate karst Marked by disappearing streams, jagged rock masses, solution depressions, and extensive cave networks; forms more slowly than tropical karst.

Tower In tropical karst landscapes, a cone-shaped, steep-sided hill that rises above a surface that may or may not be pocked with solution depressions.

Tropical karst Dominated by steep-sided, vegetation-covered hill terrain; solution features are larger than in slower-forming temperate karst landscapes.

Uvala In karst terrain, a large surface depression created by the coalescence of two or more neighboring sinkholes.

UNIT OUTLINE

I. Karst
  A. Associated with rock (limestone) removal by solution
  B. Globally widespread

II. Karst processes
  A. Karst landscape only develops where soluble limestone rich in calcite forms the stratigraphy
    1. limestone poor in calcite much less soluble
    2. dolomite can also form karst topography
    3. more porous and permeable rock more susceptible to solution
  B. The role of water: three processes contribute to erosion
    1. surface streams
    2. underground drainage flows
    3. groundwater
    4. together, these waters create karst landforms in limestone rock—water and carbon dioxide form carbonic acid, which dissolves the limestone
  C. Relief
    1. karst formation is inhibited in flat areas, promoted when limestone under relief
    2. water erodes longer if it moves rapidly, less erosional power if moving slowly

D. Groundwater
  1. occupies openings in limestone
  2. water, in the form of carbonic acid, changes the calcium carbonate in limestone to calcium bicarbonate
  3. karst areas often contain perched aquifers, groundwater at levels above the local water table

III. Karst landforms and landscapes (Fig. 44.5)

A. Temperate karst forms relatively slowly, contains disappearing streams, solution depressions, cave networks
B. Tropical karst develops quickly because of greater rainfall and humidity, contains steep-sided hills and larger karst features than temperate karst
C. Caribbean karst is found in Florida and Mexico in very flat areas, contains underground springs and large surface depressions
D. Disappearing streams and sinkholes
  1. when a surface stream disappears it does so through a swallow hole
  2. low-lying places become solution holes, and expand into solution sinkholes
  3. collapse sinkholes are created when an overlying cave, cavern, or channel collapses
       a. a collapse sink is the result when a rock ceiling collapses
       b. a suffosion sink is the result when an unconsolidated ceiling collapses
  4. an uvala is formed when two or more sinkholes coalesce, usually humid areas
E. Karst towers
  1. dominate tropical karst areas; cone-shaped, steep-sided hills
       a. cockpit karst in tropical areas—alternating towers and depressions
       b. towers are remains of thick bedrock

IV. Karst and caves

A. A cave must be large enough for an adult person to enter (any substantial opening leading to an interior open space)
B. Fully developed cave has several features
  1. entrance (portal)
  2. one or more chambers
  3. passages
  4. terminations (a place beyond which a person cannot crawl further)
C. Caves have many forms
  1. linear
  2. sinuous
  3. angulate
D. Dripping water saturated with calcium carbonate forms precipitates with calcite in the form of travertine, produces many features on cavern ceilings
  1. stalactites

      2. stalagmites

      3. columns

  E. Cave networks

      1. many unmapped networks under water

REVIEW QUESTIONS

1. Compare and contrast a stalactite and a stalagmite.

2. What is cockpit karst and how does it form?

3. List some of the surface and underground features of temperate karst, using Fig. 44.5 as a guide.

SELF-TEST

Multiple-Choice Questions

1. _____ dissolves limestone and forms karst topography.

    (a) Calcium carbonate (b) Calcium bicarbonate (c) Carbonic acid (d) Carbon (e) Dolomite

2. A rock type, other than limestone, which is soluble and forms karst topography is:

    (a) sandstone (b) shale (c) dolomite (d) quartzite (e) basalt

3. Which of the following is not a type of karst landscape?

    (a) Caribbean karst (b) tropical karst (c) temperate karst (d) subpolar karst (e) all are types of karst landscapes

4. Karst landscapes are associated with:

    (a) sunken aquifers (b) perched aquifers (c) collapsed aquifers (d) suffosion aquifers (e) an absence of aquifers

5. When neighboring sinkholes coalesce, the resulting landscape feature is called a(n):

(a) cave (b) solution sinkhole (c) swallow hole (d) cockpit (e) uvala

6. A karst tower is formed from the weathered remains of:

(a) thin sedimentary rock (b) thick bedrock (c) shale (d) granite (e) volcanic ash

True-False Questions

___ 1. In order to be considered a true cave, there must be an entrance, chamber(s), passages, and a termination.
___ 2. Stalactites, stalagmites, and columns are all features found in caves.
___ 3. Temperate karst forms more rapidly than tropical karst.
___ 4. Surface streams have no effect on the formation of karst topography.
___ 5. Karst topography forms more quickly when it is situated under some form of relief.
___ 6. Cockpit karst refers to karst landscapes large enough to be seen from high-flying aircraft.

UNIT 45: GLACIAL DEGRADATION AND AGGRADATION

UNIT SUMMARY

This unit introduces the physical geography of glaciers, setting the stage for a review of glaciers as sculptors of landscape (Units 46 and 47). A glacier is defined as a body of ice, formed on land, that is in motion. Glaciers are classified either as mountain (alpine) glaciers or continental glaciers (ice sheets). Glaciers of the geologic past are then examined, and some important concepts are introduced: ice age, glaciation, deglaciation, and interglacial. The Late Cenozoic Ice Age is highlighted, and the broader question of what causes ice ages is confronted in the Perspective box. Next comes a discussion of the formation of glaciers and their evolution as an open system, which balances ice accumulation against ablation (ice loss). The unit then concludes with an overview of glacial movement and erosion, underscoring internal temperature variations, ice-bedrock interactions, glacier-surface configurations, and the erosional mechanisms of abrasion and plucking.

UNIT OBJECTIVES

1. To discuss the different categories of glaciers.

2. To give a brief history of how glaciation has influenced the Earth's surface.

3. To outline how glaciers form, move, and erode the landscape.

GLOSSARY OF KEY TERMS

Abrasion A glacial erosion process of scraping, produced by the impact of rock debris carried in the ice upon the bedrock surface below.

Basal ice The bottom ice layer of a glacier.

Continental glacier Huge masses of ice that bury whole countrysides beneath them.

Crevasse One of the huge vertical cracks that frequently cut the rigid, brittle upper layer of a mountain glacier.

Cryosphere The collective name for the ice system of the Earth.

Deglaciation The melting and receding of glaciers that accompanies the climatic warmup after the peak of a glaciation has been reached.

Firn Granular, compacted snow.

Glacial creep One of the two mechanisms by which glaciers flow; involves the internal deformation of the ice, with crystals slipping over one another as a result of downslope movement.

Glacial sliding One of the two mechanisms by which glaciers flow; involves the movement of the entire glacier over the rocks below it, lubricated by a thin film of water between the basal ice and the bedrock floor.

Glacial surge Episode of rapid movement in a mountain glacier, as much as one meter per hour, that can last for a year or more.

Glaciation A period of global cooling during which continental icesheets and mountain glaciers expand.

Glacier A body of ice, formed on land, that exhibits motion.

Ice age A stretch of geologic time during which the Earth's average atmospheric temperature is lowered; causes the expansion of glacial ice in the high latitudes and the growth of mountain glaciers in lower latitudes.

Ice sheet See **continental glacier**.

Interglacial A period of warmer global temperatures between the most recent deglaciation and the onset of the next glaciation.

Late Cenozoic Ice Age The last great ice age that ended 10,000 years ago; spanned the entire Pleistocene Epoch (2,000,000 to 10,000 years ago) plus the latter portion of the preceding Pliocene Epoch, possibly beginning as far back as 3 million years ago.

Mountain (alpine) glacier River of ice that forms in mountainous regions; confined in valleys that usually have steep slopes.

Plucking A glacial erosion process in which fragments of bedrock beneath the glacier are extracted from the surface as the ice advances.

Rouche moutonneé The most common landform associated with glacial plucking; an asymmetrical mound.

Striation Scratches made on underlying rock layers by boulders or pebbles dragged by a glacier.

Surge Rapid movement by a mountain glacier, as fast as one meter per hour, sustained for a month or more; produces overall movement of several kilometers in a season.

Zone of ablation A glacier's lower zone of loss; *ablation* refers to all forms of loss at the lower end, including melting and evaporation.

Zone of accumulation A glacier's upper zone of growth, where new snow is added.

UNIT OUTLINE

I. Glacier definitions
  A. A glacier is a moving body of ice, formed on land
  B. Glaciers of Switzerland and Alaska are mountain (alpine) glaciers
  C. Glaciers of Antarctica and Greenland are continental (sheet) glaciers

II. Glaciers of the past
  A. An ice age is a long period of geologic time with lower average temperature, resulting in expansion and growth of glaciers
  B. A glaciation is a cooling period when ice sheets advance, deglaciation then follows
  C. Interglacials are periods of time in-between deglaciation and the next glaciation
  D. Earth at present is in an interglacial
  E. The most recent ice age is the Late Cenozoic
  F. Glaciation associated with falling sea levels, deglaciation with rising sea levels

III. The formation of glaciers
  A. Glaciers consist of ice, which is recrystallized snow
  B. When summer snow loss is less than winter snow gain, conditions favorable for glacier formation
  C. Snow is converted to ice in stages
    1. newly fallen snow flakes
    2. melting occurs or later snowfall compacts earlier snowfall
    3. firn (compacted snow) undergoes further compaction

IV. The glacier as a system
  A. An open system, gaining snow in its zone of accumulation, losing ice in its zone of ablation
    1. matter enters in solid state as snow, undergoes two changes to granular and crystalline states, and exits as liquid or vapor
  B. When mass balance is positive, glacier advances with steep icy edge
  C. When mass balance is negative, glacier is slushy and edge is less pronounced

V. Glacial movement and erosion
  A. The temperature of ice does not decrease steadily with depth
  B. Basal ice is affected by several factors, including:
    1. pressure exerted by weight of overlying ice
    2. temperature of underlying bedrock

    C. When basal ice is at the melting temperature, glaciers move faster and erode more effectively
        1. mountain glaciers in temperate areas are therefore more effective erosional agents than ice sheets
    D. The movement of ice (Fig. 45.6)
        1. glaciers move very slowly
        2. continental glaciers move slower than alpine glaciers
        3. a surge is an occasional period of rapid movement (up to 1 m/hr)
        4. crevasses are long cracks in the brittle upper layer of a glacier
        5. ice is plastic-like below upper layers of a glacier, with crystals slipping over each other due to downslope movement; results in glacial creep
        6. glacial sliding is the movement of the glacier as a whole over rock
            a. enhanced by thin film of water between glacier and rock
    E. Glacial erosion
        1. plucking (or quarrying) is glacial erosion in which blocks of bedrock are pulled up as the glacier slides (Fig. 45.8)
        2. abrasion is the process by which a glacier erodes by scraping the bedrock below
            a. when glacial debris fine but hard and bedrock hard, a polished result
            b. when glacial rocks larger, striations (grooved scratches) produced in eroded bedrock

REVIEW QUESTIONS

1. Describe the cycle of glaciations and interglacials, and list general climatic conditions associated with each.

2. How are glaciers formed from snow – what are the steps involved in this process? See Fig. 45.2.

3. What are glacial surges? Which type of glacier are they associated with?

SELF-TEST

Multiple-Choice Questions

1. A cooling period, in which ice expands is known as a(n):

(a) ice age (b) glaciation (c) deglaciation (d) interglacial (e) cryospheration

2. Granular, compacted snow that undergoes further compression in glacial formation is called:

    (a) firn (b) basal ice (c) *roche moutonnée* (d) karst (e) foehn

3. In order to remain in equilibrium, a glacier loses ice in its zone of:

    (a) accumulation (b) precipitation (c) ablation (d) compression (e) phreation

4. Which factor does not affect the temperature of basal ice?

    (a) bedrock temperature (b) weight of overlying ice (c) pressure (d) direction of flow (e) all of these factors affect basal ice temperature

5. An occasional rapid, sustained movement of a glacier is known as a(n):

    (a) glaciation (b) advance (c) slide (d) ablation (e) surge

6. The glacier process associated with erosion by pulling up blocks of rock is:

    (a) abrasion (b) plucking (c) scouring (d) glacial creep (e) surging

True-False Questions

__ 1. Glacial creep refers to the movement of the entire glacier over rock.
__ 2. Temperature does not decrease evenly with increasing depth in a glacier.
__ 3. The most common landform associated with abrasion is the *roche moutonnée*.
__ 4. The upper, rigid layer of a glacier is often cut by large cracks called crevasses.
__ 5. The ice age of the present is the Late Cenozoic Ice Age.
__ 6. A glacier receives moisture inputs in its zone of ablation.

UNIT 46: LANDFORMS AND LANDSCAPES OF CONTINENTAL GLACIERS

UNIT SUMMARY

The landforms and landscapes associated with continental glaciers (ice sheets) constitute the theme of this unit. The first half of the unit explores the two present-day continental glaciers: the Antarctic and Greenland Ice Sheets. The Antarctic Ice Sheet is examined in some detail and many salient concepts are introduced, including nunataks (reminders of the landmass that underlies the ice sheet), ice volume and weight relationships, ice-flow regimes, and ice shelves as well as related ice features that wax and wane with the seasons in the waters of the Southern Ocean that surround Antarctica. A retrospect on the Late Cenozoic Ice Sheets then introduces a review of North America's most recent glaciations. Degradational landforms and landscapes are discussed in the context of glacial lakes, and a case study highlights the formation of the five Great Lakes (see Fig. 46.11). The unit concludes with an exploration of aggradational landforms, including glacial drift, terminal and other moraines, and lesser depositional landforms--all illustrated in Fig. 46.15.

UNIT OBJECTIVES

1. To delineate contemporary continental glaciers and define their former extent during the Late Cenozoic Ice Age.

2. To identify typical landforms produced by continental glaciers.

GLOSSARY OF KEY TERMS

Calving When an icesheet enters the sea, the repeated breaking away of the leading edge of that glacier into huge, flat-topped, tabular icebergs.

Drumlin A smooth elliptical mound created when an icesheet overrides and reshapes preexisting glacial till; long axis lies parallel to direction of ice movement.

Esker A glacial outwash landform that appears as a long ribbon-like ridge in the landscape because it was formed by the clogging of a river course within a glacier, the debris from which remains after the ice melts.

Flow regime A discrete region of outward ice flow in a continental glacier; possesses its own rates of snow accumulation, ice formation, and velocity.

Glacial drift Comprised of unsorted till and stratified drift.

Glacial outwash Meltwater-deposited sand and gravel that are sorted into layers.

Ground moraine Blanket of unsorted glacial till that was laid down at the base of a melting glacier.

Ice cap A regional mass of ice smaller than a continent-sized icesheet. While the Laurentide Icesheet covered much of North America east of the Rocky Mountains, an ice cap covered the Rockies themselves.

Ice shelf Smaller ice sheet that is floating, seaward extension of a continental glacier, such as Antarctica's Ross Ice Shelf.

Kame A ridge or mound of glacial debris or stratified drift at the edge of a glacier; often found as deltaic deposits where meltwater streams flowed into temporary lakes near the receding glacier.

Kettle Steep-sided depression formed in glacial till that is the result of the melting of a buried block of ice.

Moraine A ridge or mound of glacial debris deposited during the melting phase of a glacier.

Nunatak A mountain peak of a buried landscape that protrudes through the overlying glacier.

Outwash plain Plain formed ahead of a receding icesheet by the removal of material carried in the glacier by meltwater; exhibits both erosional and depositional features.

Pack ice Floating sea ice that forms from the freezing of ocean water.

Pluvial lake A lake that developed in a presently dry area during times of heavier precipitation associated with glaciations; Glacial Lake Bonneville, the (much larger) forerunner of Utah's Great Salt Lake, is a classic example.

Recessional moraine A moraine ridge marking a place where glacial retreat was temporarily halted.

Stratified drift One of the two types of glacial drift; the material transported by glaciers and later sorted and deposited by the action of running water, either within the glacier or as it melts.

Terminal moraine The rock debris, carried in and just ahead of the leading front of a glacier, that is deposited as an irregular ridge when the ice's forward progress stops; these ridges are important to Earth scientists because they mark the farthest extent of an ice lobe.

Till One of the two types of glacial drift; the solid material (ranging in size from boulders to clay particles) carried at the base of a glacier that is deposited as an unsorted mass when the ice melts back.

UNIT OUTLINE

I. The Antarctic Ice Sheet
    A. Continental landmass lies below glacier, with mountain ranges and a huge plateau
    B. Nunataks are exposed mountain peaks that protrude through the ice and snow
    C. Volume and weight of the ice sheet
        1. about 65 percent of fresh water on Earth is locked in this ice sheet
        2. landmass below is depressed isostatically from weight of ice
    D. Features of the Antarctic Ice Sheet
        1. ice dome is divided into flow regimes
        2. ice tongues are glaciers that let out into the sea
        3. ice shelves are floating extensions of the main glacier, attached to continent
        4. ice shelves break off into icebergs at their outer edges, a process called calving
        5. icebergs float because they have lower density than the cold seawater
        6. zone of floating pack ice surrounds zone of icebergs

II. The Greenland Ice Sheet
    A. Much smaller than Antarctic Ice Sheet
    B. Greenland is only about 11 percent free of ice cover
    C. Northern hemisphere has no polar ice sheets

III. Age of the present ice sheets
    A. Analyze microorganisms of sediment to measure age of ice sheets
    B. There have been more than 30 glaciations since the Late Cenozoic began
    C. Antarctic Ice Sheet appears older, possibly 15 million years old

IV. Other Cenozoic ice sheets
    A. Former Northern Hemisphere ice sheets
        1. Laurentide Ice Sheet
        2. Scandanavian (Fennoscandian) Ice Sheet
        3. Siberian (Barents) Ice Sheet
    B. Former Southern Hemisphere ice sheets
        1. smaller ice caps formed, in southern South America and South Island of New Zealand

V. North America's glaciation: the final four (Table 46.1)
    A. Last four glaciations actually represent the last dozen of the Late Cenozoic
        1. Nebraskan (most distant)
        2. Illinoisan
        3. Kansan Complex

4. Wisconsinan (most recent)

VI. Landscapes of continental glaciers
    A. Sheet glaciers create massive, erosional landscapes
    B. Glacial lakes
        1. lake bottoms contain bands of sediment from each year's deposition
        2. water trapped when glaciers recede, leaving a huge deposit of soil and rock, from what used to be their leading edges
        3. pluvial lakes develop in areas that receive a lot of precipitation during glaciations
            a. Glacial Lake Bonneville, forerunner of Utah's Great Salt Lake
        4. The Great Lakes were also created by receding Late Cenozoic glaciers

VII. Aggradational landforms of ice sheets
    A. Glacial drift
        1. when glaciers recede, deposition of material begins as an unsorted till
        2. material sorted by water to from stratified drift
        3. glacial drift refers to till and stratified drift together
    B. Moraines (Fig. 46.12)
        1. a terminal moraine is the outermost ridge of debris left by a glacier
        2. a recessional moraine is differentiated as a ridge where an already receding glacier temporarily stops and deposits additional material
    C. Drumlins (whalebacks)
        1. smooth, elliptical hills that rise from the till plain, may be from ice sheets that override preexisting till
    D. Glacial meltwater deposits (Fig. 46.15)
        1. meltwater flows in channels in several directions away from a glacier
            a. glacial outwash is unsorted debris left by meltwater
            b. eskers are former tunnels that formed when water flowed out of a glacier; debris eventually clogs them, and the landform remains
            c. an outwash plain forms in front of a melting glacier
            d. kettles are created when large blocks of ice are initially buried in the outwash plain, and create a depression as they melt
                i. if may kettles, outwash plain is considered pitted
            e. a kame is the remains of a glacial outwash delta

---

REVIEW QUESTIONS

1. Name five landforms associated with a receding ice sheet, using Fig. 46.15 as a reference.

2. What were the most recent glaciations in North America?

3. How were the Great Lakes formed?

SELF-TEST

Multiple-Choice Questions

1. Which of the following was not one of North America's most recent glaciations?

   (a) Wisconsinan (b) Kansan complex (c) Illinoisan (d) Idahoan (e) all were recent glaciations

2. Which of the following was not a Northern Hemisphere ice sheet?

   (a) Siberian (b) Scandanavian (c) European (d) Laurentide (e) all were Northern Hemisphere ice sheets

3. Pluvial lakes form from an increase in:

   (a) atmospheric pressure (b) temperature (c) glacial melting (d) river formation (e) precipitation

4. Which type of material is deposited first when a deglaciation begins?

   (a) stratified drift (b) till (c) drumlins (d) eskers (e) moraines

5. Which landform is not the result of glacial meltwater?

   (a) drumlin (b) esker (c) outwash plain (d) kettles (e) all are meltwater features

6. Steep-sided, water-filled depressions on outwash plains are known as:

   (a) drumlins (b) kames (c) eskers (d) moraines (e) kettles

True-False Questions

___ 1. Kettles are created by buried blocks of ice on outwash plains.
___ 2. Stratified drift is a combination of till and glacial drift.
___ 3. The Great Lakes were formed by Late Cenozoic ice sheets.
___ 4. It is theorized that there were approximately five glaciations in the Late Cenozoic Ice Age.
___ 5. The Greenland Ice Sheet is much larger than the Antarctic Ice Sheet.
___ 6. A drumlin is formed by an ice sheet overriding preexisting till.

UNIT 47: LANDFORMS AND LANDSCAPES OF MOUNTAIN GLACIERS

UNIT SUMMARY

The landforms and landscapes associated with mountain (alpine) glaciers constitute the theme of this unit. The first half of the unit examines the global distribution of mountain glaciers. This is followed by an overview of the degradational landforms of mountain glaciers, highlighting such landscape features as glacial troughs, truncated spurs, hanging valleys, and fjords. The focus then shifts to high-mountain terrain: assisted by Figure 47.7, an additional set of landforms is introduced that includes cirques, horns, arêtes, rock steps, and tarns. The unit then turns to consider the aggradational landforms of mountain glaciers, comprehensively illustrated in Fig. 47.9. These include several varieties of moraines as well as the meltwater deposits that progressively evolve as the postglacial landscape emerges and matures.

UNIT OBJECTIVES

1. To examine the current distribution of mountain glaciers and to comment on the Late Cenozoic extent of these glaciers.

2. To discuss the landforms produced by mountain glacier erosion and deposition.

GLOSSARY OF KEY TERMS

Arête A knife-like, jagged ridge that separates two adjacent glaciers or glacial valleys.

Cirque An amphitheater-like basin, high up on a mountain, that is the source area of a mountain glacier.

Finger lake An elongated lake that fills much of an even longer, fairly narrow glacial trough.

Fjord A narrow, steep-sided, elongated estuary formed from a glacial trough inundated by seawater.

Glacial trough A valley that has been eroded by a glacier; distinctively U-shaped in cross-sectional profile.

Ground moraine Blanket of unsorted glacial till that was laid down at the base of a melting glacier.

Hanging valley A valley formed by the intersection of a tributary glacier with a trunk glacier; when the ice melts away, the tributary valley floor usually is at a higher elevation and thus "hangs" above the main valley's floor.

Horn The sharp-pointed, Matterhorn-like mountain peak that remains when several cirques attain their maximum growth by headward erosion and intersect.

Lateral moraine Moraine situated along the edge of a mountain glacier, consisting of debris that fell from the adjacent valley wall.

Medial moraine A moraine – situated well away from a glacier's edges – formed by the intersection of two lateral moraines when a substantial tributary glacier meets and joins a tributary glacier.

Moraine A ridge or mound of glacial debris deposited during the melting phase of a glacier.

Rock flour The very finely-ground up debris carried downslope by a mountain glacier; when deposited, often blown away by the wind.

Rock step The step-like mountainside profile (in the postglacial landscape) often created as an eroding alpine glacier moved dwonslope.

Tarn Small circular lake on the floor of a cirque basin.

Truncated spur Spurs of hillsides that have been cut off by a glacier, thereby straightening the glacially eroded valley.

Valley train Meltwater-deposited alluvium in a glacial trough; derived from the morainal material left behind by a receding mountain glacier.

UNIT OUTLINE

I. Mountain glaciers today
A. Global distribution
1. every landmass except Australia has alpine glaciers
2. may be as many as 100,000 glaciers at present
3. North America
a. Alaska
b. Canada's Yukon Territory and British Columbia
4. South America
a. southern Andes
5. Africa
a. Mount Kilimanjaro and Mount Kenya
6. Australia-New Zealand
a. Southern Alps, South Island of New Zealand
7. Europe
a. Alps
8. Asia
a. Mount Everest and other high Himalaya peaks, Nepal
b. certain ranges across south-central Asia

II. Degradational landforms of mountain glacier

    A. Glacial valleys

        1. typically a **V**-shaped valley, widened into a **U**-shaped trough by glacier (Fig. 47.6)

        2. truncated spurs are mountain edges that have been sheared off by glaciers

        3. hanging valleys, formed by large and small glaciers joining together that have different base levels

    B. High-mountain landforms (Fig. 47.7)

        1. initial landscape has ridges and peaks

        2. glacial erosion begins, and ice hollows out cirques, steep-sided depressions

        3. as cirques intersect over time, their edges form knifelike ridges (arêtes) that eventually are eroded away to form a single jagged peak (horn)

        4. rock steps show local effects of frost wedging and jointing

    C. Lakes (Fig. 47.7)

        1. in warmer areas, cirque basins filled with water during interglacials; called tarns

        2. lakes also form in glacial troughs; many are elongated finger lakes

    D. Fjords

        1. a narrow, steep-sided estuary formed by a glacial trough that filled with ocean water

III. Aggradational landforms of mountain glaciers (Fig. 47.9)

    A. Finely ground particles of glacial debris called rock flour

    B. Moraines

        1. larger fragments deposited in terminal moraines, the stalled edge of a moving glacier

        2. recessional moraines and associated debris formed during glacial retreat

        3. both terminal and recessional moraines form dams to create lakes

        4. material that falls first from valley wall becomes lateral moraine

        5. when a trunk glacier is jointed by a tributary one, their lateral moraines join to become a medial moraine

        6. erosion at the base of the valley forms a ground moraine, which is thickened by deposits when the glacier recedes

    C. Postglacial landscape change

        1. river action modifies glacial action when glaciers retreat

        2. a valley train is left when meltwater fills the valley floor

        3. glacial lakes often drained when glaciers recede, and deposits redistributed

        4. areas modified by glaciers at risk for mass movements

REVIEW QUESTIONS

1. Describe how lateral, medial, and terminal moraines form.

2. Name and discuss the main features of three degradational landforms of mountain glaciers.

3. List four features of a mountain landscape that has been transformed by alpine glaciation, using Fig. 47.7 as a guide.

SELF-TEST

Multiple-Choice Questions

1. Which landmass does not contain alpine glaciers?

   (a) Australia (b) Antarctica (c) Europe (d) South America (e) North America

2. Glacial valleys tend to be:

   (a) V-shaped (b) S-shaped (c) U-shaped (d) L-shaped (e) T-shaped

3. The erosional remnant of a cirque is called a(n):

   (a) hanging valley (b) glacial trough (c) fjord (d) horn (e) O-shaped valley

4. Narrow, steep estuaries formed when a glacier reaches the sea are called:

   (a) moraines (b) eskers (c) finger lakes (d) rock steps (e) fjords

5. What type of moraine forms from material that falls from a valley wall first?

   (a) lateral moraine (b) medial moraine (c) ground moraine (d) valley train (e) bottomset moraine

6. Meltwater deposits from morainal material left behind by a receding glacier are called:

   (a) medial moraines (b) valley trains (c) lateral moraines (d) ground moraines (e) arêtes

True-False Questions

__ 1. A medial moraine forms when a trunk glacier is joined by a tributary glacier.
__ 2. Lakes formed from water dammed up in a cirque are called tarns.
__ 3. A hanging valley forms when glaciers with identical base levels converge in an
       area.
__ 4. Africa contains no alpine glaciers.
__ 5. Glacial debris that is ground into very fine particles is called rock flour.
__ 6. Finger lakes may form on rock steps.

UNIT 48: PERIGLACIAL ENVIRONMENTS AND LANDSCAPES

UNIT SUMMARY

Periglacial environments are widespread throughout the broad high-latitude zones that lie on the perimeter of glaciation. The most effective way to identify periglacial regions is to link them to the distribution of permafrost (see Fig. 48.3). Two subsurface layers mark periglacial environments--the upper active layer and lower permafrost layer--and they are diagrammed in Fig. 48.2. The geomorphic processes that shape periglacial landscapes are reviewed next, and focus on the mechanisms of frost wedging, frost heaving, frost thrusting, frost creep, and solifluction. The often-strange landforms produced by these processes are now introduced: ice-wedge polygons, patterned ground, and pingos. To these are added the products of gravity-induced mass movements, particularly the boulder fields that are commonly found in high-relief periglacial regions. The unit concludes with a reminder of the fragility of periglacial environments as the outside world increasingly penetrates them in the search for energy and mineral resources; the consequences of the 1989 Exxon Valdez oil spill in Alaska's Prince William Sound, the subject of the Perspective box, underscores this threat emphatically.

UNIT OBJECTIVES

1. To discuss the unique landscapes that develop under near-glacial conditions at high latitudes and high altitudes.

2. To highlight the important weathering and mass-movement processes that shape periglacial landscapes.

GLOSSARY OF KEY TERMS

Active layer The soil above the permafrost table that is subject to annual freezing and thawing.

Boulder field The area of blocky rock fragments formed when weathered rocks – particularly from frost wedging – remain near their original location; also known as a *blockfield or felsenmeer*.

Frost creep The movement of particles within the active layer above the permafrost under the influence of gravity; on the surface, rocks will move downslope during the thawing phase.

Frost heaving The upward displacement of rocks and rock fragments within the active layer above the permafrost after they have been loosened by frost wedging; triggered by the formation of ice in the ground that expands the total mass of rock materials.

Frost thrusting The horizontal movement of rocks and rock fragments within the active layer above the permafrost.

Frost wedging The forcing apart of a rock when the expansion stress created by the freezing of its internal water into ice exceeds the cohesive strength of that rock body.

Ice-wedge polygon Polygonal features formed by the freezing and thawing of sediments that fill surface cracks caused by very cold winter temperatures in periglacial zones.

Patterned ground Periglacial rock and soil debris shaped or sorted in such a manner that it forms designs on the surface resembling rings, polygons, lines, and the like.

Periglacial A high-latitude or high-altitude environment on the perimeter of a glaciated area.

Permafrost The permanently frozen layer of subsoil that is characteristic of the colder portions of the **D**-climate zone as well as the entire **E**-climate zone; can exceed 300m in depth.

Pingo A mound-like, elliptical hill in a periglacial zone whose core consists of ice rather than rock or soil.

Solifluction A special kind of soil creep in which soil and rock debris are saturated with water and flow in bulk as a single mass; most common in periglacial zones.

UNIT OUTLINE

I. Permafrost
    A. Periglacial areas are on the periphery of glaciation
        1. Dfc, Dfd, E climates
        2. Gravity is the main mover of loosened materials in these areas
    B. Permafrost is permanently frozen ground (Fig. 48.2)
        1. usually extends from 15 cm (6 in.) to 5m (16.5 ft) below surface
        2. upper surface called permafrost table
        3. active layer is the soil layer above the permafrost table, freezes and thaws annually
        4. continuous permafrost in more northerly latitudes, discontinuous (alpine) permafrost further south

II. Geomorphic processes in periglacial environments
    A. Frost action
        1. frost wedging (shattering) occurs when stress of freezing and thawing breaks down the strength of rock
            a. produces patterned ground

    2. after frost wedging, frost heaving causes vertical rock displacement when ice expands

    3. frost thrusting moves material horizontally

    4. frost creep occurs when particles in the active layer move due to gravity

  B. Solifluction (Fig. 48.5)

    1. actually a form of soil creep, slow flowing of saturated soil when water cannot infiltrate soil due to permafrost

    2. vegetation in more moderate areas stabilizes solifluction

III. Landforms of periglacial regions

  A. Ice wedges

    1. created when ground becomes cold and cracks, filling with mud, ice, etc. and then expands each time it refreezes, widening the cracks

      a. can form ice-wedge polygons over large areas

  B. Patterned ground

    1. rock and other solid debris sorted to form patterns such as rings or polygons

  C. Pingos

    1. mounds consisting of ice that form under permafrost conditions, possibly from drained lakes where the permafrost level rises to the surface

  D. Boulder fields (felsenmeers)

    1. slopes covered by blocks of rock that have been removed from rock faces by frost wedging

    2. some believe that ice may have filled the openings between the boulders, creating a moving rock glacier

IV. Resource development in periglacial environments

  A. Search for resources has lead to further investigation of remote periglacial areas

---

REVIEW QUESTIONS

1. Name and elaborate on three of the major landforms associated with periglacial regions.

2. Define frost wedging, frost heaving, and frost thrusting.

3. Draw the layers of permafrost, using Fig. 48.2 as a guide.

SELF-TEST

Multiple-Choice Questions

1. Which of the following climate types would not be associated with periglacial environments?

   (a) Dfc (b) Dfd (c) Cfa (d) E (e) all of these are associated with periglacial environments

2. When stress created by freezing of water breaks the strength of rock, which occurs first?

   (a) frost wedging (b) frost heaving (c) frost thrusting (d) frost creep (e) frost faulting

3. What is the form of soil creep in which saturated soil flows very slowly?

   (a) frost thrusting (b) solifluction (c) frost heaving (d) infiltration (e) extrusion

4. Sorted rock and soil debris in periglacial areas can form:

   (a) soil blocks (b) frost wedging (c) block fields (d) felsenmeers (e) patterned ground

5. Which landform is a round or elliptical mound formed from a drained lake?

   (a) boulder field (b) patterned ground (c) pingo (d) felsenmeer (e) crevasse

6. Frost thrusting moves material in which direction?

   (a) horizontally (b) vertically (c) diagonally (d) does not move material (e) a, b, and c

True-False Questions

___ 1. When ground cracks, fills with materials, and alternately freezes and thaws, ice wedge-polygons form.
___ 2. Gravity does not play much of a role in moving materials in periglacial environments.
___ 3. Another name for a boulder field is a felsenmeer.
___ 4. Permafrost conditions are not always necessary in the formation of pingos.
___ 5. Soil in permafrost areas is often saturated because water cannot drain well through permafrost.
___ 6. The soil above the permafrost layer, subjected to freezing and thawing, forms the active layer.

UNIT 49: WIND AS A GEOMORPHIC AGENT

UNIT SUMMARY

The role of wind as a sculptor of landscapes is more subtle and difficult to measure than the effects of the other geomorphic agents. But in arid environments with little vegetation, windflow does indeed play an important part in shaping surface topography. Wind is both a degradational and aggradational agent. Wind erosion takes place through wind abrasion, whose effectiveness is directly related to the speed of the airflow. Common degradational landforms (see Figs. 49.2 and 49.3) shaped by wind are deflation hollows (shallow basins often marked by desert-pavement surfaces) and yardangs (low ridges formed parallel to the prevailing wind direction). Wind-transportation processes of different-sized particles, as shown in Fig. 49.4, include suspension, saltatation ,and surface creep. The most widely distributed aggradational landforms produced by wind-deposited materials are sand dunes. Dunes are accumulations of sand shaped by wind action. They may be active or fixed, and their structural profile is marked by a windward-facing backslope, a crest, and a leeward-facing slip face (Fig. 49.6). The most common dune forms are barchans, parabolic dunes, transverse dunes, and longitudinal dunes (Fig. 49.7). The unit concludes with an introduction to *loess*, fine-grained dust deposits laid down after having been blown some distance by prevailing winds. Most of the world's loess accumulations (Figs. 49.9 and 49.10) were deposited downwind from receding continental ice sheets, whose periglacial margins yielded huge quantities of rock flour carried away by frequent high winds. Loess is noted both for its natural fertility (which produces bountiful crop yields) and its vertical strength (which allows people to excavate cavelike dwellings in China's Loess Plateau).

UNIT OBJECTIVES

1. To examine the mechanisms of wind erosion and the landforms produced by this process.

2. To relate various types of sand dunes to environmental controls.

3. To note the importance and environmental significance of loess.

GLOSSARY OF KEY TERMS

Backslope The windward slope of a sand dune.

Barchan A crescent-shaped sand dune with its points lying downwind; convex side of this dune is the windward side.

Deflation The process whereby wind sweeps along a surface and carries away the finest particles.

Deflation hollow Shallow desert basin created by the wind erosion process of deflation.

Desert pavement A smoothly weathered, varnish-like surface of closely packed pebbles that has developed on the upper part of an alluvial fan or bajada; no longer subject to stream braiding, such a surface is stable and may support desert vegetation.

Dune An accumulation of sand that is shaped by wind action.

Eolian Pertaining to the action of the wind.

Erg A sand sea; a large expanse of sandy desert.

Loess A deposit of very fine silt or dust laid down after having been blown some distance (perhaps hundreds of kilometers) by the wind; characterized by its fertility and ability to stand in steep vertical walls.

Longitudinal dune A long ridge-like sand dune that lies parallel to the prevailing wind.

Parabolic dune A crescent-shaped sand dune with its points lying upwind; concave side of this dune is the windward side.

Slip face The leeward slope of a sand dune.

Surface creep The movement of fairly large rock fragments by the wind, actually pushing them along the ground, especially during windstorms.

Transverse dune A ridge-like sand dune that is positioned at a right angle to the prevailing wind; usually straight or slightly curved.

Wind abrasion The erosion of rock surfaces by windborne sand particles.

Yardang A desert landform shaped by wind abrasion in the form of a low ridge lying parallel to the prevailing wind direction; most common in dry sandy areas underlain by soft bedrock.

UNIT OUTLINE

I. Wind erosion
  A. Eolian processes are wind-related and shape the Earth's surface
  B. Wind is both an aggradational and degradational force
  C. Wind is only an erosive agent when it carries sand particles and performs wind abrasion

II. Degradational landforms
  A. Deflation is the process of wind sweeping away fine particles of sand
    1. deflation hollows are produced by this process

      2. desert pavement is the remaining closely-packed pebbles on the surface

      3. yardangs are low ridges that form parallel to wind direction, due to abrasion

  B. Wind transportation (Fig. 49.4)

      1. finest particles carried high in the air in suspension

      2. larger particles bounce between the air and the ground, in saltation

      3. largest rock fragments pushed along at the surface by surface creep

III. Aggradational landforms

  A. Erg, or sand sea, is the main feature in arid environments

  B. Ripples may be formed by saltation or surface creep

IIII.. Sand dunes

  A. An accumulation of sand that is shaped by the wind

  B. Dune is active when the wind is constantly moving it, and it has no vegetation

  C. Dunes become stable (fixed) when they enter a moister area, and support vegetation

  D. Dune features (Fig. 49.6)

      1. backslope (or windward slope)

      2. crest (or top)

      3. slip face (or leeward slope)

  E. Dune forms (Fig. 49.7)

      1. barchans are crescent-shaped dunes, the windward side is convex

      2. parabolic dunes are crescent-shaped dunes, the windward side is concave

      3. transverse dunes are straight or slightly curved, at right angles to wind direction, the windward side is concave

      4. longitudinal dunes are long ridges, parallel to wind direction

  F. Dune landscape research

      1. dune morphology can provide information about past climates

IV. Loess

  A. Fine-grained sedimentary deposits originally left by glaciers, then picked up by wind

  B. Distribution of loess deposits

      1. extensive in Eurasia, some in North America, southern South America

  C. Properties of loess

      1. loess produces very fertile soil for agriculture

      2. consists of quartz, feldspars, carbonates, clays, and other minerals

      3. fertile through its entire profile, not just its upper layer

      4. a homogeneous, porous substance that has vertical strength once water has developed passages within it

        a. China's Loess Plateau

REVIEW QUESTIONS

1. Name the four major forms of sand dunes, using Fig. 49.7.

2. Describe the processes of suspension, saltation, and soil creep.

3. Explain the global distribution of loess, using 49.9 as a guide.

SELF-TEST

Multiple-Choice Questions

1. Which of the following is not a feature resulting from a wind-related degradational process?

    (a) desert pavement (b) yardang (c) dune (d) deflection hollow (e) all are degradational landforms

2. The finest windborne sand particles are carried by:

    (a) saltation (b) solution (c) surface creep (d) suspension (e) stratification

3. The largest, heaviest, windborne rock fragments are moved by:

    (a) surface creep (b) saltation (c) suspension (d) solution (e) stratification

4. Which type of sand dune lies at right angles to the prevailing wind direction?

    (a) longitudinal (b) recumbent (c) parabolic (d) barchan (e) transverse

5. Which type of sand dune is crescent-shaped, with its concave side pointed in the windward direction?

    (a) parabolic (b) transverse (c) barchan (d) longitudinal (e) none of these

6. Loess is considered what type of deposit?

    (a) heterogeneous and impermeable (b) homogeneous and impermeable (c) heterogeneous and porous (d) homogeneous and porous (e) heterogeneous or homogeneous and porous

True-False Questions

___ 1. A longitudinal dune forms ridges parallel to the prevailing wind direction.
___ 2. Loess is composed of quartz, feldspar, carbonates, and other minerals.
___ 3. Saltation carries the finest particles high in the atmosphere.
___ 4. The erg is the dominant landform in sandy desert.
___ 5. The backslope is the leeward side of the dune.
___ 6. When dunes become active they usually support extensive vegetation.

UNIT 50: COASTAL PROCESSES

UNIT SUMMARY

This is the first of a pair of units on the role of coastal waves as a geomorphic agent. The focus here is on coastal processes, particularly the action of waves and related water motions in the narrow littoral zone where sea and land constantly interact. The properties of waves of oscillation in the open sea are displayed (see Figs. 50.1 and 50.2). The actions of waves breaking against the shore are then reviewed in detail, introducing the concepts of waves of translation, shoaling, wave refraction, and the generation of longshore currents. The discussion widens to incorporate the processes that shape beaches, especially longshore drift. Next comes an overview of the degradational and aggradational effects of waves, and the conceptual framework expands to include the hydraulic actions of waves, corrasion, corrosion, and attrition. Tides and shore zone currents are now considered. The effects of tides are elaborated with the aid of the Perspective box. We are introduced to tidal ranges and the actions of tidal currents, and the specialized roles of longshore currents and rip currents are delineated. The unit concludes with an examination of the effects of storms and crustal movement on the coastal landscape.

UNIT OBJECTIVES

1. To establish the importance of coastal zones as areas of interaction between physical processes and human settlement.

2. To examine the physical properties of waves and their significance in the operation of coastal processes.

3. To discuss other sources of energy in the coastal zone and their erosional and depositional significance.

GLOSSARY OF KEY TERMS

Backwash The return flow to the sea of the thinning sheet of water that slid up the beach as swash.

Barrier island A permanent, offshore, elongated ridge of sand, positioned parallel to the shoreline and separated by a lagoon from it; may have originally formed as an offshore bar during the last glaciation, migrated coastward, and grew as it shifted.

Beach drift The larger process associated with longshore drift that operates to move huge amounts of beach sand downshore in the direction of the longshore current.

Coast General reference to the strip of land and sea where the various coastal processes combine to create characteristic landscapes.

Corrasion The mechanical coastal-erosion process whereby waves break off pieces of rock from the surface under attack; the rock-fragment-loaded water, now a much more powerful erosive agent, continues to be hurled against the surface.

Littoral zone Coastal zone.

Longshore current A shore-paralleling water current, similar to the longshore drift of sand, that is generated by the refracted, oblique-angled arrival of waves onshore.

Longshore drift The movement of sand along the shoreline in the flow of water (*longshore current*) generated by the refacted, oblique-angled arrival of waves onshore.

Rip current Narrow, short-distance stream-like current that moves seaward from the shoreline cutting directly across the oncoming surf.

Shoaling The near-shore impact of ever shallower water on an advancing, incoming wave.

Shore Has a more specific meaning the *coast*; denotes the narrower belt of land bordering a body of water, the most seaward portion of a coast.

Storm surge The wind-driven wall of water hurled ashore by the approaching center of a hurricane, which can surpass normal high tide levels by more than 5 m (16 ft): often associated with a hurricane's greatest destruction.

Surf The water zone just offshore dominated by the development and forward collapse of breaking waves.

Swash The thinning sheet of water that slides up the beach after a wave reaches shore and has lost its form.

Tide The cyclical rise and fall of sea level controlled by the Earth's rotation and the gravitational pull of the moon and sun: daily, two high tides and two low tides occur within a period slightly longer than 24 hours.

Wave height The vertical distance between the wave crest (top) and the wave trough (bottom).

Wave length The horizontal distance between one wave crest (or wave trough) and the next.

Wave refraction The near-shore bending of waves coming in at an oblique angle to the shoreline; shoaling slows part of the wave, which proressively bends as the faster end "catches up".

Waves of oscillation Waves that move water particles in a circular up-and-down path; their depth is one-half their length.

UNIT OUTLINE

I. Coasts and shores
    A. Land meets sea in the littoral zone
    B. Coast refers to a strip of land and sea where coastal processes occur
    C. Shore refers to a narrower strip of land bordering the water
    D. Shoreline is the actual contact boundary between land and sea

II. Waves and their properties (Fig. 50.1)
    A. Waves are the real erosional agents of the coast
    B. Large waves form when several criteria are met
        1. high wind velocity
        2. persistent wind direction
        3. fetch is long
        4. wind duration long
    C. Wave height is the distance between a wave crest and a wave trough
    D. Wave length is the horizontal distance between two wave crests (or two troughs)
    E. Wave period is the time between the passing of two successive crests
    F. Waves of oscillation move water particles in a circular up-and-down motion
        1. the depth of this type of wave is half of its length

III. Waves against the shore (Fig. 50.3)
    A. As waves enter shallow water near a coastline, become waves of translation
        1. water particles do not return to their original positions in orbital motion, begin to erode
        2. wave becomes so steep that its crest collapses, becomes a breaker
        3. surf is the continual breaking of waves against the coastline
        4. swash is the thin flow of water that slides up the beach when a wave breaks
        5. backwash is when swash flows back into the water
    B. Wave refraction (Fig. 50.5)
        1. Shoaling is when an advancing wave is affected by shallow water
        2. wave refraction is the process by which waves approach the coast at an oblique angle, the leading edge is slowed, and the wave is bent to an angle parallel with the coastline
    C. Longshore drift (Fig. 50.6)
        1. sand is moved along the beach by arriving waves bringing material to shore at an angle, and the backwash returning materials to sea at a right angle
        2. beach drift is the movement of huge amounts of sand along the shore
        3. longshore drift can create ridges that eventually form barrier islands

IV. Degradation and aggradation by waves
    A. Erosion by hydraulic action
    B. Corrasion is the mechanical process of wave erosion
    C. Corrosion is the breakdown of rock by solution or chemical methods
    D. Low relief dominates most coastlines
        1. beaches
        2. dunes
        3. sandy islands

V. Tides and shore zone currents
    A. Effects of tides
        1. high tide
        2. low tide
        3. tidal range is the average vertical distance between low and high tide
        4. tidal currents refer to the changing water levels associated with tides
        5. tidal bore created when rapid high tide creates a wave front that runs into a river or bay
    B. Shore zone currents
        1. longshore current parallel to shore
        2. rip currents are stream-like, high velocity currents that move materials toward the ocean (Fig. 50.11)

VI. The role of storms
    A. Storms create powerful winds, creating waves called the storm surge when colliding with the shoreline

VII. Crustal movement
    A. Coastlines rise and fall in the long run due to isostatic rebound and sea level fluctuation

---

REVIEW QUESTIONS

1. Define the term longshore drift, and describe how it occurs.

2. What is a storm surge?

3. Describe the conditions necessary for the formation of large waves.

SELF-TEST

Multiple-Choice Questions

1. The actual contact plane between the land and the sea is the:

   (a) littoral zone (b) coast (c) shore (d) shoreline (e) beachfront

2. Wave height is the vertical distance between:

   (a) wave crest and trough (b) ocean surface and bottom (c) two wave crests (d) wave length (e) two wave troughs

3. The thin layer of water that flows up on the beach is called:

   (a) surf (b) wash (c) backwash (d) drift (e) swash

4. Longshore drift is a process combining waves arriving at oblique angles and water returning to the ocean at what type of angle?

   (a) oblique angles (b) acute angles (c) right angles (d) does not involve returning water (e) parallel angles

5. Mechanical erosion at the shoreline is called:

   (a) corrasion (b) corrosion (c) scouring (d) attrition (e) sand abrasion

6. When a rapidly rising high tide's wave front runs up a river or bay this is called a:

   (a) tidal current (b) tidal bore (c) rip current (d) longshore current (e) tidal flood

True-False Questions

___ 1. A rip current exhibits high velocity and is stream-like.
___ 2. Crustal movement has no effect on the shape of coastlines.
___ 3. Beach drift is a weaker form of longshore drift, which carries massive amounts of sand.
___ 4. As a wave approaches the shore, it becomes a wave of translation.
___ 5. Waves of oscillation move water particles in a circular up-and-down fashion.
___ 6. Waves are refracted as they approach the shoreline, so they appear to be on a straight approach.

UNIT 51: COASTAL LANDFORMS AND LANDSCAPES

UNIT SUMMARY

This second unit on coastal waves as a geomorphic agent treats the landforms and landscapes that mark the zone where sea and land interact. Aggradational landforms are covered first, and the survey begins with an exploration of beach dynamics. The parts of a beach are highlighted (Fig. 51.1), and the concepts of foreshore, nearshore, backshore, longshore bars, berms, coastal dunes, and beach formation are discussed. Next, with the aid of the block diagram shown in Fig. 51.4, comes an introduction to the major depositional landforms of the coastal zone, which include sandspits, baymouth bars, and tombolos. Offshore bars and barrier islands are singled out for further elaboration; the significant human impact on barrier islands is underscored in the Perspective box. The unit then turns to a consideration of degradational coastal landforms and we are reintroduced to the erosional processes first encountered in Unit 50: hydraulic action of waves, corrasion, corrosion, and attrition. Assembling the combined effects of these degradational forces, a three-stage model of the straightening of a coastline is presented in Fig. 51.9, which familiarizes us with sea cliffs, sea caves, sea arches, stacks, and wave-cut platforms. A broader discussion of coastal landscapes distinguishes between emergent (uplifted) and submergent (drowning) coastlines. The unit concludes with a section on living shorelines, highlighted by an evolutionary model of a coral atoll reef (Fig. 51.12).

UNIT OBJECTIVES

1. To examine the characteristics of a beach.

2. To relate beaches to the coastline's topographic and tectonic setting.

3. To recognize related coastal landforms of aggradation, such as sand dunes, offshore bars, and barrier islands.

4. To identify landforms typical of erosional coastlines.

5. To relate erosional and depositional processes to a general classification of coastlines.

GLOSSARY OF KEY TERMS

Atoll   Ring-like coral reef surrounding empty lagoons; grew on the rims of eroded volcanic cones.

Backshore   The beach zone that lies landward of the foreshore; extends from the high-water line to the dune line.

Barrier island A permanent, offshore, elongated ridge of sand, positioned parallel to the shoreline and separated by a lagoon from it; may have originally formed as an offshore bar during the last glaciation, migrated coastward, and grew as it shifted.

Baymouth bar A sandspit that has grown all the way across the mouth of a bay.

Beach A coastal zone of sediment that is shaped by the action of waves; constructed of sand and other materials, derived from both local and distant sources.

Berm A flat sandy beach that lies in the backshore beach zone; deposited during storms and beyond the reach of normal daily wave action.

Coral reef An aggradational reef formed from the skeletal remains of marine organisms.

Emergent coast A coastal zone whose landforms have recently emerged from the sea, either through tectonic uplift, a drop in sea level, or both.

Foreshore The beach zone that is alternatively water-covered during high tide and exposed during low tide; the zone of beach drift and related processes.

Longshore Bar A ridge of sand parallel to the shoreline that develops in the nearshore beach zone.

Nearshore The beach zone that is located seaward of the foreshore, submerged even during an average low tide; longshore bars and troughs develop here in this zone of complex, ever-changing topography.

Offshore bar An offshore sandbar that lies some distance from the beach and is not connected to land; a longshore bar is an examaple.

Sand spit An elongated extension of a beach into open water where the shoreline reaches a bay or bend; built and maintained by a longshore drift.

Sea arch A small island penetrated by the sea at its base; island originated as an especially resistant portion of a headland that was eroded away by waves.

Sea cave Cave carved by undercutting waves that are eroding the base of a sea cliff.

Sea cliff An especially steep coastal escarpment that develops when headlands are eroded by waves.

Stack A column-like island that is a remnant of a headland eroded away by waves.

Submergent coast A drowned coastal zone, more common than uplifted, emergent coasts; submergence caused in large part by the rise in sea level of the past 10,000 years.

Tombolo A sandspit that forms a link between the mainland and an offshore island.

Uplifted marine terrace In an emergent coastal zone, a wave-cut platform that has been exposed and elevated by tectonic uplift or a lowering of sea level (or both).

Wave-cut platform The abrasion platform that develops at the foot of a sea cliff, marking its recession; its nearly flat bedrock surface slopes seaward.

UNIT OUTLINE

I. Aggradational landforms
    A. A beach is a coastal zone of sediment, shaped by wave action
        1. begins at the foot of dunes and continues beneath the water
    B. Beach dynamics (Figs. 51.1 & 51.2)
        1. foreshore is the zone that is submerged at high tide and exposed at low tide
        2. the nearshore (offshore) is seaward of the foreshore, and is submerged even at low tide
            a. longshore bars (parallel ridges) form in this zone
        3. the backshore is landward of the foreshore, extends from the high-water line to dunes
            a. area contains berms, beaches that were deposited during storms or unusually high wave action
        4. beaches have different seasonal profiles
        5. beaches are open systems with inputs and outputs
        6. location of beaches related to available sediment and wave energy
    C. Coastal dunes
        1. wind is the primary builder of dunes
        2. strong sea breezes build up berms and dunes
    D. Sandspits and sandbars (Fig. 51.4)
        1. sandspits occur when longshore drift moves materials into an area with a bend or bay, where the material forms an extension into the water
            a. baymouth bars are sandspits that grow all the way across the mouth of a bay
            b. a tombolo may form if a sandspit connects an island to the mainland
    E. Offshore bars and barrier islands
        1. offshore (sand) bars are not connected to the land, interfere with wave action
        2. barrier islands (Fig. 51.7) are permanent offshore bars, may have glacial origins

a. contain dunes and vegetation, such as grasses and mangrove

b. Miami Beach, Atlantic City, Galveston

II. Degradational landforms (Figs. 51.9 & 51.11)
A. Wave erosion is the dominant process
B. Headlands are eroded by waves, create sea cliffs
C. Sea caves often eroded at the bases of sea cliffs
D. Wave-cut platform can form at the base of the sea cliff, as it continues to be eroded
E. Last remaining remnants of sea cliff are sea arches and stacks, both temporary features

III. Coastal landscapes
A. Emergent coasts
    1. elevated by tectonic forces
    2. cliffs and wave-cut platforms are elevated above sea level
    3. uplifted marine terraces form
B. Submergent coasts
    1. lowered by rising sea levels over the past 10,000 years
    2. tops of some submerged hills exposed as islands

IV. Living shorelines (Fig. 51.12)
A. Corals, algae, and mangroves can shape a coastline
    1. coral reef is built by tiny marine organisms, discharge calcium carbonate
    2. can be attached to shoreline or free-floating
    3. atolls are circular coral reefs that surround a lagoon
B. Mangrove is a shoreline builder, creates vegetated mud flats

REVIEW QUESTIONS

1. Define the terms sandspit and baymouth bar, and describe their formation.

2. Name several of the degradational landforms associated with wave erosion, using Fig. 51.9.

3. How are submergent coastlines formed?

SELF-TEST

Multiple-Choice Questions

1. The coastal zone that lies landward of the foreshore is the:

   (a) backshore (b) nearshore (c) offshore (d) longshore (e) farshore

2. Which portion of the coast is submerged even at average low tide?

   (a) backshore (b) nearshore (c) longshore (d) foreshore (e) midshore

3. When sediment carried by longshore drift extends into open water, this can form a(an):

   (a) atoll bar (b) sandspit (c) barrier island (d) offshore bar (e) coral reef

4. A landform that connects an island and the mainland is a(n):

   (a) offshore bar (b) barrier island (c) tombolo (d) stack (e) atoll

5. The last standing remains of eroded sea cliffs are:

   (a) sea caves and platforms (b) sea arches and sea caves
   (c) headlands (d) sea arches and stacks (e) coral reefs and atolls

6. Coastlines that are being uplifted by tectonic forces are known as

   (a) divergent coasts (b) submergent coasts (c) stacks (d) isostatic coastlines (e) emergent coasts

True-False Questions

__ 1. Mangrove, coral reefs, and atolls shape coastlines.
__ 2. Uplifted marine terraces are associated with submergent coasts.
__ 3. Sea caves are eroded out of the bases of sea cliffs.
__ 4. Offshore bars are formed by degradational processes.
__ 5. Longshore bars are ridges of sand that lie at right angles to the beach.
__ 6. A coastal zone of sediment shaped by wave action is called a beach.

UNIT 52: PHYSIOGRAPHIC REALMS AND REGIONS: THE SPATIAL VARIATION OF LANDSCAPES

UNIT SUMMARY

This final unit covers the physiographic realms that blanket North America and several of the key physiographic regions that mark the conterminous United States. The survey begins with a discussion of terminology that introduces the regional framework that will be pursued (see maps in Figs. 52.1, 52.4, and 52.5) and also reviews important aspects of regional criteria and boundary characteristics. The first of the six physiographic realms is the *Canadian Shield*, the geologic core of the North American landmass that bears the strongest imprint of the Late Cenozoic Ice Age. The second realm is the *Interior Plains*, the heart of the continent with a northwest extension that reaches the Arctic Ocean. Third is the *Appalachian Highlands*, the first of the realms that are also explored at the second-order, regional level; the five constituent regions highlighted are the Appalachian Plateau, the "Newer" Appalachians (dominated by ridge-and-valley terrain), the Blue Ridge Section, the Piedmont, and the New England/Maritime Province. The fourth realm, the *Western Mountains*, is also singled out for internal regional coverage; the seven profiled physiographic regions include the Southern, Middle, and Northern Rocky Mountains, the Columbia Plateau, the Colorado Plateau, the Basin-and-Range Province, and the Pacific Mountains and Valleys. The fifth physiographic realm is the *Gulf-Atlantic Coastal Plain*, which lines the continent's eastern fringe from New York City southward to Costa Rica in southern Central America. The sixth realm is the *Central American Mountains*, the highland spine that marks North America's southernmost section and extends from west-central Mexico to Panama's border with the South America landmass. A closing statement summarizes the overall physiographic imprint on the landscape.

UNIT OBJECTIVES

1. To introduce the physiographic realms and regions.

2. To briefly discuss the six physiographic realms of North America.

3. To discuss in greater detail the regions that constitute two of the physiographic realms of the conterminous United States.

GLOSSARY OF KEY TERMS

Appalachian Highlands Extend northeastward from Georgia and Alabama through New England into Maritime Canada; actually a complex of several physiographic provinces.

Appalachian Plateau Eastern edge defined by the Allegheny Front in the north and the Cumberland Escarpment in the south; area of coal deposits and irregular topography.

Basin-and-Range Province Lies south of the Columbia Plateau in the intermontane region between the Rocky Mountains to the east and the Pacific Mountains and Valleys to the west; a region of basins and arid climate.

Blue Ridge Mountains Lie east of the Great Valley, extend north from Georgia to Gettysburg, Pennsylvania; underlain by much older crystalline rock than the other areas of the Appalachians.

Canadian Shield The original core of the North American landmass, heavily glaciated; characterized by low relief, unproductive soils, and large mineral deposits.

Central American Mountains Area to the south and west of the southern extension of the Gulf-Atlantic Coastal Plain; the contact zone between the Cocos and Caribbean lithospheric plates, dominated by volcanic landforms.

Colorado Plateau Area to the west of the Southern Rockies; exhibits few strong topographic contrasts, and is underlain by flat-lying sedimentary strata.

Columbia Plateau Area wedged between the Northern Rockies and the Cascade Range; one of the largest lava surfaces in the world, lies as high as 1800 m (6000 ft) above sea level.

Gulf-Atlantic Coastal Plain Extends along North America's eastern seaboard from New York City southward to the Caribbean coast of Costa Rica; lies below 300 m (1000 ft) in elevation, underlain by gently sloping, sedimentary rocks.

Interior Plains Extend eastward from the Rocky Mountains to the western edge of the Appalachians; generally an area of low relief.

Middle Rocky Mountains Area of ranges and wide valleys, less congested topography than in the Southern Rockies.

New England/Maritime Province The rugged northeastern region of the Appalachians; strongly affected by glaciation and dotted with lakes.

"Newer" Appalachians Contains ridge-and-valley topography and the fertile Great Valley.

Northern Rocky Mountains Area northwest of Yellowstone Park; a confused topography of generally lower relief than the Middle and Southern Rockies.

Pacific Mountains and Valleys Lies west of the Columbia Plateau and the Basin-and-Range province; orientation is north-south, a region of complex physiography, containing the Sierra Nevada and Cascades as well as California's central valley and other major lowlands.

Physiographic realm A first-order subdivision of the North American continent at the broadest scale; characterized by an appropriate uniformity of landscapes, landforms, and other physiographic elements.

Physiographic region A second-order subdivision of the North American continent at a more detailed scale than the physiographic realm; characterized by an appropriate uniformity of landscapes, landforms, and other physiographic elements. Also sometimes called *physiographic provinces*, an older geographic term still in use.

Physiography Literally means *landscape description*; refers to all of the natural features on the Earth's surface, including landscapes, landforms, climate, soils, vegetation, and hydrography.

Piedmont Low, hilly area east of the Blue Ridge section of the Appalachians.

Regional concept Used to classify and categorize spatial information; regions are artificial constructs developed by geographers to delineate portions of the Earth's surface that are marked by an overriding sameness or homogeneity (in our case, physiography).

Southern Rocky Mountains Province lying across the center of Colorado; mountains rising sharply out of the western border of the Great Plains.

Western Mountains Region bordering the Interior Plains to the west, that extends to the pacific coast; an area of rugged mountain topography and high plateaus.

UNIT OUTLINE

I. Defining physiographic realms and regions
   A. Largest physiographic subdivisions are called realms (first-order units)
   B. Realms subdivided into regions (second-order units)
   C. Regions further subdivided into subregions (third-order units)
   D. Physiography relates to all natural features on Earth, including
      1. landforms
      2. climate
      3. soil
      4. vegetation
      5. hydrography
   E. Boundaries of physiographic regions established by whatever criteria (as mentioned above) are being used to define a region; broad transitional zones much more common than sharp borders

II. Physiographic realms of North America
   A. The Canadian Shield
      1. low relief, igneous and crystalline rock, thin soils
   B. The Interior Plains

           1. from Rocky Mountains to Appalachians, sedimentary rock, rich soils for agriculture

    C. The Appalachian Highlands

           1. from Georgia to Maritime Canada, rolling and rugged hills, folded sedimentary rock

    D. The Western Mountains

           1. dominated by high relief, varied topography, from New Mexico to Alaska, igneous, sedimentary, and metamorphic rock; Pacific region is mostly marked by rugged, high-relief terrain

    E. The Gulf-Atlantic Coastal Plain

           1. seaboard coastal North America, running south from New York City to Costa Rica; barrier islands, lagoons, beaches; low relief, little topographic variety

    F. The Central American Mountains

           1. Gulf-Atlantic Coastal Plain reaches southward to Mexico and Central America; to the south and west are the Central American Mountains volcanic landforms, earthquakes, altitudinal zonation of environments

III. The Physiographic Imprint

    A. Today's landscape reflects all of the building forces and erosional systems covered in this text.

REVIEW QUESTIONS

1. Draw a generalized diagram of the six physiographic realms of North America, using Fig. 52.1

2. Compare and contrast the various physiographic provinces within the Appalachians.

3. What is the extent of the Gulf-Atlantic Coastal Plain?

SELF-TEST

Multiple-Choice Questions

1. Which of these is not a physiographic region of North America?

    (a) Canadian Shield (b) Great Plains (c) Colorado Plateau (d) Appalachian Plateau (e) Southern Rocky Mountains

2. The Pacific Northwest region of North America exhibits:

   (a) high relief (b) arid conditions (c) low relief (d) extreme high temperatures (e) little relief

3. The Gulf-Atlantic Coastal Plain extends as far south as:

   (a) Antarctica (b) Florida (c) Mississippi (d) Costa Rica (e) Virginia

4. Which of the following is not one of the criteria used to define a physiographic realm?

   (a) vegetation (b) population density (c) climate (d) landforms (e) all are usable criteria

5. Which of the following is a second-order unit in the geographical classification hierarchy?

   (a) landmass (b) realm (c) subregion (d) province (e) region

6. The Interior Plains extend from the Rocky Mountains eastward to:

   (a) the Appalachians (b) the Mississippi River (c) New York City (d) the Atlantic Ocean (e) the Cascade Mountains

True-False Questions

___ 1. The realm is a third-order unit in the geographical classification scheme.
___ 2. The Canadian Shield is composed largely of igneous and crystalline rock.
___ 3. The Gulf-Atlantic Coastal Plain is an area of generally high relief.
___ 4. Physiography involves the integration of climate, vegetation, urbanization, and economy of a place.
___ 5. The Central American Mountains are largely volcanic in origin.
___ 6. The Appalachians' Ridge-and-Valley section is largely composed of folded sedimentary rocks

UNIT 1

MC

1 C
2 B
3 A
4 E
5 C
6 A

T/F

1 T
2 T
3 F
4 T
5 F
6 T

UNIT 2

MC

1 D
2 E
3 A
4 B
5 C
6 E

T/F

1 T
2 T
3 F
4 T
5 T
6 F

UNIT 3

MC

1 B
2 A
3 E
4 A
5 A
6 B

T/F

1 F
2 T
3 T
4 T
5 T
6 F

UNIT 4

MC

1 C
2 B
3 A
4 A
5 A
6 D

T/F

1 F
2 T
3 T
5 F
5 T
6 T

UNIT 5

MC

1 A
2 C
3 E
4 B
5 B
6 D

T/F

1 T
2 T
3 F
4 T
5 T
6 F

UNIT 6

MC

1 D
2 C
3 B
4 C
5 E
6 B

T/F

1 T
2 F
3 F
4 T
5 T
6 F

UNIT 7

MC

1 A
2 B
3 E
4 C
5 A
6 B

T/F

1 T
2 F
3 T
4 F
5 T
6 T

UNIT 8

MC

1 B
2 C
3 D
4 E
5 A
6 C

T/F

1 F
2 T
3 F
5 T
5 T
6 F

UNIT 9		UNIT 10		UNIT 11		UNIT 12	
MC		*MC*		*MC*		*MC*	
1	A	1	A	1	D	1	A
2	C	2	B	2	B	2	D
3	B	3	E	3	A	3	B
4	A	4	B	4	E	4	C
5	E	5	C	5	A	5	A
6	D	6	B	6	C	6	E
T/F		*T/F*		*T/F*		*T/F*	
1	F	1	T	1	T	1	T
2	T	2	F	2	T	2	F
3	F	3	T	3	T	3	F
4	F	4	F	4	F	5	F
5	F	5	F	5	T	5	T
6	T	6	T	6	T	6	T

UNIT 13		UNIT 14		UNIT 15		UNIT 16	
MC		*MC*		*MC*		*MC*	
1	B	1	A	1	A	1	B
2	A	2	E	2	C	2	E
3	E	3	C	3	B	3	A
4	C	4	A	4	A	4	B
5	D	5	B	5	E	5	A
6	D	6	D	6	D	6	D
T/F		*T/F*		*T/F*		*T/F*	
1	T	1	F	1	F	1	T
2	F	2	F	2	F	2	F
3	T	3	T	3	T	3	F
4	F	4	T	4	F	5	T
5	T	5	T	5	T	5	F
6	F	6	T	6	T	6	T

UNIT 17		UNIT 18		UNIT 19		UNIT 20	
MC		*MC*		*MC*		*MC*	
1	A	1	C	1	B	1	D
2	D	2	B	2	A	2	B
3	A	3	A	3	E	3	A
4	E	4	E	4	D	4	C
5	B	5	B	5	A	5	D
6	C	6	C	6	A	6	B
T/F		*T/F*		*T/F*		*T/F*	
1	F	1	F	1	T	1	T
2	T	2	F	2	T	2	T
3	T	3	T	3	T	3	F
4	F	4	T	4	F	5	T
5	F	5	T	5	F	5	F
6	T	6	F	6	T	6	F

UNIT 21		UNIT 22		UNIT 23		UNIT 24	
MC		*MC*		*MC*		*MC*	
1	A	1	A	1	B	1	C
2	D	2	D	2	A	2	A
3	B	3	E	3	C	3	B
4	B	4	B	4	C	4	C
5	C	5	C	5	B	5	E
6	E	6	E	6	C	6	D
T/F		*T/F*		*T/F*		*T/F*	
1	F	1	T	1	T	1	T
2	T	2	T	2	F	2	F
3	F	3	F	3	F	3	T
4	T	4	F	4	F	5	T
5	T	5	F	5	T	5	T
6	T	6	F	6	F	6	F

UNIT 25		UNIT 26		UNIT 27		UNIT 28	
MC		*MC*		*MC*		*MC*	
1	B	1	C	1	C	1	A
2	D	2	A	2	E	2	B
3	E	3	D	3	A	3	D
4	D	4	E	4	E	4	E
5	E	5	A	5	C	5	B
6	A	6	B	6	D	6	C
T/F		*T/F*		*T/F*		*T/F*	
1	T	1	T	1	T	1	F
2	F	2	F	2	F	2	T
3	F	3	T	3	T	3	T
4	T	4	T	4	F	5	F
5	F	5	T	5	T	5	T
6	T	6	T	6	T	6	T

UNIT 29		UNIT 30		UNIT 31		UNIT 32	
MC		*MC*		*MC*		*MC*	
1	A	1	C	1	A	1	B
2	C	2	A	2	B	2	A
3	C	3	D	3	A	3	C
4	E	4	E	4	D	4	D
5	D	5	B	5	E	5	E
6	A	6	A	6	C	6	B
T/F		*T/F*		*T/F*		*T/F*	
1	F	1	T	1	F	1	T
2	T	2	T	2	F	2	T
3	F	3	F	3	T	3	F
4	T	4	F	4	T	5	T
5	T	5	T	5	F	5	F
6	T	6	T	6	T	6	T

UNIT 33		**UNIT 34**		**UNIT 35**		**UNIT 36**	
MC		*MC*		*MC*		*MC*	
1	A	1	D	1	B	1	A
2	C	2	A	2	A	2	B
3	B	3	E	3	E	3	E
4	E	4	B	4	C	4	C
5	C	5	B	5	D	5	D
6	A	6	C	6	B	6	A
T/F		*T/F*		*T/F*		*T/F*	
1	T	1	T	1	T	1	T
2	F	2	T	2	F	2	F
3	F	3	F	3	F	3	T
4	T	4	T	4	F	5	F
5	F	5	T	5	T	5	T
6	F	6	F	6	T	6	F

UNIT 37		**UNIT 38**		**UNIT 39**		**UNIT 40**	
MC		*MC*		*MC*		*MC*	
1	D	1	B	1	A	1	D
2	C	2	A	2	B	2	C
3	E	3	B	3	C	3	A
4	A	4	E	4	E	4	B
5	B	5	D	5	D	5	E
6	C	6	D	6	A	6	C
T/F		*T/F*		*T/F*		*T/F*	
1	T	1	T	1	F	1	T
2	T	2	T	2	T	2	F
3	T	3	F	3	T	3	F
4	F	4	T	4	T	5	T
5	F	5	F	5	F	5	T
6	T	6	T	6	T	6	T

UNIT 41
MC

1   B
2   C
3   E
4   A
5   B
6   A

T/F

1   F
2   T
3   F
4   T
5   T
6   F

UNIT 42
MC

1   D
2   A
3   B
4   E
5   B
6   B

T/F

1   T
2   T
3   T
4   F
5   F
6   T

UNIT 43
MC

1   B
2   E
3   B
4   C
5   A
6   D

T/F

1   F
2   T
3   T
4   F
5   T
6   T

UNIT 44
MC

1   C
2   C
3   D
4   B
5   E
6   B

T/F

1   T
2   T
3   F
5   F
5   T
6   F

UNIT 45
MC

1   B
2   A
3   C
4   D
5   E
6   B

T/F

1   F
2   T
3   F
4   T
5   T
6   F

UNIT 46
MC

1   D
2   C
3   E
4   B
5   A
6   E

T/F

1   T
2   F
3   T
4   F
5   F
6   T

UNIT 47
MC

1   A
2   C
3   D
4   E
5   A
6   B

T/F

1   T
2   T
3   F
4   F
5   T
6   T

UNIT 48
MC

1   C
2   A
3   B
4   E
5   C
6   A

T/F

1   T
2   F
3   T
5   F
5   T
6   T

UNIT 49		**UNIT 50**		**UNIT 51**		**UNIT 52**	
MC		*MC*		*MC*		*MC*	
1	C	1	D	1	A	1	A
2	D	2	A	2	B	2	A
3	A	3	E	3	B	3	D
4	E	4	C	4	C	4	B
5	A	5	A	5	D	5	E
6	D	6	B	6	E	6	A
T/F		*T/F*		*T/F*		*T/F*	
1	T	1	T	1	T	1	F
2	T	2	F	2	F	2	T
3	F	3	F	3	T	3	F
4	T	4	T	4	F	5	F
5	F	5	T	5	F	5	T
6	F	6	T	6	T	6	T